SEX AND THE EMPIRE THAT IS NO MORE

With much gratitude
to my friends in the
Princeton Anthropology
Department.

Randy

9/17/94

Gender and

the Politics of

Metaphor

SEX AND THE EMPIRE THAT IS NO MORE

in Oyo Yoruba

Religion

J. LORAND MATORY

University of Minnesota Press

Minneapolis
London

Figure 1 was originally published in Henry John Drewal, John Pemberton III, and Roland Abiodun, *Yoruba: Nine Centuries of African Art and Thought,* ed. Alan Wardwell (New York: Center for African Art/Henry Abrams, 1989). Reprinted with permission of the Museum for African Art.

Published by the University of Minnesota Press
2037 University Avenue Southeast, Minneapolis, MN 55455–3092
Printed in the United States of America on acid-free paper

Library of Congress Cataloging-in-Publication Data

Matory, James Lorand.
    Sex and the empire that is no more : gender and the politics of metaphor in Oyo
  Yoruba religion / J. Lorand Matory.
      p.   cm.
    Revision of thesis (Ph. D.)—University of Chicago, 1991.
    Includes bibliographical references and index.
    ISBN 0-8166-2226-4 (alk. paper).—ISBN 0-8166-2227-2 (pbk. : alk. paper)
    1. Yoruba (African people)—Religion.   2. Sex role—Nigeria.   3. Nigeria—Religion.
  I. Title.
  BL2480.Y6M37   1994
  306.6'9968333—dc20   93-37980

The University of Minnesota is an
equal-opportunity educator and employer.

for my dearest Bunmi

Contents

Foreword

I reached Yorubaland accidentally, much as Columbus reached America, and found out more than I had expected to. Of course, my voyage was in the opposite direction and, though well precedented in its motives, was of concern to fewer people. My guide had been Bastide's *African Religions of Brazil* (1978), one of many books rightly or wrongly privileging the Yorùbá influence on Africa's American diaspora. So, in a way, I had reached Brazil accidentally, too, in my pursuit of what made me *Afro*-American, inside and apart from the brownness of my skin, the fullness of my lips, and a range of social disadvantages or (mal)adaptations that generations of sociologists and policymakers had attributed to others of my complexion. The sort of *cultural* origins that seemed so obvious to Afro-Brazilianists and Afro-Cubanists and is so readily named by Brazilians and Cubans has been subject to vigorous contention among North Americans.

My choice to study the Yoruba and, eventually, to live for just over two years in Nigeria arose, therefore, not from inevitability but from an aspiration. That aspired-to quality makes my ethnic self and my pride in being an African no less authentic, postmodern deconstructions of identity notwithstanding. It is true that my idealism about Africa has diminished considerably over these decades, but the same must be said of my feelings for Brazil and the other place I call home, the United States of America. Not only did I marry Nigerian, but I love Nigeria with both anger and joy.

Herein lies, for me, the importance of metaphor. Metaphors, and tropes generally, are not simply literary fabrications that take license with the literal truths of the world. Rather, they are models according to which we daily think about and act upon the world (Lakoff and

Johnson 1980). So much in social life depends on one's ability to see oneself in others—individually in the process of psychological development and collectively in the process of political action. Personal and social predications of equivalence across time and space (metaphor proper) make us who we are. Such predications interlock with equally powerful assertions of who and what we are *not* (negation), our relations to others within the group (metonymy), and the choice of representatives of the group (synecdoche).

Obviously, tropes do not always refer explicitly to social order. Nor do the ritual forms of trope that will concern us in this book. However, by definition, rituals and their constituent tropes take place in a social context. Through minimal verbal and material figurations, Yoruba rituals of worship and healing posit certain metaphors upon the world that structure conceptions of human possibility. Moreover, rituals themselves require the orderly mobilization of human bodies. I am not concerned here to reaffirm the usefulness of structural-functionalism but to demonstrate the "dialogic" (Bakhtin 1981) sense of rituals in an age of highly unsettled moral principles. Therefore, I will treat Ọ̀yọ́-Yorùbá rituals as prescriptions and as forms of conduct that may alter or undermine rival conceptions of social order. Endemic to this tropic rivalry and to all efforts at social change are ritual predications that some will regard as *ironic*.

Amid the diverse ideological currents of colonial and postcolonial Nigerian national society, few personae seem more ironic than the priestesses and transvestite priests of the Oyo-Yoruba gods. It is for us to figure out the logical and social order of which they form a consonant and, in this case, a crucial element. Feminist ethnography has opened our eyes to women's extraordinary contribution to African agricultural production, as well as the conditions of their marginalization and exploitation in colonial and postcolonial states. Feminist scholarship on the Yoruba and other coastal West African peoples has revealed a distinctive case, in which women dominate important spheres of commercial exchange. The following ethnography concerns an interstitial case, where women once assumed power at the heights of the royal state, not as traders but as priestesses, and have transformed that power into an important voice in postcolonial rural communities.

What is not clear is that the women so empowered speak *as* women or *for* women as a class.

It is a given in feminist scholarship that women suffer political and social disadvantages across cultures because of their sex. The challenge for international feminist activism has been to grasp the structures of consciousness and identity that have so often divided Western from black, brown, and Third World women equally concerned about political inequality (see, e.g., Amadiume 1987:1–10; A. Davis 1985). This study is not about the independently wealthy market women so much discussed in the Yoruba lore and Yorubanist ethnography. Nor is it about women as such. Rather, it takes as its point of departure the metaphoric likeness, shared political roles, and ritual cooperation among male transvestite and female possession priests—apical exemplars and executive managers of communities made oppositional by the development of the Nigerian postcolonial state. This metaphoric conjunction of characters not only resists the Islamic and capitalist hegemony of the Nigerian metropolis but confounds the most common feminist and scholarly constructions of gender.

I will argue that gender is not simply the cultural elaboration on a "naturally" given dichotomy between biological "men" and "women" (see also Collier and Yanagisako 1987:7). Much American folk reasoning, including its academic elaborations, is grounded in the ideological centrality of the "male"/"female" heterosexual dyad, which is taken implicitly as the program for an overall division of social labor. Women's marginalization in the "public" sphere seems to arise as the natural sequel of their reproductive role in the "domestic" sphere. Moreover, as we collectively wax nostalgic about "domestic" life, its central categories often become popular justifications for the vilification of people who do not conform to supposedly "natural" reproductive priorities—such as "homosexuals" and "transsexuals." In scholarly circles, they tend to be relegated to footnotes or, strangely enough, used to prove the ultimate and cross-cultural dualism of human gender roles.

In Yoruba society, the heterosexual dyad is neither the unique foundation of social reproduction nor even the most privileged site in the manufacture of hegemonic gender categories. Historical changes in a range of lineage, class, ethnic, religious, national, and racial hierarchies

have overdetermined the innermost nature of Yoruba gender categories, leaving them inexplicable to any investigator who supposes that
gender is simply the cultural elaboration of biologically given "sex." As
we shall see, both male wives and female husbands are central actors in
the Oyo-Yoruba kingdom and village. To understand the life of such
communities in modern Nigeria, we must understand both the internally perceived logic and the externally perceived irony of these gendered roles. In a sense, then, what follows is a history of irony.

And who could be better suited to write it? The anthropologist himself is an ironic character—heroic to some, ridiculous to others, and
dastardly to more than a few—because she or he traverses geographical and semantic boundaries. The anthropologist is par excellence a
cross-dresser, an outsider who wears insider's clothes and gradually
acquires the language, eating habits, and behaviors that conventionally
go along with them. Then she or he must go back someplace to report
what lies beyond the boundary so crossed. Yet, the best of ethnography
upsets such expectations and muddies old boundaries rather than
reproducing them. Ethnography is a monument to the irony of cross-
linguistic dialogue, cross-cultural cooperation, and transpsychic understanding.

Many have participated in the dialogue, cooperation, and understanding of which this book is a momentary rendering. Foremost I
must thank those who have sustained me emotionally through my
multiple crossings: my wife, Bunmi Fatoye-Matory, as well as my dear
friends Nico Jacob, Amilton Costa, Christina Gomez, Michael Fitz-
gerald, Chris Dunn, and Jerry Doyle. They have shown a love, patience,
and generosity whose practical worth I can only begin to acknowledge
here. In particular, the companionship of my wife has stilled much of
the loneliness that comes with repeated departures. At the same time,
she keeps alive my affective sense of the places and people we have
temporarily left behind.

Doyin Ṣoyibọ of the University of Ibadan met me on the first day I set
foot in Nigeria. The good luck of knowing him and his family have followed us through the years. I thank him first as my friend and then as
my teacher. There are few people to whom I owe more than to Ọmọ-Ọba
Oluremi Olubadejọ Adebọnọjọ, who not only introduced my parents to
each other but, two decades later, became my Nigerian father in the

fullest sense, watching over me from my first months in his country to my wedding day and beyond. I thank my mother and father for their confidence in me through trials and adventures that only parents strong of heart could have borne. My brothers, sisters, and stepmother too deserve thanks for their loyalty through the years. I thank Baba and Mutti Jacob for their incomparable warmth and welcome.

The success of my research in Yorubaland would have been impossible without the guidance of S. O. Babayẹmi, once my teacher and now the King of Gbọ̀ngán, as well as the other outstanding scholars of the Institute of African Studies, University of Ibadan. I am highly indebted to Ìyá Yemọja Omilẹyẹ of Ibára, Abẹ̀òkúta, and Bàbá Yemọja Ogunnikẹ Mosadogun of Ìdí Arere, Ìbàdàn—who taught me with humor and patience that good fieldwork flows from friendship, and vice versa. The Olúbára of Ibára, the Alákétu of Kétu, and the late Onígbòho of Ìgbòho, Jeremiah Afọlabi, kindly opened many doors for me, as did the Aláàfin of Ọ̀yọ́. That I could not rightfully have expected the welcome of these powerful men makes my gratitude all the more serious and heartfelt.

John Ọmọoyè Bọlarinwa deserves much of the credit for my decade-old friendship with the Ṣàngó and Yemọja priests of Igboho. Not only did his hospitality and generosity take me repeatedly to Igboho, but his introduction brought me into the trust of my most important informants. I thank also the Alépàtà of Igboho, Solomon Oyediran, who displayed the highest Yoruba ideals of character (ìwà) during my stay in the town. He was open and kind when mistrust might have been a lesser man's instinct. Without the help of both men, I would never have experienced the love and assistance of my friends Ajitoni Oyediran, the late mọ́gbà Yemọja Ìyá Elégbo, and the three ẹlégùn Ṣàngó Ṣangobunmi, Ṣangodara, and Adeniran—all of whom deserve superlative gratitude and recognition here. I thank my assistant Elizabeth Akinọla for revealing to me the world of local women in purdah. My eyes would have seen everything differently were it not for the education I received from Santera Ollochundé Guadalupe of Lawrence, Massachusetts, Santera (Dra.) Aleyda Portuondo of Silver Spring, Maryland, and, most of all, Pai-de-Santo Amilton Costa of Bahia, Brazil.

This book began as a dissertation for the Department of Anthropology, University of Chicago. Hence, what I have said about Mr. Costa, I must say equally about my dissertation committee chairperson,

Jean Comaroff. Throughout my fieldwork, the words and perspectives of these two friends came to me daily. I often asked myself what they would make of the complex ritual and social phenomena before me. I must thank Jean in particular for encouraging and bolstering my intellectual independence through her gift for impeccable guidance without dictation.

I thank Nancy Munn for her conscientious reading and critique of the many lengthy works in progress I have placed before her, despite the weight and urgency of her other responsibilities. Few scholars combine classical method and wit so well as Raymond Smith, whose caring was never lost to me. Nor can I overstate my good fortune in having as a friend Karin Barber, who contributed her vast expertise to the refinement and correction of several lengthy Yoruba transcriptions and their translations. Wande Abimbọla and Andrew Apter too deserve the warmest thanks for their careful reading and insightful replies to this work in progress.

Bọlanle Awẹ of the University of Ibadan has been a source of inspiration for so long that pinpointing all my debts to her might tax the reader's patience. More recently, I have benefited from comments on portions of this work by colleagues in the Department of Anthropology at Princeton University and the Departments of Anthropology and Afro-American Studies at Harvard University: Larry Rosen, Gananath Obeyesekere, Henry Louis Gates, Jr., Sally Falk Moore, James Watson, Kwame Anthony Appiah, Henry Finder, Michael Herzfeld, Ronald Niezen, Mary Steedly, and Nur Yalman. Although I cite several of these friends and colleagues extensively, this Foreword must stand in lieu of the complete and proper citation of their contributions, which would otherwise lengthen this book considerably. Cited or uncited, they are not to be held responsible for any error in my interpretations or ethnographic reports.

Finally, I thank Connie Sutton of New York University for offering me the unexpected encouragement to publish my dissertation and for having guided me to so marvelous a publishing house. I could not have dreamt of a more perfect fit than the one I have found with my editor, Janaki Bakhle, and her assistant, Robert Mosimann. I thank them for all the things that editors do and they have done so well, but especially for their wise choice of anonymous readers, without whose praise and provocation this would be a very different work. They deserve not only gratitude but more than a small measure of credit for this book as it stands now.

Acknowledgments to institutions may seem to lack the warmth and immediacy evident in thanks to individuals, but the several institutions that have most assisted my work and growth are remembered here because they inspire not only my gratitude but my great respect for the ideals they represent and for the individuals without whom those ideals would have no life. I mention the Rotary Foundation, which sponsored my first Nigerian field research under the Scholarship for Graduate Studies Abroad (September 1982-August 1983). The Committee for Institutional Cooperation supported my summer training in Yoruba language, my second trip to Nigeria (July-September 1985), and part of my first Brazilian fieldwork (August-December 1987) under the C.I.C. International Studies Fellowship. The National Science Foundation financed the balance of my first Brazilian fieldwork under a Fellowship for Graduate Study. The Social Science Research Council supported my second trip to Brazil (February-September 1992), with the additional assistance of the W. E. B. Du Bois Institute for Afro-American Research at Harvard University.

Most crucial to the actual production of this document have been the U.S. Department of Education, which funded my third stint in Nigeria (April 1988-April 1989) under a Fulbright-Hays Fellowship; the Institute of African Studies at the University of Ibadan, which hosted both my yearlong sojourns in Yorubaland; Williams College, which supported my dissertation write-up with incomparable generosity and scholarly support; the Princeton Anthropology Department, where a postdoctoral fellowship allowed me to recover my sense, after a year of highly specialized ethnographic writing, of the broader issues in a fast-changing discipline; and the Du Bois Institute, which sponsored the final preparation of this book and exposed me to the most international and interdisciplinary gathering of Afro-Americanists on the planet. My sense of gratitude is both overwhelming and diffuse, like awe. For these are the foremost among the people and places that have structured my sense of possibility and guided my crossing. Without them, I would not be who I am.

Note on Orthography

Yoruba consonants are pronounced much like their English counter-parts, with the exception of

[p]   which resembles an imploded [kp];
[gb]   which is an imploded [gb];
[y]   which is pronounced at times like the English [y] and at times like [ny]; and
[ṣ]   which is pronounced like [sh].

Vowels are pronounced as in Spanish, except when marked under-neath with dots, which indicate an *open* sound.

[a]   resembles the vowel in the North American pronunciation of "pot" and "rock";
[e]   resembles the vowel sound in "date" and "cake";
[ẹ]   sounds like the vowel in "pet" and "nest";
[i]   resembles the vowel sound in "meat" and "green";
[o]   resembles the vowel sound in "coat" and "rove";
[ọ]   resembles the vowel sound in "raw" and "fought";
[u]   represents the vowel sound in "groove" and "shoe"; and
[n]   is sometimes a syllabic nasal vowel, in which case it will be marked for mid [̄], low [`], or high [´] tone. In some words, the syllabic nasal will appear as [m].

At the beginning of a syllable, [n] represents the same sound as in English. At the end of a syllable, it simply indicates the nasalization of the preceding vowel.

Yoruba is a tonal language, in which low- and descending-tone syllables are marked with the grave accent [`] over the vowel, high- and rising-tone syllables are marked with the acute accent [´], and mid-tone syllables are unmarked. Although dramatic divergences from the recognized tones of a word can distort their meaning, speech is characterized by continual unrecognized glides between these levels (Barber 1991:10).

I have done my best to transcribe songs and poetry according to contemporary orthographic norms, as represented, somewhat differently, by Abraham (1962) and Barber's definitive work on *oríkì*, or panegyrics. However, many of the colonial and contemporary written texts I use employ nonscholarly but perfectly comprehensible popular orthographies, which I preserve in all direct quotes. Such texts are seldom tone-marked. I tone-mark and provide subdiacritica in all phrases and lengthy quotations of the oral texts I recorded and upon the first isolated mention of any given Yoruba word. In order to avoid confusion and to preserve the sanity of the typesetter, subsequent isolated words are unmarked, except when they appear in lists containing other marked words, or when the absence of diacritica would leave the word's meaning ambiguous. Except in transcriptions of poetry, I follow the Nigerian convention of marking personal names with subdiacritica only, but I do so only at the first mention of any given name. Some spellings in the lengthier texts may vary from those now conventional in "standard Yoruba," for I have tried in every way possible to respect and accurately capture the local dialects of Oyo North and Oyo town.

Chapter 1

A Ritual History

In the 1970s, anthropology quickly took advantage of the victories Western feminists had won in the streets and in the popular press. The study of women's *roles* in other societies was not without its precedents. What would "kinship" be, after all, without women? Following Ardener (1972) and Ortner (1974), however, came a plethora of excellent edited volumes and monographs specifically devoted to the *experiences* and *perspectives* of women in other societies and the *symbolic structures* that define their collective activities (e.g., Ortner and Whitehead 1981; Rosaldo and Lamphere 1974; Hoch-Smith and Spring 1978; MacCormack and Strathern 1980; Schlegel 1977). The effort to redress our own deficits as a discipline and as a sexist society made it obvious that "women" elsewhere should be studied as a distinct social class, defined, implicitly, by contrast to "men."

Hence, the major precedent to the discussion of gender in Africa, from the 1950s to the 1980s, is really about *women* in Africa. It addresses variously women's economic options and resources, their political rights, the legal construction of their sexual relations to men, and witchcraft beliefs (Oppong 1983; Hafkin and Bay 1976; see esp. Potash 1989). Much has been written about the economic independence of Yoruba women (Sudarkasa 1973, 1977; H. U. Beier 1955; Mabogunję 1961), their prominence as chiefs in some kingdoms (Awę 1972, 1977; Biobaku 1960; Abiọdun 1989), and the witchcraft (*àjé*), or potentially destructive power, attributed to some of them (Prince 1961; Hoch-Smith 1978; Morton-Williams 1956; Idowu 1970).

However, various important anomalies challenge the realism of "women" and "men" as salient classes of social experience. For example, marriages between "women" are documented in a wide array of

1

African societies, requiring ethnographers to reclassify some "women" as "men" (see Oboler 1980; O'Brien 1977; Krige 1974). In other cases, like the present one, *all* "women" are husbands to somebody and simultaneously wives to multiple others (see also Amadiume 1987). "Women" who express points of view with oppressive implications for "women" somehow elude our analytic pursuit of the "woman's" perspective (consider, e.g., Kandiyoti 1988). Then there are the numerous cases of "men"—studied more frequently in Europe, the Pacific, and the Middle East than in Africa—who present themselves sexually or sartorially as "women" and are therefore classified as such in some cases (Wikan 1977; Whitehead 1981; Mageo 1992). There are marginal and little-analyzed exceptions to Africanists' neglect of this last phenomenon. For example, Evans-Pritchard (1970), Shepherd (1987), Smith and Dale (1920), Besmer (1983:18), Boddy (1989:210–11 n. 4), Beattie and Middleton (1969:xxv), Berger (1976:170), Turner (1967:223, 254), Baum (1993:25–31), and Brain (1976) mention symbolically significant instances in Africa of what Westerners have described as "homosexuality."[1] As such cases accumulate, one wonders if some fundamental question has not been skipped by conventional investigative premises in the study of gender, particularly in Africa.

Undoubtedly, approximately half of the persons in every society, not including minors, satisfy our Anglo-Saxon biological indices of "womanhood." Even if they do not define *themselves* by the same indices—physical, psychic, social, symbolic, or what have you—we can legitimately ask what events tend to befall them as a set. However, we must not then convince ourselves that the answer to that question aptly describes their *experience* and *perspective* or the local social and symbolic conventions that unite and divide "women" socially. The virtue of such a question in many cases lies in its very *disregard* of local categories. The foundation of gender categories in any given society and their distinguishing features require specific investigation, for the people we call "women" necessarily identify and act corporately with groups of persons that either subdivide or crosscut "womanhood."

The discussion of gender may usefully detail what "women" versus "men" do and think. However, we must also ask, without prejudice, what complementary roles structure the reproduction of society and which among them are truly illuminated by the analytic concept of gender. The importance of studies on the significant economic and political accomplishments of "Yoruba women" is not to be diminished. Indeed, they have furnished both the incentive and the essential tools of the present effort, which is to assess the historically specific definitions and manipulations of gender that potentiate certain women's accomplishments, place them beyond the reach of most women, and give form to male achievement as well.

Thus, this book will begin and end with contextual discussions of the male transvestite. Before this study, Drewal (1986) and Abiodun (1989) considered instances of Yoruba male transvestism as reflections of the status and moral qualities of the women so imitated, and Matory (1986; 1988) treated them as reflections of the gendered idiom of domination generally in Yoruba polity and religion. Here I will argue that transvestites not only illustrate the independence of salient Oyo-Yoruba gender categories from sex but are key political actors whose involvement in specific political projects has *transformed* existing gender categories.

Strathern (1987:6–7) has argued that in Pacific societies, sexual/gender inequality is the irreducible "idiom" in which even inequality between persons of the same sex and gender is understood, implying that the gender difference between biological men and women is simply given and is therefore not constructed, historically or logically, according to nonsexual axes of inequality. On the contrary, I will argue that in the Oyo-Yoruba case the creation and inscription of gender are themselves extensive projects in social coordination. As such, they are subject to enactment and resistance by parties with diverse interests. Not only individual gender transformation but changes in collective conceptions of gender are *negotiated* according to the divergent political interests of royals and commoners, the rulers and the ruled, the urban and the rural. Gender concepts are subject to influence from various realms of ideological and social production, just as gender concepts influence them.

The ethnographic focus of this study is a set of politically influential possession religions. In modern Oyo-Yoruba religion, there are both gods who possess people and gods who do not. The former are regularly associated with royal dynasties of pre-nineteenth-century origin and, by extension, with dimensions of the broader civil society that have potentiated and accompanied royal sovereignty. On the other

hand, certain extant nonpossession religions stood at the center of the
nonroyal polity that dominated the Oyo Yoruba in the nineteenth century and revolutionized local norms of gender hierarchy and political
inclusion. Thus, modern Oyo-Yoruba religious practice is imbued with
contrasting images of gender in the devolution of power, which, in this
chapter, we will use to illuminate the mechanisms of change in regional
political history.

Sahlins (1985:53–72) contrasts the Philippine Ilongot and North
American sense of history as an ongoing improvisation of collective life
with the Maori sense that present events simply recapitulate the highly
structured past events recounted and objectified in local mythical tales,
songs, and poems. Maori oral literature thus not only explains the
unfolding of present events but guides Maori responses to them.
Sahlins designates the process by which myths thus structure the action
of the Maori and similar peoples as "mytho-praxis." Yet, even in societies where historical actors and raconteurs are imbued with the ideology of freedom from cultural constraint, Sahlins maintains, action is
structured by both a local habitus (Bourdieu 1977) and a set of local
assumptions about the world.

My sense is that Oyo-Yoruba actors and historians are generally
wedded neither to the Ilongot and North American ideology of self-
invention nor to the rigid mythic templates Sahlins attributes to Maori
history and action. Yet, particular objective semiotic practices widespread among the Oyo Yoruba are so closely and repeatedly wedded to
rival forms of political action that their value as *templates* of action begs
for investigation. The uses to which Sahlins has put myth in his study
of "mytho-praxis" will here be put to ritual, in what one might call
"icono-praxis."

Sango versus Ogun: Rival Ritual Templates of Gender and Polity

The Yoruba gods, or òrìṣà, are often worshiped in groups, sharing the
same altars and being feted on the same occasions. However, sites and
occasions of worship for possessing gods like Ṣàngó, on the one hand,
and the nonpossessing god Ògún, on the other, are almost invariably
separate in Oyo North, the historical heartland of the Oyo kingdom

and of the Oyo dialect of Yoruba. This contrast illuminates a dichotomy not only between approaches to the divine but between historical concepts of sociopolitical order and the function of women in the state.

Ifá oracular texts suggest the intensity with which the contrast between Sango- and Ogun-worship in the region under discussion reflects contrasting values concerning the conduct of women in the political process:

> From Ifa we learn that long ago, when women used to terrorize their man folk with their knowledge of spirit possession, the men consulted Ifa, and were told to sacrifice to Ogun. On the day the women were preparing to call out the spirit of their departed elder, Ogun suddenly appeared in their midst . . . and, followed by the braver men, he chased the women into the bush. (Euba 1985:14)

The Ifa priesthood and the oracular texts it has generated are focused on the non-Oyo kingdom of Ifẹ̀ (Peel 1990:342). Yet, perhaps because the cult long ago expanded into Oyo-Yoruba regions, certain texts bear strong hints of the values and controversies enshrined in Oyo politics and religion.

The following discussion will focus on the implications of this highly ramified conflict for female participation in the Oyo-Yoruba polities of the eighteenth and nineteenth centuries. Although highly gendered in its hierarchies, Oyo-Yoruba polity adds myriad complexities and a subtle metaphoric logic to this "battle of the sexes."

Sango was reportedly an early ruler of the Oyo Empire, and he remains a symbol of Oyo royal might. According to Johnson, he was the son of Oyo's founder, Ọ̀rányàn, by a Tápà princess, who was given in marriage by her father to cement an alliance between the two kingdoms.[2] Oranyan's son and immediate successor was deposed for his weakness, having submitted Oyo to the rule of the neighboring kingdom of Òwu. Replacing his brother on the throne, Sango refused to render the accustomed tribute to the King of Owu, who then threatened, significantly, to deprive Sango of his wives and children. Using his remarkable "medicinal" powers (*oògùn*), Sango produced smoke from his mouth and nostrils, frightening the Owu king and his army into flight. Many tales report that Sango's great power led him to conquest and tyranny. He is also said to have accidentally destroyed his own compound (Johnson 1921:149–51), whereupon he either abdicated voluntarily or was forced to commit suicide. Abimbọla (personal communication, 19 October 1990) and Iṣọla (1991) attribute some of these tales to Christian propaganda, thereby questioning the premise that Sango is tragically flawed and suicidal.[3] What appears consistently in these tales is that upon his death he ascended to the sky and proclaimed his continuing power in the form of thunder and lightning, the incendiary force with which he is still identified.

Ogun, on the other hand, was a hunter who proved inept in the projects of government and marriage—not only slaying his own subjects but losing or driving away his wives. Indeed, various tales recall that Sango seduced Ogun's wives Ọya and Ọṣun, persuading one or the other to leave him. Rather than being an administrator, Ogun is a path maker. His purview extends not only to hunting but to all iron-related endeavors, such as warfare and road building. In Oyo territory, his contemporary priests are hunters and blacksmiths. Drivers as well sacrifice to him. Historically and mythically, he is far more closely associated with warriors and itinerant entrepreneurs than with kings. In the nineteenth century, his foremost clients were the plebeian military commanders who displaced kings in the seat of power. The Ife-centered Ifa oracle, as we have seen, codifies this contrast explicitly as a contest between men's power and women's. However, the rites and vocabulary of Oyo-based religions present the contrast in terms more specific and complex.

Unlike Sango-worship, Ogun-worship is expressly divorced from spirit possession (òrìṣà gígùn), which is associated chiefly with women.[4] Although possession by Ogun is reported outside the Oyo-Yoruba region, I have heard of but one uncertain exception to the overwhelming rule that Ogun in Oyo North does not possess people.[5] Suggestively, Abraham (1962:456) reports that only men worship Ogun. His overstatement contains the kernel of truth that women are not common, much less paradigmatic, among his priests. The exclusion of women is a stated ideal and a former reality in some towns (e.g., Òǹdó; see Akinrinṣọla 1965:90). In Ìrè, the women at the festival generally remain in separate groups, and while making offerings they may not face the god (Ibigbami 1978:53, 56).

The ranking god of the military empires—Ibadan and the

Èkìtìparapò Alliance—ritualized and ritualizes not women's singular role in the service of gods and kings but the divinity of men in groups. Oyo-Yoruba priesthoods of Ogun are exclusively male. Hence, the logic of complementary gender opposition that, as we shall see, dominates Sango iconography is absent from shrines of Ogun and his priests' accoutrements. Ogun priests wear the male-coded attire of their professions—the charm-laden shirts and trousers of hunters and blacksmiths. Whereas all Ogun priests are male, Sango priests are *mostly* female. The many who are male don women's coiffures, jewelry, cosmetics, and clothing.[6] The ritual metaphors of Sango-worship, in opposition to those enlisted in Ogun-worship in Oyo country, represent relations to the divine in sartorial images of femininity. Yet "femininity" only partially captures the character of the relationship thereby invoked.

The vocabulary and dress code of the possession religions—including the Sango cult—illuminate the structure of that relationship. Recent initiates of Yemoja, Òṣun, Obàtálá, and Ṣàngó—to name a few of the gods that possess people—are known specifically as "brides of the god" (*ìyàwó òrìṣà*). They wear women's blouses (*bùbá*), skirts (*ìró*), and slings of the sort that mothers use to carry their babies (*òjá*). The god is said to "mount" (*gùn*) those he possesses. The term "mount" is rather polysemic. It refers not only to possession but to the action of a rider mounting a horse (suggesting an extreme form of control) and an act of copulation almost animal-like in its violence or vulgarity. Indeed, the behavior of those mounted by Sango, the paradigmatic possessing god, is expected to be violent. The mounted priest may be called a "horse" (*eṣin*), recalling the importance of cavalry in Oyo's imperial expansion, a matter discussed in the following section. These parallel verbal associations suggest the suitability of women and cross-dressing men to a violent and sexually redolent subordination to the royal god. As one might expect, the "brideliness" of the initiand implies the character of the god, whom female devotees do praise as their "Husband (and Lord)" (*Oko*). We might expect this juxtaposition of divinity and husbandliness to affect the symbolic standing of worldly husbands as well. This ritual protocol manifests a logic strikingly different from that of the male cross-dressing found among the Ondo Yoruba, for example, where the female attire of the king (*oba*) on certain ritual occasions commemorates the founding of the kingdom by a woman (Olupona 1983;

Abiodun 1989). The cross-dressing of male possession priests in the Oyo-Yoruba context seems to represent, instead, the male adoption of a style of productive and reproductive servitude attributed typically to the fecund *wives* of mighty husbands.

The Age of Sango: History and the Cult of Wifely Authority

The gendered political structures of Sango- and Ogun-worship stand not simply in a static opposition but in a historical dialectic. They have rivaled and given form to each other across at least two hundred years of traceable history. I will demonstrate this dialectic primarily in the context of a single paradigmatic transition in Oyo-Yoruba history: the collapse of the royal empire and the rise of the warrior state in the nineteenth century. Oyo imperial methods and gender metaphors did not arise sui generis. The symbolic consonances and homologies that appear simultaneously in contemporary Sango-worship condense a history of gender-related political strategies, which can be partially reconstructed from oral and written records. Royal strategies developed in tandem with (1) geopolitical and commercial opportunities and (2) challenges from usurpers and nonroyal aspirants to state power.

Old Oyo was the northernmost of the Yoruba kingdoms (see fig. 1 in chapter 3). It intervened in the trade between the Sahel and the forest. Hence, Oyo was uniquely situated to make cavalry a major instrument of conquest. With the aid of Hausa veterinarians, Oyo maintained a cavalry that, in the forest kingdoms, would have died of trypanosomiasis. Oyo owes much of the success of its imperial expansion over the southern savannah to its unique access to horses from the north (Johnson 1921:161; Smith 1965:67–68). Oyo's cavalry conquered Ègbá, Ègbádò, Òwu, and Dahomey. The equestrian means of Oyo conquest would imprint itself permanently on the symbolism of political and religious delegation in the region.

Expansionism presented nonroyal military chiefs with the means to enhance their own power over the king. Only a highly extended and efficient palace organization could assure continued royal control. As blood kinsmen, other royals might have been loyal staffers in the palace administration. However, the consanguineal kin of royalty naturally posed a special threat to any reigning king: they were qualified to usurp the throne. An implicit concern throughout Oyo royal ritual and policy was the palace's mistrust of the royal family. In order to deter parricide, the àrèmo (crown prince) was, until King (Alaafin) Atiba's reform in 1858, killed upon the king's death (Johnson 1921:41–42; Abraham 1962:63). However, even Atiba kept the princes away from the palace (Babayemi 1979:151–52). Likewise, the king's royal kinsmen were expressly excluded from appointments to the highest military title—Basòrun—lest they take the crown through martial force.

Outsiders without any natal claim to the throne, the ayaba—wives of the reigning king and his predecessors—were entrusted somewhat more safely with administrative functions and prerogatives. They served as the heads of empire-wide priesthoods, as royal advisers, as intermediaries between the king and subject chiefs, and provincial representatives of the palace. Some of the ayaba were "wives" of the apotheosized king Sango as well (Alaafin Adeyemi III, personal communication, 17 October 1988; see also Morton-Williams 1964a:255). Other wifelike palace delegates, known as ilàrí, served as diplomatic observers, toll collectors, messengers, cavaliers, royal guards, and priests (Biobaku 1952:40). Female ilari were regularly classified as "wives of the king" (ayaba). Oral histories from various sources report that male ilari cross-dressed and declared themselves "wives of the king" as well (Atanda 1979:203; Aderele 1982:163; Smith 1965:60). Hence, ritual manipulations of gender created a corps of male "wives" who were free to move around the country, at a time when many of the king's female wives were, in principle, secluded. It may have been this very principle that required the creation and proliferation of male "wives."

The Oyo historical record preserves scattered but numerous references to gender transformation in the context of political activity. The oral accounts recorded by Johnson date the convergence of key ritual concepts at the eve of Oyo's imperial expansion, during the kingship's residence in the city of Igboho—dated by Robert Smith (1965:74) in the latter half of the sixteenth and the beginning of the seventeenth centuries. Johnson's sources report that cavalry became important to the Oyo army during this period. It was also during this period that castration became a requirement for the highest palace officials—the iwèfà (Johnson 1921:163). This procedure reflects far more than concern over the paternity of royal children, for the functions of some iwefa were primarily outside the palace, and certain high-ranking ritual officials had only one testicle removed (Lander and Lander 1832, 1:129; Johnson 1921:30). Symbolic concerns about the *wifeliness* of royal auxiliaries in relation to the palace account far more comprehensively for these practices.

The Alaafin, or Oyo king, credited with developing Oyo's formidable cavalry was Qrọ̄mpọtọ (ca. 1560) (Smith 1965:67–68; Johnson 1921:161), whose transformation from female to male (discussed in chapter 3) has become a key point of reference in the royal history of Igboho. The increasing importance of horsemanship in this period recommends the Igboho period as a precursor to Oyo's imperial expansion and a time when the subsequently successful political arrangements of the kingdom were first forged. These politically charged instances of horsemanship and gender transformation must be taken as ancestral to the polysemic ritual image of "mounting" (*gígùn*) in modern Sango-worship—a view confirmed by the direct involvement of Sango priests in the pre-nineteenth-century system of political and religious delegation.

Although wives were unable to usurp the throne, they presented a distinctive threat. An extensive Yoruba lore questions their trustworthiness and understands their loyalties to be inevitably divided. They favor their own children over others in the polygynous household and, according to that lore, undermine their husbands' material interests in favor of their own.[7] The palace went to considerable lengths to redress the structural conflicts of interest between the king and the palace wives. For example, royal wives who were potentially too powerful might be killed. According to Johnson (1921:63), the king's very own mother (a wife of the royal patrilineage) was put to death on the grounds that the monarch must be supreme in the land and owe obedience to no one. One suspects that a queen mother would have compromised his expected obedience to the interests of the royal lineage itself.[8]

The *ilari* palace deputies were prepared by Sango cult officials (*mogba*), much after the manner of possession priests and priestesses (*elegun*), whose defining characteristic is the periodic displacement of their personal will. Like male possession priests, many male *ilari* were transvestites. So closely were they identified with the king's consciousness and will that they bore as names various attributes, prayers, intentions, and potential directives of the Alaafin. For example:

> Ìlúsìnmí ("The-country-worships-me"),
> Báṁwówó ("Bring-me-money"),
> Ọbakòṣetán ("The-King-is-not-ready"),
> Mádáríkàn ("Do-not-oppose-him"),
> Kòsíjà ("There-is-no-fight"),
> Káfilégbọn-in ("No-compromise"),
> Mákọhùn ("Do-not-refuse")
>> (Johnson 1921:60–63; Oroge 1971:64; Babayemi
>> 1979:139; Abraham 1962:19)

Each king who comes to the throne renames all the *ilari* according to his preferences (Abraham 1962:20). In order to invest them with the royal will, the senior palace priestess of Sango—the *Ìyá Kéré*—initiated *ilari* in her palace apartment. Their heads were shaved, incised, and planted with powerful substances (Johnson 1921:63, 74). The *ilari* manifested multiple signs of their investment in the ancient political hierarchy of "mounting" (*gigun*). The first is precisely that they were prepared by the same personnel who initiated Sango possession priests. Second, male *ilari* regularly *cross-dressed* and female *ilari* were classified as *royal wives*. Third, many *ilari* exercised their duties on *horseback*.

Yet, certain aspects of their late eighteenth-century role seem clearly innovative. In the last quarter of the eighteenth century, writes Babayemi (1979:62), "[King] Abiodun altered the nature of the *ilari*; they were converted from religious representatives, possessing indirect religious authority, into political and economic officers possessing direct authority over the politics of the provinces." It is difficult, in my opinion, to separate the "religious" functions of the palace personnel neatly from their "political and economic" ones, particularly prior to British colonization, but this contemporary Western analytic distinction has caused some researchers, like Atanda, to overlook sacred dimensions of Oyo royalism under Indirect Rule as well, a point to which we will return in the next chapter. Nonetheless, the late eighteenth-century change that Babayemi describes merits close attention.

Partly owing to the economic and military changes wrought by the transatlantic trade, the eighteenth century saw the steady aggrandizement of nonroyal political institutions and the decline of royal control over the empire. Numerous kings reigned under the darkening eclipse of nonroyal chiefs' authority. That eclipse culminated in the long reign of the *Basorun*, or Prime Minister, Gáà, who had derived his early power from control over Oyo's trade corridor to the Atlantic ports (Babayemi 1979:57). Beginning around 1754, the Prime Minister installed and deposed successive Alaafin at his personal pleasure. Under the pretense of defending Alaafin's honor, Gaa brutally suppressed provincial rulers and allowed his own sons to rule arbitrarily all over the empire (ibid.: 54–57; Johnson 1921:178–86).

The eclipse of royal power in the metropolis did not compromise Oyo imperial authority in the provinces. Provincial rulers came to experience the most direct forms of imperial domination ever instituted. Although Prime Minister Gaa made this political centralism possible, the palace finally found in Abiodun a *king* who could take direct advantage of it. Abiodun ordered the assassination of Gaa and the provincial partisans through whom he had in effect ruled, replacing the latter with the *ilari* messengers. With his expanded corps of "wives"— *ayaba* (royal wives), *elegun* (possession priests), *iwefa* (eunuchs), and *ilari* (messengers)—Abiodun surpassed all of his forefathers in unifying a sprawling empire under direct royal control.

We have no way of knowing precisely when the *ilari* came to bear names identifying them so directly with the king's personal will, but it seems that Abiodun established the exemplary reign of the Age of Sango by submitting the ideology and technology of "mounting" to his *personal* interests. On the one hand, the *ayaba* (royal wives), the possession priests, and the cavalry represented various collective institutions, which either regulated or opposed the king's personal prerogatives. The *ayaba* collectively represented royal husbands—living, dead, and divinized—as did the priests of Sango and of other possessing gods. Horses seem to have enhanced the power of the king and the military chiefs alike. By contrast, the conditions of Abiodun's innovation, which redressed a progressive takeover of the state by military chiefs, and the very names of the *ilari* recommend these messengers as pillars of an unprecedented centralization of authority in the king himself. Rather than embodying the power and will of possessing gods, the *ilari* seem to have embodied, as if through "mounting," the will of the living king.[9] In chapter 5, we will explore the precedents of this royal political

assertion in both Oyo-Yoruba conceptions of descent and the possession religions.

Hence, the Age of Sango is not a period of unmitigated supremacy
for the Oyo monarchy. Instead, it is a period of recurrent challenges—
from royal kinsmen and plebeian chiefs—answered with increasing
degrees of success through royal ritual strategies resonating with the
signs and deeds of horsemanship, marriage, and gender transformation. Most consistently, the palace expanded the symbolic potentials of
marriage and harnessed them in its service, bolstering these with various other socially and historically salient images of conquest, domination, penetration, loyalty, and delegation. After Abiodun's unprecedented success at projecting the gendered hierarchy of "mounting," a
century would pass before another Oyo king surpassed his degree of
autocracy. And the *ilari* would be right there to demonstrate it.

The extant iconography of the Sango cult reflects various conceptual dimensions of pre-nineteenth-century Oyo political practice,
whose material details, as we shall see in chapter 2, are often found in
the interstices of nonindigenous narrative and explanatory frame-
works. In particular, the social and symbolic role of women in contemporary Sango-worship enlightens us to the historical character—
including the limits—of women's and wives' participation in Oyo royal
administration.

The Age of Ogun: History and the Cult of Male Solidarity

The circumstances of the Oyo's fall, around 1830, fatally confirmed the
virtue of precautions against usurpation by royal kinsmen. Following
King Abiodun's late eighteenth-century reign, Oyo chiefly councils had
repeatedly appointed weak kings in an effort to preserve their own
authority. The last king to reign in Old Oyo was Aọlẹ, who was coerced
into assigning the highest military office—ordinarily forbidden to royals—to his kinsman Àfọ̀njá. Greedy for power, the latter colluded with
Fulani jihadists in his own efforts to secure the throne. The result was
the destruction of the old capital. Before taking the poison that would
end his reign, King Aole immortalized in Yoruba literature a sacred
image that had accompanied the symbolism of wifeliness, horsemanship, and gender transformation in the Oyo-Yoruba possession reli-

gions and would follow them in their transatlantic diffusion—pots and calabashes:

> He stepped into the palace quadrangle with face stern and resolute, carrying in his hands an earthenware dish and three arrows. He shot one to the North, one to the South, and one to the West uttering those ever-memorable imprecations, "My curse be on ye for your disloyalty and disobedience, so let your children disobey you. If you send them on an errand, let them never return to bring you word again. To all the points I shot my arrows will ye be carried as slaves. My curse will carry you to the sea and beyond the seas, slaves will rule over you, and you their masters will become slaves."
>
> With this he raised and dashed the earthenware dish on the ground smashing it into pieces, saying "Igba la isọa ki isọ awo, bẹhẹni ki ọrọ mi o ṣe to! to!" (a broken calabash can be mended but not a broken dish; so let my words be—irrevocable!). (Johnson 1921:192)

By the 1840s, former imperial subjects had fled southward in large numbers, and slave traders had captured tens of thousands of refugees, many of whom reached Cuba and Brazil (Curtin et al. 1978:243–44; Morton-Williams 1967:42–43; Johnson 1921:188–90; Atanda 1979:37).

The flight from Old Oyo prompted the founding of three new political centers in lieu of the once-mighty and singular imperial capital. The headquarters of Oyo's leading generals, nonroyals themselves—at Ibadan and Ìjàyè—immediately proved mightier than the new royal headquarters at Àgọ́ D'Ọ́yọ̀ọ́, or New Oyo. The rivalry between the two military centers ended in Ijaye's defeat. Under the command of the Oyo-Yoruba general Oluyọle, Ibadan became an expansionist center in its own right, relying little on the sanction of New Oyo. Any of the dozen-odd multiethnic armies confederated at Ibadan was stronger than Alaafin's. Ibadan's southward expansion kept its armies fully occupied, forestalling any immediate threat to New Oyo and its remaining loyalist domains—Egbado and the upper reaches of the River Ògùn, known as Oyo North. Yet Ibadan became the vortex of changes in regional political ideology and practice sufficient to merit description as a "revolution" (Akintoye 1971; see also Falọla 1984). The conduct of this revolution found precedents in preexisting tensions within the Oyo political order, and it found prior mythic and ritual representations there as well.

What I have denominated the Age of Ogun was a period of vast human mobility, warfare, and de-emphasis on marital and kinship metaphors in the constitution of the state.[10] Generals and armies ruled in the place of kings and their "wives." The Age of Ogun commences with the failure of the Oyo state apparatus to unify against Fulani jihadists, followed by the overshadowing of royalty by the nonroyal military and commercial elites. Clearly, military force and trade had always been important features of the Oyo polity. Nonetheless, the personnel, the economic means, and the foci of these dimensions of statecraft had shifted. Whereas the Oyo kingdom had grown up substantially around a trans-Saharan trade, in which the royal state monopolized key trade items such as horses, the transatlantic trade in slaves, guns, and European iron had progressively changed the nature of warfare and become the sine qua non of statecraft in the region. Particularly in the nineteenth century, this southern trade not only marginalized the Oyo palace, which was based farther north than virtually any of its former domains.[11] Over a much longer period, that trade had introduced vast quantities of cowries, in a way that greatly facilitated the monetization and professionalization of commerce (Belasco 1980; Hogendorn and Johnson 1986; Falola 1984:106–7). By the mid-nineteenth century, entrepreneurial warriors and traders had completely taken over the state and its defensive responsibilities. The armies of Ibadan were all that stood between Oyo and the predacious armies of Dahomey and of Fulani jihadists from Ìlọrin.

In the mid-nineteenth century, town after town was overrun by enemy troops and forced to regroup in huge new urban centers like Ibadan and Abẹ̀òkúta. In Ibadan, paradigmatically, the abandonment of royal capitals and ancestral towns coincided with the abandonment of an old order of politics, religion, and gender relations. Private traders—many of them women—and military commanders each established their private fiefdoms without the authorization or supervision of royal elites. Ibadan recognized Alaafin as its sovereign only in the most perfunctory way. Personal leadership (rather than birth) and the services of war captives (rather than of wives and "mounted" men) determined the extent of one's authority. In this age of endemic warfare, mobility, and nonethnic, non-kin-based, non-marriage-based authority, the god Ogun reigned supreme.[12]

Ogun is the god of iron, one of the major imports of the transatlantic trade. He is closely associated with guns, warfare, and mobility, all of which were central features of life in this region during the nineteenth century. In the Oyo territories best shielded from the nineteenth-century warfare, including Oyo North, Ogun is now associated primarily with hunters. Neither in the number of shrines nor in the number of worshipers is Ogun well represented there. The area known as Oyo North includes Igboho and other towns that never came under the rule of any polity rivaling the Oyo kingdom—not Dahomey, not the Fulani Emirate of Ilorin, and not Ibadan. By contrast, in the Ibadan sphere of influence, where the generals ruled in the nineteenth century, Ogun altars featured prominently at the headquarters of the mighty. These altars stood in the smithies and at the center of the war camp—which became, in turn, the center of many a populous new town. Akintoye writes:

> Perhaps one of the most important and most frequented spots in the camp was the shrine of Ogun, the god of war and iron. This was a wooded grove right in the center of the camp where sacrifices were frequently offered. . . . (The Ogun grove can still be seen near the walls of Ogedemgbe's [an important general's] hut. . . .)
>
> A short distance from the Ogun shrine and situated amidst rocks and boulders on a small promontory was the hut occupied by the Commander-in-Chief. (1971:135)[13]

By 1886, the camps of the new military empires boasted populations of up to sixty thousand people—a large proportion of them the wives, children, and attendants of the fighting men. Yet, from the 1850s until the British colonization, slavery was the characteristic mode of labor and warfare the characteristic mode of its recruitment in Ibadan (Falola 1984:63–64). The rise of Ibadan represented a major reorientation of the Oyo-Yoruba sociopolitical order, not without the guidance of its own religious forms and concomitant changes in the relations of gender to political power. Ibadan's military techniques and government hierarchy were imitated throughout what would become Yorubaland (Akintoye 1971:44–45).

The Ogun of the blacksmiths and of the war boys reigned during the nineteenth century. The horses that had become emblematic of Sango and the Oyo royal empire—as well as the *ilari* (ritually prepared messengers) and the *elegun* ("mounts" of Sango)—showed decreasing utility in the project of empire. Ibadan carried its war of conquest into tsetse-ridden zones where horses quickly fell ill (Smith 1988:101). So useless was cavalry in Ibadan's expansionist policy that horses roamed free in that city and served more often as food and sources of talismans than as military transport (Johnson 1921:288). Ibadan's own counter-parts to the *ilari* were the nontransvestite *ajele*. They were warriors rather than priestly initiates (Awe 1964:54). They were often killed for the despotic behavior of which Oyo's palace messengers had probably been equally guilty. Ibadan presided over the lapse of the credibly inte-grated administrative and symbolic system that Oyo had cultivated into a national politico-religious norm.

Ogun's Women

Ogun is not only a fixture but a metaphor of Ibadan's reign. Myth-ically, Ogun inevitably abandons the political and judicial duties of government, for he is less an administrator than a pathfinder, road maker, and warrior. Just as myths seldom depict Sango on the battle-field, the Ogun of myth seldom stays long on the throne or at the hearth. When, occasionally, marriage appears in Ogun mythology, it is failed marriage:

Yemanja [Yemoja] was a woman of great beauty. But she had only one breast. Because of this, she did not want to marry, because she feared that her husband might ridicule her and expose her secret to the world.

One day she was walking home sadly from the market and she said to herself: "How sad it is to be lonely; to return to a childless house; to have no husband to cook for."

Ogun overheard what she said, because he was walking along the same road. He felt a strong desire to marry her and he seized her and said: "Do not be afraid. I know I look fierce and all the world fears me. But I will do you no harm. I will look after you and protect you; but here is one thing you must promise me: you must never make fun of my bloodshot eyes."

Yemanja agreed to marry him. She confessed that she had only one breast and she said: "You must promise me one thing, never touch my breast."

For a long time they kept each other's promise. Yemanja bore many chil-dren to Ogun.

One day Ogun wanted to please Yemanja and he went into the kitchen to cook soup for her. But being unused to a woman's work, he dropped *the pot*, broke it and he spilled the food all over the floor. Yemanja, who had been resting, woke up at the noise. She rushed into the kitchen; and as she did not realize how the accident happened she cried angrily: "What are you doing in my kitchen! You with your blood shot eyes!"

Ogun could not control himself, when he heard this. He struck her and she fell to the ground. But he felt sorry for her and he knelt beside her and stroked her breast.

At this Yemanja began to tremble. She turned into water and slipped through his fingers.

Ogun was sad to lose his wife. But then he said to himself: "Gentleness is not for me!" And he left his house to go out and fight many more wars, as he used to do. (U. Beier 1980:45–46—emphasis mine)

Ogun's relations with wives are clumsy. Ogun fails to recognize the complementary distinctness of the wifely role. Indeed, when he tries to fill that role, he destroys the primary icon of both the kitchen and the altar of gods that "mount"—the pot. On the other hand, numerous myths associate Sango with servile and loyal wives, suggesting both the inseparability of marital metaphors from Sango's relation to his worshipers and the indispensability of wives in Oyo royal strategies. Even when Sango's subjects reject him, his wife Oya accompanies him into exile. Idowu (1963:91) writes that Sango has "a help meet for him in his wife the goddess Oya . . . who is absolutely indispensable to her husband in every way. It is said that without Oya, there is nothing that Sango can accomplish." Corollary to Ogun's path breaking, on the other hand, is the escape and autonomy of women. The nineteenth-century Age of Ogun is indeed noted for the unprecedented rise of powerful and independent women.

Iyalode

Post-Oyo strategies of domination marginalized marital symbolism and made way for new female roles. It is partly in this light that we must view the rise of the Ìyálóde, the women-chiefs justly famous in discussions of "precolonial Yoruba society." Yet their prominence clearly does not span the entire precolonial period. The historian Bolanle Awe says that the power of the Iyalode originated in the nineteenth century and that it was "in defiance of what was customary and traditional among the Oyo-Yoruba" (1972:271–72; 1977:150). The most powerful women of the previous age had been the Oyo palace wives. In the nineteenth century, the famous Ọmọṣa and Ẹfunṣetan of Ibadan and Tinubu of Abeokuta rose to power as traders and war financiers in these cities created by imperial dislocation. The Iyalode represented themselves and other market women in collective action and on the councils of state. Their role in nineteenth-century Yoruba society coincides with then-current mythic templates of personal conduct and social order (or disorder, from the royalist perspective), which appear "untraditional" for the same reasons that the Age of Ogun in general appears so.

Reports of their unwifely and antireproductive conduct recommend for them a gender classification quite different from that of the royal "wives." The great female entrepreneurs of the nineteenth century were often childless—as were Tinubu and Efunsetan—and without what Awe describes as a "normal domestic life" (1972:271–72; see also Biobaku 1960:40). Freed from Sango-style metaphors of marriage as their chief political function and means to power, these women enriched and empowered themselves through the command of numerous slaves and the exploitation of the new forms of trade generated by nineteenth-century militarism. Tinubu, for example, acted as an intermediary for Brazilian slave dealers.

Over two thousand slaves worked the farms of Madam Efunsetan of Ibadan, while others served in her urban compound, which was one of the 104 large compounds in the city. An Egba by birth, she went to Ibadan sometime before 1860. Her trade and her farms flourished, such that she commanded her own large army (I. B. Akinyele, cited in Oroge 1971:181; Johnson 1921:393). Her character was not only unwifely and militaristic but legendarily antireproductive. She bore only one daughter, who died while delivering Efunsetan's grandchild. Thereafter, according to the roughly contemporaneous account by Johnson, Efunsetan became strangely cruel to her pregnant female slaves. Efunsetan saw that such cruel means were used to induce abortion that her pregnant slaves usually died. Her own life ended in 1874 by the hand of her adopted son and by order of Ibadan's leading general, who had become jealous of this Iyalode's wealth and influence (Johnson 1921:391–94).

Like the powerful men of their age, the Iyalode of Lagos, Ibadan, and Abeokuta were mobile, militarized, and more in control of than under control by royal institutions. They were authorities in their own right, up from humble parentage, and engaged in the competitive politics of nineteenth-century commercial and military leadership. Not only their gender but their fame distinguishes them sharply from the generations of anonymous palace men and women who exercised power as the "wives" of Alaafin and Sango. In their own names, the nineteenth-century entrepreneurs recruited servants and auxiliaries through adoption and enslavement. However, historical accounts of the Age of Ogun suggest that these women's leadership was tenuous and at odds with that of men, who more effectively commanded the instruments of war. The lapse of Oyo royal hegemony freed women from gender-specific role prescriptions in the political economy but also eliminated their reserved place at the heights of the state, as kings' "wives" and delegates.

Sango's Women in the Age of Ogun

What integrity remained in the Oyo king's jurisdiction during the Age of Ogun was still constituted primarily in idioms of marriage. Marriage continued to be deployed not only in the consolidation of the internal hierarchies of the palace but in projects of political representation and legitimization among loyalist plebeians:

> From the time of Atiba [founder of New Oyo, who reigned ca. 1838–51], chiefs particularly from the Upper Ogun towns [i.e., the Oyo-North towns of Ìgbòho, Ṣẹ̀pẹ̀tẹ̀rí, Ṣakí, Ìséyìn, Òkèihò, etc.] gave their daughters as wives to the Alaafin through the priestesses. In this way, such priestesses became the "patronesses" of such chiefs in the palace. (Babayemi 1982:6)

Conversely, several chiefly houses in Oyo North—those of the Iba of Kísí and the Ọ̀nà Oníbodè of Igboho, for instance—claim that their male founders married Oyo princesses, thereby legitimizing their local hereditary lines through marriage to female Oyo royals. The nineteenth century thus witnessed, in Oyo North, the growth of marriage practices integrating conquering and conquered aristocracies into a common political bloc, practices probably of considerable antiquity.

By the end of the Age of Sango, symbolically feminized men had long served the Oyo palace. Male *ilari* and eunuchs (*iwefa*) had been in charge of the king's private commerce and collected tribute and tolls on his behalf. The administrative duties of the royal wives (*ayaba*) had kept them largely within the palace. During the nineteenth-century Age of Ogun, the Oyo king needed to compete for access to supplies and revenues from the Atlantic coastal trade. He therefore discontinued the systematic seclusion of the female "wives" and made them his agents in the trade (Awe 1972:269–70). By the early nineteenth century, palace women had become prominent in long-distance commerce. Oroge (1971:205) maintains that these so-called royal wives (*ayaba*) were simply slaves given that marital title fictitiously. In either case, the preexisting royal pattern of defining the palace's delegates as "wives" was adapted to the circumstances of the nineteenth century, when royalty could no longer automatically claim privileged access to the most important foreign resources. Indeed, the entry of guns from the south dealt the ultimate blow to the military value of horses from the north.

European travelers in the first half of the nineteenth century reportedly encountered Alaafin's wives "every place trading for him" (Clapperton 1829:21). In 1830, the Lander brothers encountered "not less than a hundred" Oyo royal wives in "Jadoo," probably in the southern province of Egbado. They describe them thus:

> They have all passed the bloom of life, and arrived here lately with loads of trona and country cloth which they barter for salt and various articles of European manufacture, particularly beads; with these they return home, and expose them for sale in the market and afterwards the profits are taken to their husbands. (Lander and Lander 1832, 1:109–10)

That these wives were all postmenopausal may mean that the social status—and, as such, the gender—of postmenopausal wives was distinctive in the conduct of royal commerce, as it is in the service of the gods.[14] Twentieth-century studies of Yoruba women in commerce may cast doubt on the contention of Clapperton and the Lander brothers that the palace "wives" handed their profits over to their husband. What is evident, though, is that a large group of women traded under the aegis and authority of the king, that they were conceived by all to be either literal or metaphorical "wives" of the king, and that the palace derived material benefit from their activities. What also remains clear is that the role and membership of the corps of palace "wives" changed to suit the palace's new economic needs and diplomatic concerns during the nineteenth century. Nonetheless, that classificatory terminology and the practice of deploying "wives" as delegates continued to be applied by the palace and to be recognized by those who informed European travelers throughout the last century. Royal marriage in the Age of Ogun constituted not only a highly ramified local political order but a commercial network of major importance.

The Geography of Gender and Polity

On one level, the ages of Sango and Ogun are temporal. They are separated by the early nineteenth-century collapse of the Oyo royal empire around 1830. Yet they possess geopolitical correlates as well. They reproduce the contrast between Oyo and Ibadan, between the imperially driven Oyo-speaking origin of Sango-worship and the relatively small-scale, seldom-unified Ogun-worshiping polities of the east—in the Èkìtì and Òǹdó regions, for example. These general, named contrasts reflect a complex and ramified divergence among styles of administration and in the broader character of relations between gender and social order. These divergences are seldom absolute or unalloyed. For example, an Ogun shrine is found in the palace at New Oyo and is the site of annual rites (Wande Abimbola, personal communication, 12 October 1990). But no one would claim that it even nearly matches in importance New Oyo's royal Sango shrine. Likewise, male cross-dressing appears in the rites for Ogun in Ìrè-Èkìtì and Ondo (Akinrinsola 1965:87, 94; Ibigbami 1978:53). It is not clear, however, whether this cross-dressing is associated with possession, political delegation, or the conjunction of the two. Among the Oyo Yoruba, at least, neither possession, nor cross-dressing, nor royal political delegation is associated with Ogun priests. Hence, it is among the Oyo Yoruba that this mythic model of history and politics applies most instructively.

The utility of the Sango/Ogun model in understanding Oyo-Yoruba historical actors and the indigenous narrators of their action does not end with the advent of colonialism. Indeed, in the project of Indirect Rule, the British endeavored to resurrect as many of the ritual signs of Oyo sovereignty as were necessary to guarantee Alaafin's legitimacy as a "paramount chief," or king (oba). For the Oyo king and his subjects, these clearly included the highly public pomp and authority of the elegun (Sango possession priests), ilari (ritually prepared palace messengers), *ayaba* (royal wives), and *iwefa* (eunuchs). The transvestite male *ilari* still moved about the country displaying, through their harsh and arbitrary exactions, the Alaafin's omnipotence. Royal "wives," *ilari* messengers, and eunuchs were still dispatched as late as the 1950s to install subordinate rulers on Alaafin's behalf.[15] Where the ritual signs of Oyo royal legitimacy failed to impress Alaafin's subjects, the British often enforced his authority with military force. However, by allowing the reemergence and growth of Oyo's gender-bending system of political delegation through "wives," the British unwittingly reestablished both the most recognizable feature of pre-nineteenth-century Oyo administrative policy and the most provocative conceivable flash point for a generation increasingly accustomed to the political marginalization of women—a marginalization enhanced by the nineteenth-century rise of not only Ogun worship but Christianity and Islam. The armed British defense of what Atanda calls "the New Oyo Empire" would forestall open rebellion only until the era of independence.

Conclusion

A significant transformation occurred among the Oyo Yoruba during the early nineteenth century, when one hegemonic style of rule and its attendant gender conceptions displaced another. What I have described as the ages of Sango and Ogun are periods in which important changes in gender concepts gave form to and were given form by changes in the Oyo-Yoruba political economy. The sacred eponyms of these ages are ancient mythic models of *contrasting gender ideologies* as well as emblems of extant politico-religious groups. The Sango and Ogun priesthoods of the late twentieth century have inherited many words, symbols, rites, and myths from predecessors directly involved in rival precolonial projects of political rule. Hence, we have used modern sacred signs as sources of an interpretive hypothesis to integrate a range of apparently stray historiographic details whose gendered implications seem, at the end of this examination, quite central to two past political orders. The hermeneutical cues furnished by modern *orisa* religions help to illuminate not only diverse historical eras but the religious and political divergence between neighboring regions of Yorubaland.

Like even the most promising hypothesis, however, this one awaits detailed testing in a range of further cases, where the extent of its applicability and its limitations will be revealed. At its most daring, this hypothesis guides an effort to reconstruct past notions of gender and politics, based on the limited primary data available to students of the African past—including the nineteenth-century accounts by European and American travelers, European and African missionaries, and royal oral historians. At its least daring, this hypothesis guides an *icono-practical* interpretation of the gendered tensions shared among modern Oyo-Yoruba ritual, myth, and historical memory. There is strong evidence for both lines of reasoning. However, we will never possess sufficient documentation to produce a complete history of gender and politics among the Oyo Yoruba. What we cannot now doubt is that any political history or ethnography of this society must take seriously the notion of gender. Students of the Yoruba and of other African peoples are encouraged to question literal and objectivist accounts of "women's" role. This time-honored and homogenizing rubric in the anthropological and Africanist literatures certainly obscures the complex realities of Oyo-Yoruba politics, in which various groups not only differ over the conduct allowed women but, by embellishing and manipulating images of "wifeliness" in the design of political options for both men and women, undermine the emic salience of "women" as a category.

The worship of the possessing gods and of Ogun among the Oyo Yoruba reflect different prescriptions for social order, endorse different historical epochs as ideal models of contemporary politico-religious order, and identify different social spaces as the foci of contemporary life. In the late twentieth century, the possessing gods sit most prominently in the palaces of Oyo, Oyo North, and Egbado, sanctioning the authority of the highly respected hereditary chieftaincies and the centripetal order of patrilineal life. Despite its male-centered genealogical charter, the symbolic and material constitution of the patrilineage depends on its relation to wives. Ogun, on the other hand, is the lord of the highways and automobiles that draw traders and young people into the urban vortex, where money and armed force now define a non-hereditary order of authority.

When Oyo-Yoruba men and women retire or seek to legitimize their urban wealth, they leave the fearsome anomie and rapacious capitalism of the metropolis and return to the village—to the ideologically integrated sphere of kingship, patriliny, and "mounting." The inescapable reality of the Nigerian national political economy, however, is that the sons of Ogun rule and women do not. Nonetheless, the gravity of Sango, his mother, and his wives continues to radiate from the Oyo-Yoruba village. The ages of Sango and Ogun do not simply belong to different times and places; they represent rival gendered outcomes of problems and potentials continuously recognized—and even contemporaneously personified—in Oyo-Yoruba politics.

Chapter 2

The Ọyọ Renaissance

Eighteen-thirty was a watershed in the shift from royal supremacy to military republicanism in the Oyo-Yoruba state. It also marked the beginning of a new gendered constitution of authority. Of equal consequence was the year 1895, when the British conquered the Oyo capital and co-opted the kingdom into the colonial project, paving the way toward a resurrection of royal sovereignty throughout and beyond Oyo's eighteenth-century domains. Precisely because Oyo North had never significantly resisted the sovereignty of the Oyo kingdom, it became the flash point of armed resistance to the British-mandated social and legal reforms that threatened Oyo's gendered political hierarchies. As will become apparent, marriage had been not only a metaphoric source in the definition of hierarchy within the palace but a focus of the kingship's regulatory responsibilities in Oyo-Yoruba civil society. Social reforms legislated at the apex of the colonial state thus transformed the symbolic and regulatory functions of Oyo kingship.

It has become normal since Boserup (1970) to observe that colonialism undermined women's "traditional" status in African societies (see, e.g., Amadiume 1987; Étienne and Leacock 1980). For even longer, it has been assumed that colonialism undermined or destroyed "traditional" religions as well (see, e.g., Parrinder 1972). However, Oyo royalism and its possession religions owe their twentieth-century renaissance to their unintended consonance with British Indirect Rule. The consequences for women's rights are more ambiguous. The Oyo Yoruba were subjected to the tandem principles of British mercantilism and liberal conceptions of individual rights. In the process, common women were liberated from oppressive marital arrangements at the heart of the royalist order. At the same time, British-sponsored reforms undermined the foremost guarantee of *some* women's participation at the heights of the state.

Under British rule in the first half of the century, Alaafin (the Oyo king) was reputed to be able almost to "turn a man into a woman" or vice versa (Atanda 1970:227), a phrase intended to evoke the extraordinary extent of his political authority, but also recalling the ritual foundations of that authority. The Oyo dynasty became, somewhat arbitrarily, the foremost institution of Yoruba government under British rule. Although the choice of Oyo royalty was less historically necessary than British political officers conceived it to be, its high status was credible to subjects in Oyo North, at least partly because the mythic and ritual formulas sanctioning that status had survived the military upheavals of the Age of Ogun. However, the force of those ritual formulas in the twentieth century must be understood in light of the precise context of Oyo's restoration to political sovereignty—British Indirect Rule.

British Penetration and the Restoration of Oyo

The Oyo Empire of the late eighteenth century had embraced territories from the River Niger in the north to the Atlantic in the south, from Ọ̀fà in the east to Popo in the west. In the 1830s under Alaafin Atiba, Oyo concluded a pact with its erstwhile generals in Ibadan and Ijaye, renouncing Oyo's hold on all but the Oyo North region, which includes Igboho and Egbado, which voluntarily remained loyal to Oyo. By 1881, Alaafin lacked the military might to protect even Oyo North from Dahomean predations (Atanda 1979:43–46).

Fearful of both Ibadan and Dahomean conquest, Oyo seemed to encourage British intervention, at first to mediate a truce in the ongoing wars. Then, in treaty after treaty, Oyo found itself engulfed in the sly progress of British overlordship. Since the bombardment and occupation of the slave port of Lagos in 1881, the British had remained content with the profits of trade between its Lagos Colony and the politically independent "hinterland." However, Lagos trade interests worried that the inland wars endangered their profits, while inland missionaries worried about the safety of their own project. Both Ibadan and the rival Ekitiparapo Alliance, weary of war, repeatedly called in the British as the only party strong enough to enforce peace accords. By

1894 the British had moved from enforcing voluntary treaties to "pacifying" the "Lagos hinterland." By 1898, all the areas that would later become Oyo Province were firmly under British control, and all of the Yoruba kingdoms became part of the "Protectorate of Southern Nigeria" in 1906 (Atanda 1979:84; Soumonni 1986:56).

The first decade or so of British rule was essentially a military project. The district commissioners were mostly young military officers, whose administrative techniques were often martial (Asiwaju 1976:95). In the early years, the administration of Oyo and Ibadan fittingly recognized Ibadan's nineteenth-century might. Based on the Anglo-Ibadan Agreement of 1893, Ibadan administered most towns in the area under British military supervision. Hence, the Resident and Travelling Commissioner, Captain R. L. Bower, posted in 1893, had his headquarters in the city of Ibadan. None of the "hinterland" polities had willingly invited British rule; so the extent of British authority was under test.[1]

In 1895, Captain Bower assumed unofficially the virtue and necessity of enforcing certain "traditional" or rightful relations among Yoruba town sovereigns, or kings (oba), and subordinate chiefs (ìjoyè).[2] For example, the town of Okeiho had come into existence when refugee chiefs and their followers abandoned their hometowns and resettled around the naturally defended town of Ijo in the nineteenth century. There they initially accepted the sovereignty of Ijo's ruler, the Onjo, over the entirety of what became the inclusive town of Okeiho. The Onjo had been by far the strongest among the chiefs. But after the menace of Fulani and Dahomean invasion ended, the other chiefs were no longer prepared to accept the Onjo's authority, and so they deposed an Onjo who would not do their bidding. Alaafin carried the moral authority to send his *ilari* messenger to restore that Onjo, quite in accord with Captain Bower's preference. However, Alaafin had no means to prevent the refugee chiefs from reversing his choice. Bower surmised, probably mistakenly, that Alaafin's *ilari* himself had underhandedly effected the dethroning of the Onjo. So Bower sought a pretext to show Alaafin his mettle (Atanda 1979:56ff.).

The practice of castrating those who committed adultery with chiefs' wives was, if my overall argument is correct, a logical punishment for a grave assault on a government institution based quite heavily on the metaphor of the king's control over his wives. Atanda says the act was regarded as "high treason." Secondarily, such castration served as a means of recruitment to the Alaafin's personal staff, which was, as we have seen, symbolically feminized by surgery and other ritual means.

A man charged with cuckolding the Aséyìn, king of the Oyo North town of Ìséyìn, had been sent to Alaafin for castration. The procedure would have violated no treaty signed by the Alaafin with the British, but Captain Bower questioned the Oyo king's right to execute the punishment and demanded custody of both the alleged adulterer and the *ilari* who had intervened in the Okeiho succession dispute. In defiance, Alaafin killed the adulterer, whom he had apparently already castrated, and refused to hand over so important a palace official as an *ilari*. Alaafin's chiefs discouraged conciliation with Bower. The captain responded by leading a contingent of sixty soldiers into Oyo, whereupon a crowd of Oyo citizens armed with guns and swords gathered to protect the palace. Bower had his troops fire on the crowd of civilians and then sent to Ibadan for more arms. He demanded:

1. That the two eunuchs who strangled the mutilated man [Bakare] be handed over to the Commissioner [Bower].
2. That one Kufu [Kudefu] who had been doing outrageous things at Okeiho be handed over to the Commissioner.
3. That all arms and ammunition be surrendered to the Commissioner.
4. That the Alafin prostrate [himself] before the Commissioner and apologize for the insult to the British Government.
5. That a Commissioner be allowed to live at Oyo henceforward and for ever. (quoted in Atanda 1979:68)

Unsatisfied with the reply of Alaafin and his chiefs, Bower bombarded the Oyo capital. On 12 November 1895, the day of the bombardment, Alaafin sent Bower "ducks with their wing feathers cut, in token of submission" (quoted in Atanda 1979:72).[3]

From then on, Oyo cooperated in the project of Indirect Rule. The spirit of that cooperation lives on in the following song:

In Oyo we don't fight
We are to enjoy life and exercise royal authority.[4]

The progress of Indirect Rule would render British military violence largely unnecessary and seal the coffin of Ibadan's plebeian military revolution. Five years after the Anglo-Ibadan Agreement of 1893, the

Governor of Lagos, Henry E. McCallum, and the Resident at Ibadan, F. C. Fuller, orchestrated the expansion of the Oyo kingdom's domain. In the half decade after Bower's bombardment, Alaafin Adéyẹmí I proved servile and loyal to British interests, whereas the Ibadan chiefs proved brashly assertive. Moreover, the British—through Crowther, Johnson, and a century of Anglophile Yoruba missionaries and British explorers—had rediscovered Oyo's ancient and noble past. Undoubtedly, the royalist tenor of the Protectorate administration owed much to Queen Victoria's renown in this age of British empire and to the gratitude of these sons of commoners, who had found a place of honor in the colonies. One senses that these factors lent some zeal to the restoration of this African royalty. At this juncture of Yoruba and British government, the upstart and nonhereditary authority of the uncrowned *Bálè*, or Town Chief, of Ibadan would not do. Scare quotes did not diminish Fuller's enthusiasm over the Oyo monarchy and monarch, whom he described as "the most 'royal' native [he had] seen in Yorubaland" (Atanda 1979:101).

Having witnessed the effectiveness of rule through hereditary chiefs in the Lagos Protectorate, Governor MacGregor favored the restoration of crowned kings to power elsewhere in Nigeria and regretted that previous colonial practice had weakened their power. Hence, according to the Native Councils Ordinance of 1901, councils of chiefs were established in each District under the presidency of the "person who is recognized by the Governor as the principal ruling chief of the District or Province" (Asiwaju 1976:99). The area directly under Alaafin's command, Oyo *District*, had already been expanded by Governor McCallum in 1898. Of the larger *Province* of Oyo, which included Ọ̀yọ́, Ifẹ̀-Iléṣà, and Ìbàdàn Districts, Alaafin was the choice of the later Governor MacGregor and the Resident at Oyo, Captain W. A. Ross, as the paramount chief and sole "native authority."

The colonial government devoted great energy to building and reconstructing the popular legitimacy and authority of natural rulers, even when they recognized the resentment the policy inspired among the Ibadan war chiefs and among literate citizens of the Province.[5] The British believed that Alaafin "possessed the 'traditional' *locus standi* which the British regarded as *sine qua non* for practicing 'ideal' Indirect Rule" (Atanda 1970:216). Governor MacGregor first enunciated an official government policy in 1903 to the effect that "the authority of the Alaafin should extend beyond its present limits, over districts formerly ruled by him and his predecessors" (Atanda 1979:104).

Thereafter, Oyo replaced Ibadan as the seat of the Resident, making it in effect the seat of provincial government. MacGregor's policy was executed maximally in Oyo and Ibadan divisions by Captain Ross, who served as Oyo's Resident from 1906 to 1931 and showed a particular interest in Oyo culture. His advocacy of Oyo paramountcy seems strongly connected to his personal friendship with the crown prince, Ladugbolu, who ascended the throne in 1911.

Until the official enactment of Lugard's policy in 1914, "native authorities" were generally regarded as keepers of the peace and mouthpieces of the British administration, transmitting orders from the Commissioner to their subordinate chiefs and organizing labor for public works (Asiwaju 1976:96–97). However, as early as 1901, MacGregor raised the political stature of Alaafin by increasing his jurisdiction over criminal cases (Atanda 1970:216). Indeed, until as late as 1931, Alaafin's authority over boundary disputes, domestic and criminal cases, and the succession of all chiefs and kings extended unchallenged over the territories of his ancestors. Oyo replaced Ibadan as the seat of the Resident of Oyo Province, affirming definitively its status as the provincial capital. So piously did Ross protect the interests of Alaafin that he is still remembered as *ajẹ̀lẹ̀ Aláàfin*—one of a class of royal messengers made up almost entirely of *ilari*. Court etiquette had hitherto so restricted others' access to Alaafin that Ross's frequent and intimate communication with the king could be understood in no other terms. Credited with engineering his own apparently autocratic powers, Alaafin Ladugbolu is praised as *Ọba tí pe èbó [òyìnbó] ránṣẹ́*—"The King who sends the white man on errands" (ibid.:109, 224).

Ritual Reform and Cooperation in the Oyo Renaissance

The early phase of Indirect Rule greatly amended Oyo's nineteenth-century authority. In keeping with Lugardian policy, the indigenous instruments of administration and delegation remained in force in important ways. However, certain features of Oyo politico-religious management proved incompatible with or abhorrent to British politico-religious norms. As in the early twentieth century, the *ilari* messengers again carried the king's authority far and wide:

> The activities of these agents of the Alafin's power took various forms. There were those messengers who claimed to be carrying the goodwill of the Alafin to various parts of his domain, notably in Oyo and Ibadan Divisions. They were known, in local parlance, as *Baba ni nki ọ* (Father, that is the Alafin, asked me to greet you). Wherever they carried such "message" of goodwill, they expected to be lavishly entertained both with food and, sometimes, [with] money. Refusal by the people to entertain these messengers in this way was counted as lack of respect for, and loyalty to, the Alafin. (Atanda 1979:203)

Ross provided Alaafin with the force to punish any disloyal chief. The conduct of the *ilari* messengers and the *ayaba* (royal wives) was frequently remarked upon. The character of their proverbial mischief was not arbitrary. The enduring wifely signs of their authority are revealing. In his critical retrospective on colonial Oyo, Atanda records an Oyo-North informant's recollection:

> One [male *ilari*] nicknamed Majengbasan (Don't let me [leave] empty-handed) had the reputation of *dressing up as an ayaba* (queen, that is Alafin's [the king of Oyo's] wife). He would then accuse any man in the town, where he and his followers visited, of either "proposing" to, or assaulting, "her"! His followers would then arrest the unfortunate victim and charge him for assaulting an ayaba. Only a handsome sum, sometimes up to £5, would save the victim from being taken to Oyo. (ibid.:203—emphasis mine)

As in the eighteenth century, Oyo royalism in the twentieth asserted its legitimacy by magnifying the ideological structure of ordinary husband-wife relations and made the king's literal and metaphorical "wives" into the public icons and agents of their "husband"'s authority.

Thus, a complex of explicitly gendered signs shaped both consent and resistance to Indirect Rule. Indeed, the health and security of the kingdom are believed to depend on equally gendered signs of the king's own subordination to superior forces. Oyo kings submitted and submit to the same head preparation as the "brides," or possession priests, of Sango (Adeyemi III, Alaafin of Oyo, personal communication, 17 October 1988). Conversely, the nickname given by a plebeian audience to this royal agent subversively reinterprets—or, to apply Gates's (1988) vernacular usage, "signifies on"—the royal directives, threats, and proposals of intention that normally make up the names of the *ilari* messengers. This satirical oral history, like the scholarly argument in which Atanda situates it, is a gender- and religion-coded assault on royal authority itself.

Complaints notwithstanding, MacGregor understood that to check the *ilari* system would "diminish the Alaafin's authority which it is the aim and desire of the Government to uphold and strengthen" (Atanda 1979:106). In response to Alaafin's complaint that a District Commissioner had interfered with his messengers in several towns, MacGregor reprimanded the Commissioner and asked that Alaafin be allowed sole authority in regulating the conduct of the *ilari*. The persistence of complaints about them from every quarter for several more decades suggests that neither MacGregor nor the Alaafin seriously tried to check their excesses.

For Atanda, over three decades of alliance between British and Oyo royal forces consolidated a "New Oyo Empire." However, in 1931, when Resident Ross left Nigeria, the new Governor, Sir Donald Cameron, took office with a new vision of Indirect Rule—that if the subjects of the regime were "not prepared to accept the order of the so-called authority, chief or otherwise, unless we [the British political officers] compel them to do so, then, of course, the administration is not indirect and the Native Authority set up on such a basis is a sham and a snare" (quoted in Atanda 1970:251).

Ross's successor as Resident, Ward-Price, complained that the "system of Government at Oyo today is highly centralized, with the Alaafin almost an absolute ruler." As late as 1934, Ward-Price wrote of widespread fear of the Alaafin among chiefs and commoners, "owing to the way in which his large retinue of servants and his wives exercise authority in his name" (ibid.:253, 254). Government hostility, along with Ibadan's ardent resistance to Oyo overrule and general complaints about the "native authorities" among educated and well-traveled Nigerians, gnawed away at Alaafin's authority, until Ward-Price demoted Oyo by moving his headquarters to Ibadan in 1934. Ibadan was not yet allowed to stop paying a sizable part of Alaafin's salary but was otherwise liberated from his overrule (Atanda 1979:273–74, 281). Nevertheless, Alaafin kept the loyalty of Oyo District, which had become a Division, and continued to wield considerable authority there through his *ilari* until around 1950, when constitutional changes anticipating decolonization began to transfer power to the new, bourgeois politicians—class descendants of the nonroyal elites whose rise the Pax Britannica had checked at the end of the Age of Ogun (Atanda 1970:225–27; 1979:291ff.).

For half a century the Oyo royal dynasty experienced unprecedented authority over subordinate chiefs and over a remarkably consolidated territory, owing not simply to the restoration of supposedly "traditional" arrangements but to a renegotiation of the sources of royal power and the deployment of ancient ritual systems in its exercise. *Ilari* (messengers) and *ayaba* (royal wives) remained important ritual guardians and the principal repositories of royal power. This deployment of power became possible because of the peculiar British interpretation of Yoruba history, Ladugbolu's friendship with Captain Ross, and considerable royal control over the marital institutions on which this ritual system of delegation was modeled. The first and the last factors (which will most concern us here) both saved and reoriented the structure of Oyo royal government.

The British interpretation of Yoruba kingship and Alaafin's friendship with Ross allowed Alaafin Ladugbolu to eviscerate the power of the Ọ̀yọ́ Mèsì, the council of nonroyal chiefs in Oyo town formerly empowered to check Alaafin's power. That council included the successor to the nemesis of many an eighteenth-century king—the *Basorun*. In an important sense, the Oyo Renaissance replicated Abiodun's late eighteenth-century revolution, and, as we have seen, the *ilari* were once again its most prominent emblems.

Not only the administrative order but also the sacred principles underlying royal delegation had shifted. Whereas the source of royal power was once visualized primarily as the *orisa*, or "gods," now it was just as much the *òyìnbó*, or "Europeans." These sources were structurally similar. Both *orisa* and *oyinbo* were personae of high prestige and material power. Both were associated with foreign places, superior knowledge, and political rule. Moreover, like the *orisa*, the *oyinbo* realized their power by sharing it with their subordinates. Nonetheless, British military support may, to some degree, have diminished royal dependency on priestly expertise. More explicitly, certain priesthoods and sacred practices proved anathema to British conceptions of health and public order.

Throughout the Oyo Renaissance, the British Crown instituted numerous religious prohibitions. British-administered treaties in 1886 and 1888 officially ended human sacrifice (Johnson 1921:663–65; Babayemi 1979:290), and a 1917 ordinance abolished the worship of Ṣọ̀npọ̀nnọ́n (god of smallpox), which includes spirit possession, amid the suspicion that Sonponnon priests had deliberately spread the disease.[6] Inspired by a concern for public security, the British also prohibited nighttime drumming and the nighttime meetings of Ogun priests and Ifa diviners in certain areas (Asiwaju 1976:212).

Under Captain Ross and King Ladugbolu, the tenor of official responses to Yoruba and British religious differences followed from Ross's respect for Oyo culture and from the official priority to restore Alaafin's authority. Particularly on matters the British classified as "religious" and social (i.e., issues whose relevance to good government was not obvious to the British), Alaafin was freely permitted to promulgate laws and enforce his judgment. He did so without reference to the Resident as long as his decision was not, in the British view, "repugnant to human justice" (Atanda 1970:221). Nevertheless, archives reveal what "religious" concerns remained important to "good government" in the eyes of Alaafin.

Women and the Christian Challenge

Christians posed a challenge to Oyo royal authority, sometimes to its very symbolic foundations. Missionaries introduced a new vocabulary of class and gender relations, which was taken up by those women intent on resisting patrilineal and royalist controls. For example, Southern Baptist missionary S. G. Pinnock had long been active in the Oyo capital. Convinced by Captain Bower's 1895 bombardment of Oyo that the British were intent on reform, Pinnock expected the colonial government to support the causes of his flock against "oppressive" indigenous government. However, his appeal to Euro-Christian conceptions of justice failed in the climate of early Indirect Rule. In 1908, Reverend Pinnock regarded the increasing power of Alaafin Lawani (Ladugbolu's father) as the revival of "harsh methods of government"

in which "the poor were oppressed, crushing fines imposed on innocent people, and cruel deeds enacted." That year he complained directly to then District Commissioner Ross about the mistreatment of one of
his parishioners. Alaafin regarded the complaint as a challenge to his
authority and wished to prevent further such challenges. Instead of
taking heed, Pinnock preached a sermon titled "The Alaafin and the
Táláká [the 'poor' or 'commoners']," in which he likened Alaafin to the
biblical King Herod. Consequently, with Ross's full backing, Alaafin
ordered Pinnock forcibly ejected from Oyo half a year later. The incident increased Alaafin's authority greatly (Atanda 1979:114–15). Yet
Pinnock's apparently democratic sentiments foreshadowed specifically
local forms of Christian opposition to the colonial state, of which
women's withdrawal from the patrilineal and royalist order would
remain a touchstone throughout the Oyo Renaissance. The very unde-
mocratic British administration could not fail to respond to this emergent resistance.

Pinnock could not have anticipated the local and popular form the
conflict would assume. Generally, mission churches' condemnation of
polygamy and witchcraft beliefs would face enduring opposition
among the Yoruba. Yet, the earliest ritual conflicts between the missions and local religions reveal a more specific set of interested positions. Although the church's own brand of justice for the poor and
socially marginalized inspired many great moral gestures on the part of
missionaries, it was the church's unprogrammatic and nearly accidental defense of women's freedom of movement that provoked the ire of
the entire royalist establishment—including kings, chiefs, priests, and
commoners. For example, in Òkè-òdàn, religious "traditionalists" im-
prisoned women in the church. "On several occasions, Christians, especially the women among them, were threatened by the Oro cult. The
oro, whom women were forbidden to see, was usually brought out
when Christians held prayer meetings in churches; and women
Christians had to be shut up until the Oro people could be persuaded to
allow them out" (Asiwaju 1976:223). In 1929 the *Bale* (Town Chief) of
the Oyo-Yoruba town of Qla scheduled the final day of the Oro (bull-
roarer) festival on a Sunday and forbade Christian women to attend
church that day.[7] As in the previous cases, Resident Ross condemned
Pinnock and conferred full authority on Alaafin Ladugbolu. Following

repeated violence, Alaafin's *ilari* ordered the church moved out of town. The royal state's authority over women became a major battleground, not only between the kingship and the church but between other local religions and the church as well. In Ola, worshipers of Egúngún masquerades and of Sango entered the fray on the Oro side.

New alliances were formed on this battleground. Oro is devoted to restraining the primarily female outlaws of the patrilineal order—the witches (*àjẹ́*) (Eades 1980:125). Yet, this bull-roarer society displays its authority and efficacy by periodically forcing *all* women to withdraw from the public sphere.

At least twice in 1913, "possessed Sango priests broke into the Methodist Church of Igan-Okoto and uttered curses at the congregation during Sunday services" (Asiwaju 1976:223). As far back as 1879, Johnson documents threats by Sango priests in Abeokuta against even non-Sango priests' conversion to Christianity.[8] The emergent gendered norms of the Christian opposition were equally threatening to Oro- and Sango-worshipers. Christian women became the targets of their reaction.

Archival documents from the early twentieth century reveal little conflict between Muslims and Christians or between Muslims and *orisa*-worshipers. Although the latter are recalled in oral histories, they were the subject of few complaints to the administration. What requires explanation is the fact that in the 1980s the battle lines have been drawn anew, between *orisa*-worship and Christianity on one side and Islam on the other. (We will discuss this subject in the next chapter.)

The frictions between Alaafin and the emergent civil society of colonial Nigeria underline the joint importance of gender issues, not only in the synthesis of new socioreligious identities and cleavages but in the reconstitution of royal authority. Whereas Muslims challenged the state little on these issues, certain gender relations proposed parenthetically by the church threatened the Oyo kingship at base and apex, particularly because the exclusion of the royal state from its former military prerogatives shifted the balance of its purpose, authority, and means further onto issues of domestic reproduction and gender-based ritual.

Other instances show how the colonial state itself could drive a wedge into gendered royalist hierarchies and inspire the collective wrath of royal and commoner alike. One of the earliest legislative

moments in the British regulation of Yoruba sociopolitical arrangements was the promulgation of the Marriage Ordinance of 1884 in the
Lagos Colony, which created a category of bindingly monogamous
marriage. Similar provisions were extended to Oyo territory in 1900
(Nwogugu 1974:23). Whereas "Ordinance," or statutory, marriages
were under the jurisdiction of the church and the Protectorate, most of
the renegotiation of marital institutions at this point in Oyo-Yoruba history occurred closer to the juncture of British and indigenous judicial
forms—in the native courts. The native courts quickly became and
remained a battleground for wifely freedom and restriction. The terms
of that battle were reformulated at the apex of local administration,
among paramount chiefs, Residents, and District Officers.

The Ìsẹyìn-Òkèihò uprising in 1916 revealed that the king's failure to
regulate marital relations in his domain undermined the efficacy of any
administrative project the British hoped to assign to him. The precolonial hierarchy of family, quarter, and town courts had been controlled
by various patriarchs, who effectively discouraged divorce and other
litigation by exacting high bribes from litigants at every level of appeal.
In lieu of the costly indigenous hierarchy of appeals, the British Native
Court system established a single court under Alaafin's administration.
"The [precolonial] socio-judicial system did not give much freedom for
divorce on flimsy grounds. Thus, the menfolk regarded the traditional
system as a check on the loss of their wives through divorce. This was
one of the securities which . . . the Native Court system inaugurated by
the British in 1914 destroyed" (Atanda 1969:501).

Under the new system, once a woman had paid the necessary sum-
mons fees to the single Native Court, no family had the legal right to
detain her. In order to prevent such detentions the British made the
head chief's home a sanctuary from which departing wives could not
be forcibly removed. British legislation had also diminished the privileges of local chiefs. Far more unsettling was local men's concern about
increasing divorce rates. These reforms led to the bloody Iseyin-Okeiho
revolt, in which the native court and the judge were burned up and the
local ruler appointed by Alaafin was murdered. The hunters and warriors who led it enjoyed great popular support. In response, Ross's
troops decimated the insurgents and, through the agency of Alaafin's
court, condemned several rebel leaders to death (ibid.:503, 513). Thus

proceeded an unequal dialogue on the justice and realpolitik of Yoruba marital and political relations. After the Iseyin-Okeiho uprising of 1916, colonial officials could never again disregard the threat that divorce posed to the royalist order. Hence, women's right to divorce would have to be carefully balanced against the political priorities of kings.

Many written correspondences among colonial officers and the noble jurors of the native courts address the changing prerogatives of husbands and kings over wives. Those correspondences detail the overlaps and contradictions between indigenous and British legal views of wives, as well as lacunae in the new synthetic system of enforcing those views. Three key features stand out in the official discourse of the 1920s, when the New Oyo Empire was at its height. First, administrators shared local husbands' fears about the potential disintegration of the preexisting patrilineage. Issues of divorce and child custody occupy the attention of these officials far more than does, say, education. Second, British-sponsored reforms *monetized* marriage and divorce negotiations to unprecedented degrees. Third, in keeping with the premise of Indirect Rule, royalty in Oyo Division (as opposed to subordinate chiefs) was given great authority in legislating and executing local sociopolitical reform.

Divorce Laws and the Challenge to Royalty

Contrary to Chanock's (1982) conclusions on the Northern Rhodesian case, British administrators were not unaware that the inauguration of a code called "Native Law and Custom" involved profound modifications of preexisting legal practice. Oyo-Yoruba litigants and kings did not generally testify capriciously, arguing whatever principle would serve their momentary moods and interests. Indeed, the legislative dialogue between Yoruba kings and British administrators reveals that both parties had long-term interests to protect and could negotiate new principles and codes according to intelligently selected precedents and careful sociological reasoning. What the Yoruba case probably shares with the Northern Rhodesian is that wives participated in these reforms more with their feet and their cash than with their policy recommendations. Yet the codification of women's rights and of the cost of release from marriage would bear considerable consequences for them.

Colonial officials acknowledged that administration policy had increased the divorce rate. The District Officer of Ife Division wrote:

> Divorce was uncommon before the British Protectorate was established, because women who showed signs of being about to leave their husbands were tied up and beaten into submission. If a lover did manage to take over another man's wife, he became an enemy of the whole family of the husband, and was liable to have to defend himself from serious assault. Such assault would now, perhaps, be punished in a court.
> A wife was a chattel and rarely had any freedom of choice whatsoever.[9]

Despite evidence that many wives were fleeing threats to their health and dignity, colonial officials focused greater attention on local husbands' concerns that village wives would now find it possible to run away whenever they found a richer man to marry.[10] Recognizing such concerns, which had been voiced both strongly and continuously since they prompted the Okeiho uprising, the state reoriented itself toward stemming the rise of women's mobility and postmarital freedom of choice. Sympathetic to the old obstacles to divorce, Provincial Resident Ross articulated the prevailing opinion to the District Officer of Oyo Division in 1927. The District Officer in turn wrote to the president and judges of the Oyo Native Court: "I am instructed by the Resident to remind you that you have power to forbid a divorce where you consider there is no good reason for granting it. . . . Do not think that every women who asks for a divorce is entitled to it."[11]

At the same time, the administration could not betray the emancipatory spirit that occasioned the British colonization of Lagos in the first place. Freedom of movement for wives was not wholly a British introduction, though. As we have seen, Alaafin's wives in the nineteenth-century Age of Ogun served not only as secluded mates and palace administrators but as long-distance traders. Their freedom of movement implies that their loyalty to Alaafin depended far more than before on harmony among their personal interests. Despite traditional contentions that the wives of the *oba* were secluded, Johnson's history of Oyo records many cases of Oyo kings' being cuckolded. Yet the might and royalist policy of the administration altered the balance of power among kings, chiefs, husbands, and wives, as well as the expressive options of all parties involved.

Administrative policy not only placed royals in charge of domestic courts but gave them virtual carte blanche in fixing legally the domestic privileges they regarded as important to their royal status. Chiefs in the Ife District of Oyo Province legislated the following:

> The wives of the reigning Oni [paramount chief, or king, of Ife] shall not be seduced and adultery with his wife or wives shall be punishable with the maximum penalty of the court and the seducer shall be banished from the District after serving his term of imprisonment. Any wife of the Oni who commits adultery may be punished.
>
> The wives of the Inner and Outer chiefs, including the Obaluaiye [sic; it should be Ọbaláayé] and the Bale of Modakeke shall not be granted divorce. If the seducer and woman continue in their wish to live together then dowry and the adultery fine shall be double and the seducer banished from the town.[12]

Administrators understood that a moral and social order was at stake. For kings and chiefs, the political order of the state was at issue in the very same "domestic" legislation. With the support of the administration, they encoded the long-established policy of meting out special punishments for adultery involving the wives of chiefs and kings.

It would be superficial to conclude that the "paramount chiefs" made their own law in their own momentary interests. Oyo-Yoruba "customary" law and the native courts extended and transformed an enduring system in which royal interests were the keystone in a hierarchy of corporate patrilineal interests. High chiefs had long been responsible for policing other men's errant daughters or wives. A man who suspected his wife's intention to leave and marry another man could marry her off first to a chief or king. The departure of such a woman from the palace would, in nineteenth-century practice, have brought down the full wrath of the royal state on the "seducer," who, as we have seen, could be castrated and perhaps even drafted subsequently into the political service of the palace. Muslim Yoruba exploited the concept of sàráà, or "charity," to give daughters to oba without requesting bridewealth, either to control their daughters' supposed promiscuity or to obtain the palace's politically useful gratitude (Fadipẹ 1970:67). Thus, women were passed upward for control by, in effect, higher husbandly authorities. By regulating the conduct of such women, the high chiefs not only bolstered the honor of a woman's previous, failed guardian but secured his further investment in the royalist state and deterred the proverbially feared flight of wives in general. By the royal-ist view, this husbandly collusion forestalled the tandem disintegration of lineage and state.

Ross stopped short of validating husbands' right to marry their adulterous wives off to kings.[13] Although forced marriages and puni-tive castrations ended legally under the colony, kings willingly exploit-ed new legislative means to regulate marital relations. However, dur-ing the long transitional period when knowledge of and respect for the new "Native Law and Custom" was poorly diffused (a period that some would say has not yet ended), the palace and its priestly agents remained a material, psychological, and religious deterrent to the flight of wives and the socially unregulated movement of women generally.[14] A persistent array of cases identified royals with the stubborn defense of the old marital order and also underlined the gendered nature of challenges by old and new rivals for control over the order of the state.

First, since kings often quietly ignored laws, the British exploited an old fissure in the Oyo-Yoruba kingdom to guarantee wives a way out. The *dìpómú* system made the houses of certain chiefs into refuges for fleeing wives.[15] In 1929, the Assistant District Officer of Òṣogbo de-scribed one woman's odyssey:

> Recently a woman named Hunmani complained to me that on taking action in Native Court, Ejigbo, for divorce against her husband, her husband had given her to Elejigbo [king of Èjìgbò] with the approval of the Judges. She did not want to be one of Elejigbo's wives. She had no father or mother and was under the protection of Jagun.[16]

The Jagun is, according to his title, a war chief. That he has implicitly acted in opposition to royal hegemony invokes—in the arena of divorce litigation—a long history of gendered ideological, political, and reli-gious opposition, detailed in chapter 1, between royals and military chiefs. Equally associated with the Age of Ogun, the houses of the Iyalode, or women-chiefs of the market, were also common *dipomu* sanctuaries.[17] Because of the administration's ultimate concerns, Alaafin was granted full jurisdiction over the case, a jurisdiction the state was willing to enforce against the will of any military chief.

Second, as we have seen, early Christians joined the opposition to the old marital and political order. The series of church invasions and

sequestrations of Christian women by Oyo-Yoruba priests, documented from 1879 to the mid-twentieth century, demonstrated an axis of
opposition that was not altogether new. Yet Christians drew the focus
of antiroyalism toward the issues of polygamy, widow inheritance, and
patrilineal principles of child custody. Although the Bishop of Lagos
recognized the danger of a rapid upheaval and avowed his patience in
the modification of indigenous social institutions, he queried the
administration's handling of cases, for example, in which children of a
Christian widow were taken from her and handed over to her "pagan"
affines, and in which a Christian widow had been claimed as a wife by
a "pagan" relation of her deceased husband. The exercise of leviratic
rights sometimes occasioned rape.[18] The bishop wrote the Attorney
General, who classified the cases as matters of "inheritance," in the
sense of Ross's definition: "The Elder brother is the next of kin and
inherits the property. . . . The wife or wives are themselves legacies."[19]
On inheritance matters the government was categorically "not prepared to interfere with native law and customs," but the District
Officers had been advised to encourage compromise.[20]

   In supporting native court decisions, the District Officer submerged
concern for Christians' or women's inalienable rights beneath concern
for the viability of native authority. He anticipated "the danger of
undermining the influence of native authorities, if those over whom
they should rightly exercise jurisdiction can easily avoid their obligations by professing to embrace Christianity."[21] If only in justifying
Lugardian policy, administrators became aware of humanitarian issues
that made liberal reform difficult. For example, Ross noted the injustice
to children of modifying Christian women's position: in the Native
Court system, the same person who inherited a dead man's wife also
inherited his children and, in his view, a strong sense of responsibility
in rearing them. A widow would almost surely marry another man,
who would likely have no interest in the children except as servants.
"Are these children to be deprived of very real and proper guardianship because the woman has embraced Christianity?" Ross asked.
Basing his recommendation on indigenous precedent rather than on
the principle of female, individual, or Christian rights, Ross proposed
that Christian women be granted the same rights as Muslim Yoruba
women—that they never be forced to marry the dead husband's kins-

man but that they be required to repay the bridewealth before leaving.[22] Colonial administrators and kings recognized the complex links between the domestic order and the polity. Husbands of the realm held the king ultimately responsible for safeguarding that order from the flight of wives, which held unclear but nonetheless frightening implications for the reproduction of the patrilineage, the guardianship of children, and the many loci of the foremost idiom of hierarchical cooperation in the royal state—marriage.

Although marriage had long been a focus of regulatory authority for the Oyo palace and a succession of lesser hereditary officeholders, the Native Court system made it an important arena, in which relations of hierarchy and opposition were renegotiated among colonial officers, kings, chiefs, and their subjects of both sexes. Reluctant to undermine the authority of kings, the British actually invested unprecedented degrees of authority in them and created unprecedented gaps between them and their subordinate chiefs. This centralization carried direct consequences for wives: although kings became uncontested masters of the overall marital order, they were legally obliged to allow every wife a hearing and a much-simplified means of divorce.

The British administration's efforts to systematize the links between domestic order and the polity involved every level of the hierarchy of "mounting" in the liberal ideology and monetary devices of the mercantile state. The colonial state gave a new idiom of action to both royal sovereignty and its opposition. The royalist system was gradually reoriented by the new forms of resistance to it. Military chieftaincy, mission Christianity, divorce laws, and the centrally issued currency of the colonial state were unlikely partners in the design of a new way of opting out of the royalist and patrilineal hierarchy of "mounting." In the Native Court system, those least privileged in that hierarchy could *buy* themselves out. Under the colony, their choice was less and less between a royalist and a military politico-religious commitment, and progressively more between a royalist and a metropolitan one.

Money, Divorce, and the Codification of Domestic Law

Although anthropologists have long been concerned to distinguish the payment of bridewealth (or bride-price) from purchase, it is difficult to ignore the implications of Yoruba parlance and the British enactment of controls upon "head prices" in the midst of the administration's active suppression of slavery and debt peonage. Much of the anthropological caution seems motivated by the fear of breaching the sharp divide that Westerners characteristically erect between commerce and moral relationships (see Mauss 1967; Parry 1986; Bloch 1989). This divide should not be assumed universally, nor should its ideological impact be ignored under conditions of large-scale slave trafficking or of British sovereignty and mercantile dominance. It is precisely the salience and meaning of that divide that were being negotiated in the native courts, with great consequence for Yoruba wives.

The Attorney General, like the officers in the field, was concerned most with preserving the integrity of the royalist system they had resurrected, reformed, and fortified amid myriad contrary forces. For administrative purposes, that system had to be liberalized, fixed, and codified. The terms of that codification arose from sometimes sensitive and sometimes gross understandings of Oyo-Yoruba culture. In what appears to be a case of the latter, the official discourse on domestic law in the 1920s monetized wives' rights of divorce to unprecedented degrees.

This codification was aimed at the clarification of wives' rights, but it also tapped local precedents and bore local consequences with the opposite political implications. Particularly at its height during the eighteenth and nineteenth centuries, the transatlantic slave trade introduced huge quantities of cowry shells into Yorubaland, which progressively became the normal medium of taxation, tolls, and myriad forms of purchase in an extensive region of West Africa. At the end of the century, cowries remained the normal medium of local commercial exchange. European coins, according to Johnson's 1899 report, were still a curiosity in areas far from the coast, probably including Oyo North, and barter remained a major mode of exchange alongside cowries (Johnson 1921 [originally written in 1899]:118). In the same era, Johnson emphasizes the rapidly increasing sums of cowry shells demanded as marital prestations. Prosperous families were demanding a maximum of twenty thousand cowries, then valued at thirty pence, along with choice condiments and clothing (ibid.:114, 118–19). The later the period one examines and the closer to the coast, the greater the demand for European coins. Otherwise, the virtual equivalence of coins and shell money was assumed.[23] In 1918, payments in coin had become important everywhere. Although standard bridewealth payments in Oyo were surely much lower, two pounds, ten shillings was a commonly recognized figure in Abeokuta (Fadipe 1970:77–78).

Oyo-Yoruba marriage and money stood together at one in a series of crossroads, and one would follow the other in transforming a range of social and political relationships. Even before the apogee of the slave trade, small numbers of highly valuable cowry shells had been present in the Oyo territories, probably having originated mainly from the trans-Saharan trade (Hogendorn and Johnson 1986:119). According to Belasco (1980:43), they had been used principally as gifts, objects of petty barter, and, especially, instruments of communion with the *orisa* (see also Nadel 1937). Although these antecedent forms of circulation are what later made them acceptable media in the coastal trade in human merchandise, Belasco argues that the later flood of shells into the local economy propelled "the assimilation of a multivalent symbol to a mere monetary signal" of commodity exchange, collapsing "communalistic categories of value into reinterpreted notions of wealth ultimately subsumed as privately counted money" (Belasco 1980:55, 59).

Although Belasco's evocation of pre-slave-trade Yoruba commerce and society requires the strongest qualification, it does suggest highly plausible dimensions of nineteenth-century social and religious change. By the eighteenth century, the West African zone of cowry money usage was coextensive with the zone called "the Slave Coast." Until 1807, cowries were the main means of purchasing slaves, and slaves were far and away the main "goods" purchased with cowries (Hogendorn and Johnson 1986:110–11). In this context and during the subsequent "legitimate" trade in palm oil, not only the quantity of cowries in the bridal prestations but their significance surely changed.

Particularly in contrast with the British metal coinage subsequently introduced, the cowry represented not one past but several. Aside from their mercurial and ultimately declining value as specie, cowries embodied symbolic allusions to several prior phases of Oyo-Yoruba sociopolitical life. They continued in a range of ancient sacred functions, all of which themselves came to bear historical associations with the large-scale capture and lucrative sale of human beings. Cowries recall an era when intra-African trade was as important as the transatlantic trade. Although European merchants paid in cowries for slaves, cloth, vegetable products, and ivory, they seldom accepted them in payment for the goods Africans bought from them. Until the great inflation at the end of the nineteenth century, cowry money traced ever-expanding networks of intra-West African commerce (ibid.:111). If new African markets for its use had not continually been found, inflation would have eliminated its value far earlier. The use of cowry money thus expressed both the users' trust and their participation in intra-African networks of sacred and nonsacred exchange, which, as we shall see, are explicit in *orisa* mythology.

Hence, a form of money preceded the introduction of European coinage by at least a century.[24] Given the meanings and uses of its antecedents, colonial monetization did not unravel the fabric of local authority and social obligations, as students of such situations often expect (see Parry and Bloch 1989:12–16). Nor did money commoditize in any simple sense the goods and relationships it was used to secure. Once finally accepted, British-issued bank notes emblemized a high degree of trust in a system of personal rights and international exchange relations thereafter sponsored and regulated by an unprecedentedly centralized state, which could variously undermine, revivify, or reorient existing local relationships. The colonial state often acted without knowing or intending the consequences. Yet, Oyo Yoruba voluntarily invested the new currency, as well as the state administrative and ideological apparatuses in its tow, in marriages and other more explicitly sacred relationships.

The British "civilizing mission" sponsored forms of exchange that progressively clarified the notion of ownership. Colonial money more easily concealed the trail of social and sacred relationships it had financed, thereby purifying the position of the owner, defined more and more exclusively by the juncture of relationships among the things (and people) owned. To put it another way: the owner was increasingly defined by opposition to the owned, rather than as a being enmeshed in the shared (cf. Mauss 1967). It is in this sense that monetization unintentionally structured new forms of personhood, as well as the new conceptions of servitude and "freedom" that came along with them.

This new capitalist negotiation of the self did not exclude the human being in her or his entirety from the objects of exchange. Rather, the alienation of labor through wages redefined the boundaries of the *subject* of exchange. Within those boundaries, in Western bourgeois understandings, lies the self or, by metaphorical extension, the corporation. In Oyo-Yoruba marriage, the subject of exchange was and is not the individual self but the corporate lineage. The monetization of bridal prestations clarified the line between the woman as vessel and the corporate subject of reproduction. As we shall see in our examination of marriage and possession rites, the space of the subject is defined by contrast to wifely bodies and the symbolic structures of uterine reproduction. Such structures, their facsimiles, and their metonyms had been negotiable property in the extension of Oyo sovereignty during the Age of Sango. Moreover, the conjunction of precolonial and state-issued currencies in the late twentieth century would be used to shift the boundaries both of the negotiable territory and of the negotiants. It is for these reasons that we look to the Oyo Renaissance and its effects on the evolving relationship between money and marriage.

The new divorce code redefined the subjects of marriage and reproduction first by redefining the media of exchange. The Native Courts reduced to monetary figures the worth of gifts with diverse symbolic meanings (discussed in chapter 4) and included those figures in refundable amounts greatly exceeding the sums of monetary bridewealth recorded in previous decades. Charts fixed the sums refundable by the wife on the occasion of divorce or liberation from the levirate (*opó ṣíṣú*). They were sufficiently high for many women to find paying them difficult.[25] Yet a substantial security in cash became prerequisite to a woman's even being heard in the courts. In the late 1920s and early 1930s, increasing numbers of betrothed girls and married women in flight were being sent to prison for nonrestitution of "dowry." Only after some years did the Resident condemn the practice, which probably continued years beyond its legal prohibition.[26]

Inevitably, the Native Authority system extended its jurisdiction from divorce to regulating bridewealth itself in marriage negotiations. The monetization of marriage, reproduction, and divorce introduced the specter of inflationary profiteering. Women's reproductive resources remained the scarce and valued goods as young men's cash earnings increased. In effect, bridewealth negotiations became an occasion for elder men and women to renegotiate the power imbalance entailed in the new cash wealth of junior men.[27] Oyo Division tended to be the last affected by all of these trends, but it reacted no less definitively to ensuing inflationary trends. A 1953 "Modification of Native Law and Custom" in Oyo Division attempted to reduce bride-wealth to a maximum of £12.10.0.[28]

The maximum "dowry or betrothal presents" recoverable after divorce in 1956 was fixed by the new Oyo Southern District Council at £20, minus £3 for each child delivered by the wife, suggesting that the fight against bridewealth inflation met with little success over the inter-vening three years. Bridewealth inflation was and is symptomatic of ever-increasing structural inequality between rural primary producers and their mobile, wage-earning sons-in-law. Bridewealth inflation remained the impetus behind continual town council debates in Oyo North well into the 1980s.

Colonial officers' description of women as "chattel" in the "tradi-tional" system contains evidence of the British critique of slavery as well as a local conception, still officially recognized, of people as capital resources with a use-value. Indeed, the diminution of women's use-value—or at least the reduction of their indenture—through the service of childbearing is implied directly in Ife's declining scale of bride-wealth restitution. Moreover, pawning and de facto slavery remained realities in the Oyo-Yoruba system of production and credit at least until the late 1930s. By way of guaranteeing the rights of debt peons, the British reclassified ìwọ̀fà (debt peons), in effect, as wage laborers. The Native Courts standardized the monetary value of their labor. For each unit of agricultural labor, the amount of the debt for which the peon, or pawn, served as collateral would be reduced.[29] The legislation ignored at least some indigenous people's view that a pawn benefited greatly from the nonpecuniary rewards of his sometimes interminable service, such as training, food, housing, clothing, protection, and the pride of membership in a rich person's house. In a parallel fashion, the amount of bridewealth a divorcée was and is required to refund dimin-ishes by a fixed sum for each child she has borne for her estranged hus-band.[30] Insofar as manual labor had been legally commoditized, so had uterine labor. Insofar as they had not been, debt peons and wives found themselves subject to a moral order now vastly transformed. The value of their choice to cooperate (albeit a choice not easily abandoned) was greatly changed by its context and its alternatives.

It is revealing that the standardization of pecuniary bridewealth and divorce restitution occurred last in the jurisdiction where royal privileges were most assiduously preserved. Probably owing to Ross's personal protection of Alaafin Ladugbolu's prerogatives, Oyo Division was delayed in standardizing its dowry-restitution figures. Alaafin asked that the law be left unwritten, maximizing his personal power and discretion.[31] Nonetheless, moved by the same exigencies that propelled Ife wives away from their affinal homes, large numbers of wives in Oyo Division were, by 1932, filing for divorce without knowing where the dowry refund would come from, casting doubt on the assumption that these divorce suits characteristically anticipated the women's marriage to the rich seducers awaiting them. These women were fleeing oppressive situations. In order to prevent overcrowding in the courts and in the *dipomu* sanctuaries, the Assistant District Officer finally ordered the fixing of bridewealth figures in Oyo Division in 1933. Fleeing wives who did not pay it made themselves vulnerable to arrest.

With an eye toward systematizing and protecting individual liberties, the Native Authority system translated liberty and domestic labor too into pecuniary terms. The new codes of the Native Authority affirmed the progress of capitalist values in domestic and reproductive economic domains. My evaluation does not posit noncapitalist terms as the natural medium of "domestic" exchanges. I mean simply to illuminate the role of the colonial state in monetizing a sphere of Yoruba social life that previously had contained but the *seeds* of the commodification of wives, children, and "domestic slaves." As a matter of policy, the options of debtors and dissatisfied wives alike became increasingly connected to the market of cash and wages.

More or less intentionally, King Ladugbolu had constructed his domain as non-Christian, uneducated (in the Western sense), and poor in money but rich in respect for "family life" (Atanda 1979:243–44). It is for these qualities that Yorubaland's disproportionately Ìjẹ̀bú and Ẹ̀gbá elites now know the Oyo Yoruba. State-issued money, individualism, monogamy, and Western bourgeois education were emblems and pillars of metropolitan society in colonial Nigeria (see Mann 1985).

In the new order of the Nigerian state, earning and saving money became the sine qua non of wives' freedom and the measure of legal self-control. Hence, high divorce rates, women's flight to the metropolis, female commerce, and prostitution remained foci of royalist trepidation and exemplary forms of resistance throughout the twentieth century. Divorce and the pecuniary forms of its negotiation placed common wives at the leading edge of new forms of social investment. They had the least to lose by their disloyalty to the patrilineal order. However, earning and saving would become everyone's means of investing in and benefiting from the metropolitan economy. Throughout this century, women have made up the majority of traders. They have also been the disproportionate source of finance for their children's education and the enterprises that liberate those children from cultivating the land and from the status hierarchies in which their fathers are invested. Thus, European coins and paper money became, in a sense, the opposite of the cowries that link the classic hierarchies of "mounting" in the kingdom and the possession cults. Colonial divorce laws reveal the centrality of women and money in the emergence of an antiroyalist petite bourgeoisie.

So, from the bombardment of Oyo town to the end of the colony in 1960, conflicting principles guided a culturally synthetic reform of women's rights and concomitant changes in the reproduction of patrilineage and the state. The explicit negotiation between colonial officers and "paramount rulers" was but one factor guiding that reform. Violent plebeian objections to administration policy—the Iseyin-Okeiho uprising, for example—oriented the fears and strategies of the New Oyo Empire for decades. At a more microscopic level, commoners' bridewealth negotiations linked wider *economic* forces to the reproduction of the lineage. The Native Authority system not only codified the terms of male corporate control over wives and children but the price of wives' self-possession and, as we shall see, the dividends wives could rightfully expect from their possession by the patrilineage.

Emergent Female Options

Oyo's reliance on the mobility of royal wives in the nineteenth century had altered wifely rights and duties at the very apex of the patrilineal system. The nineteenth-century rise of the Iyalode circumvented the husband-dependent basis of the *ayaba's* authority and exemplified symbolic forces that the British-sponsored Oyo Renaissance could not easily suppress, no more easily than it could suppress Ibadan itself.

Almost all able-bodied and healthy Yoruba eventually married during the Oyo Renaissance, much as they do now. However, the liberating precedent of the nineteenth-century Iyalode women-chiefs affected younger women in the twentieth. Ordinary girls could and did simply take to the road before marriage, away from father's or fiancé's surveillance. Many young women traveled and engaged in premarital affairs, but, according to Fadipe (1970:66), even professional prostitutes probably ultimately found a place in marriage since, among the mobile population of colonial Nigeria, they could easily find a man who knew nothing of their history. When a girl chose—or was chosen by—a partner, her family generally carried out investigations to assure that the husband's family bore no hereditary flaws, which, to the Yoruba, included leprosy, epilepsy, alcoholism, insanity, criminality, chronic indebtedness, laziness, or moral turpitude. Ultimately, a girl was more or less obligated to marry the man favored by her parents, and "elopement" was officially illegal.[32]

Once wedded, a woman possessed within the Native Authority system clear rights in marriage and rights of divorce from a nonroyal husband—the foremost grounds for which replicate the concerns of the usual parental investigation but also include, at the top of every local codification, "impotency." Nothing bespeaks more eloquently the foremost article of a wife's bill of rights—the right to motherhood. Like pre- and postmarital prayers of the present era, the official grounds for divorce suggest the foremost recognized function of Yoruba marriage and what is commonly viewed as the principal dividend for the wife—that is, the children. Children are regarded as blessings and as a form of wealth. Among other advantages of well-reared children is the support they can offer for their mother's comfort in dotage and widowhood.[33]

Under Indirect Rule, women who for any reason needed to leave their marriages could take refuge in the houses of chiefs—like the Jagun of Ejigbo, the Iyalode of Osogbo, or other designated agents of the *dipomu* system. Even if bridewealth repayment was onerous, women could at least invoke the rule of law in opposition to the personal law of affines, patrilineage authorities, and kings bent on forestalling divorce.

If women lacked bridewealth or the new system failed to meet their needs, they possessed the means to foil enforcement efforts. In the 1920s, if the Native Court denied divorce, a wife might leave town. If traced, she could legally be brought back, but the limits of enforceability made chiefs "nervous of being too strict."[34] Men also feared *mágùn* medicine. Yoruba generally believe that women's bodies can be prepared ritually to kill a man who penetrates her. Hence the name of the ritual preparation: *magun* means "don't mount." In discussing the difficulty of enforcing the Native Court's decisions against divorce, the District Officer of Ife Division wrote in 1927:

> I believe . . . that Magun poisoning has still to be taken into consideration. If they force a woman to sleep with a husband and so make her desperate, means may be found of killing the husband by this method. This possibility is often present in the native mind.[35]

We have no way of assessing the literal reality of *magun* as a means of killing men. But we can affirm that it constitutes a living and elaborate part of the Yoruba lore on gender relations and the struggle to possess wives' bodies. Whereas *magun* is believed nowadays to be applied mainly by husbands to their possibly adulterous wives, this evidence from 1927 suggests its use by wives wishing freedom from their husbands. In either case, the belief in *magun* evokes metaphorically the unhinging of patrilineal authority, as well as its dangers to life itself.[36]

The Oyo Renaissance represented a resurrection of "mounting" metaphors at the heights of the Oyo-Yoruba state and their intersection with British missionary, commercial, and colonial projects. The royal wives, the *ilari* messengers, the eunuchs, and the Sango possession priests remained active in the display of royal sovereignty. The New Oyo Empire was antagonistic toward women's emerging social and pecuniary independence precisely because the empire remained so dependent upon its wives in the exercise of authority. Yet *magun* was not the only, or even the foremost, female assertion that preoccupied kings during the Oyo Renaissance.

The questions raised by Oro and Sango's antagonism toward Christianity earlier in the century and high divorce rates forever after were never fully resolved by the legal machinations of the Native Courts. Indeed, they were compounded by the vast expansion and popularization of women's commercial activity under the colony. As among the Nupe, studied by Nadel (1954:172ff.), women's financial and social independence from the husbandly patrilineage evoked popular fears of witchcraft. One more often hears that a woman "*has* witchcraft" (*ní àjẹ́*) than that she "is a witch" (*àjẹ́ ni*). The substantial object she has is usually conceived of as a bird that resides in her stomach but flies about at night to devour the "blood," "inside," or "head" of her co-wives, her husband, his kinsmen, or his children—including the ones she herself delivered. A "witch" can cause impotency and turn fetuses into stone. She is the personified threat to the patrilineage, "death within the house." "*Bì ikú ilé kò bá pa ẹni, ikú òde kò lè paá,*" says a Yoruba proverb— "If death within the house fails to kill a person, death from outside cannot kill him either." The enemy who knows your secrets is best able to kill you, and the elderly widow knows more of the lineage secrets than do most sons of the house.

The king's ritual paraphernalia mark him out as the realm's main defender against the witches. Many royal crowns (*adé*) depict birds gathered in a circle around one bird higher than all the rest. The central bird represents the king himself, whose leadership forestalls the chaos that these free and powerful women can cause (Thompson 1972:254; Babayemi 1982:10; Abimbọla, personal communication, 19 October 1990). The controlled movement of the *ayaba* (royal wives), *elegun* (possession priests), *iwefa* (eunuchs), and *ilari* (ritually prepared royal messengers) centers itself on the *oba*, who is structurally the husband to them all. By contrast, when undirected, the witches fly out of control, devouring the kingdom's people and destroying the order of the patrilineage from within.

The witches meet at the marketplace by night. Their daytime counterparts are the market women, who are known for hoarding money, circumventing husbandly authority, and undermining the authority of the patrilineage over its sons and daughters. Ritually circumscribed by British law and servile to guarantees of wives' rights to divorce, Yoruba kings showed themselves unable to forestall some highly public female threats to the patrilineal order. In one of the transitional moments in the rise of the Nigerian bourgeoisie, the king's failure invited others to sponsor the Atinga witch-finding movement. The next chapter will consider this gender-coded harbinger of class revolution.

However, the progressive retrenchment of Indirect Rule as a colonial policy posed the definitive challenge to Oyo royalty. From 1931 onward, the incoming Governor of Nigeria, Sir Donald Cameron, and the new Resident of Oyo Province made moves to diminish the geographical breadth and political range of Alaafin's authority. In the 1950s, the Native Authority system, under the increasingly titular headship of Alaafin, suffered further setbacks in the constitutional shift toward rule by nonroyal politicians. The progressive loss of the colonial state's backing and the British withdrawal in 1960 relegated the palace's authority to a rural margin, geographically replicating its jurisdiction in the nineteenth-century Age of Ogun, but even more distant from the center of regional economic and political power, now in Lagos. Yet Oyo and related royal communities continued to host the worship of possessing gods like Sango, Yemoja, Oya, and Obatala.

Conclusion

Not only did the British restore Oyo royal power, but they used the Native Court system to transform Sango's kingdom and the mode of its gendered projection into civil society. "Mounting" remained at the core of royal hegemony. However, British conceptions of individual rights and the inescapable logic of the British commercial project appear to have inscribed a bourgeois concept of ownership and selfhood upon already complex bridal and divorce transactions, an inscription that will carry serious implications for the ritual construction of personhood in the modern possession priesthoods (discussed in chapters 5 and 6).

Of nearly equal importance was resistance to the royalist order by Euro-American and Yoruba Christians. Together, common Yoruba women and Christians generally demonstrated the incipient forms of withdrawal from the royalist order and its corporate patrilineal foundations. Moreover, they powerfully influenced the form of a new metropolitan social sphere with its own gravity, which would, by contrast, forevermore define the ruralized kingdom. Although Christians had led in the fight for Nigerian independence, Christianity ceased to be the exemplary antithesis of royal authority and its attendant sacred forms.

The Oyo-Yoruba church itself came to manifest the divisions inherent in the ancient antagonism between Sango and Ogun, between the politico-religious order of "mounting" and the order of autonomous male leadership. The rapidly growing African independent churches, steeped in their own gender-marked forms of spirit possession, contrasted sharply with mission Christianity and the other nonpossession religions characterizing the heights of the Nigerian bourgeois state. For the possession priests and the citizens of Oyo North generally, Islam in particular grew in its power to emblemize their marginalization in the postcolonial apparatus of state power. Yet the possession religions have been sufficiently adaptable as to make Islam into the instrument of their reempowerment as well.

Chapter 3

Igboho in the Age of Abiọla

Independence marked the latest eclipse of Oyo royal sovereignty by the forces of Ogun. During the First Republic (1960–66) and the Second Republic (1979–83), bourgeois political candidates sought the support of local people by courting their kings. Once elected, the politicians prevailed, with the power to punish or reward Yoruba kings' political choices. During the remainder of Nigeria's years of independence, the military has reigned supreme. Ogun is not only the god of war and iron but the cutter of paths, the lord of human mobility. During the oil boom of the 1970s and 1980s, the proliferation of private minibuses and taxis created a transport revolution. So common and unregulated was private transport that Nigeria reported the highest highway mortality rates in the world. To protect themselves from Ogun's thirst for blood, southern Nigerian transport workers regularly offered Ogun his favorite food—dogs. Canine corpses were seen frequently along highways.

Barnes (1980:42–45) attributes the present growth in Ogun's popularity to his symbolic representation of mobility and military action, of technological and social change. In the 1970s, Yoruba Nobel laureate Wọle Ṣoyinka denominated Ogun the god of technology, destruction and creativity, war, and revolution (see Soyinka 1976a and 1976b)—an emblem nonpareil of changes wrought by independence and oil wealth. The omnipresence of his canine nourishment and automobile altars on the highways of Oyo State evokes specific parallels with the nineteenth-century Age of Ogun, associated as it was with both the revolutionary rise of nonroyal military and trade elites and the marginalization of wifely tropes of delegation.

Yet, in Nigeria's lively popular press, it is members of a Muslim and Christian political elite who command the renown—dare I say glory?—

once reserved for gods and long-dead, mythic heroes. It is difficult to say who deserves top billing in the postcolonial pantheon—M. K. O. Abiọla or Ọbafẹmi Awolọwọ. For many Yoruba, the heroic and exemplary status of "Awo" has long been obvious for reasons that I will detail shortly, and the importance of this popular *ideological* endorsement is not to be underestimated. However, notwithstanding the critical moral posture of some of my Nigerian friends toward him, I initially chose Abiola as the eponym of this Ogun Restoration (Matory 1991:63ff.) because his religion, Islam, and the forms of acquisition attributed to him conjointly represent an Oyo-North vision of royalty's current nemesis. Indeed, the present Oyo king made a highly significant and ambiguous effort to co-opt Abiọla's symbolic power. In 1988, King Adeyemi III conferred upon Abiola the military chieftaincy title of *Ààrẹ Ọ̀nà Kakanfò*, the very title held in 1830 by Afonja, who, by conspiring with Fulani jihadists, precipitated the collapse of the royal empire (Johnson 1921:188–90). We are not in a position to judge the accuracy of rumors—both celebratory and critical—that Abiola took enough kickbacks in connection with ITT's construction of Nigeria's half-functional telephone system to make him the richest man in the country.

My initial nomination of Abiola as the eponym of this age has, in the 1990s, acquired an additional historical resonance. Vowing to restore Nigeria to civilian rule, the current military ruler, General Ibrahim Babangida, established a political party framework and scheduled presidential elections. In June 1993, the duly nominated candidate of the Social Democratic party, Abiola, won the plurality of votes in an election recognized as fair by the international community, making him the first Yoruba ever elected as head of state. However, Babangida canceled the results and vowed to schedule new elections, from which both Abiola and his former rival will be excluded. Scores of people were killed in the rioting and military repression that followed. As of August 1993, the outcome of this political crisis remained unclear. Whatever the outcome, Abiola's place in history is assured, as is his emblematic value in the present study.

This contemporary study of gender, religion, and politics unfolds both at the margins of the Nigerian state and at the center of the vividly remembered Oyo Empire—in the savannah town of Igboho, Oyo State (see figure 1). Many details of religious practice and economic condi-

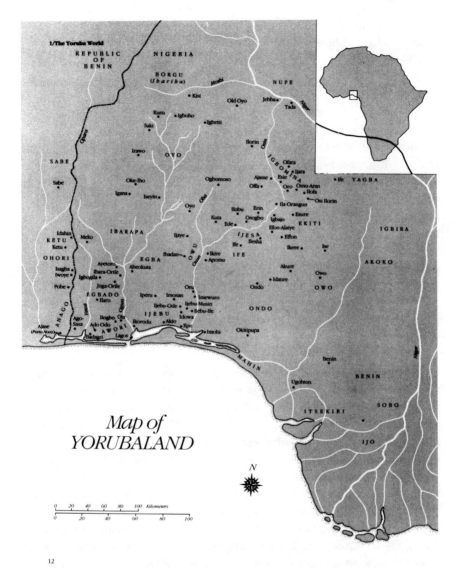

Fig. 1. Map of Yorubaland. Entirely capitalized words indicate Yoruba sub-groups, like the Oyo Yoruba. From Drewal, Pemberton, and Abiodun (1989:12); used with permission.

tion here bear general application to the towns surrounding the upper reaches of the River Ògùn, collectively known as Oyo North. These towns share a fairly homogeneous dialect with Oyo town (the present seat of the kingdom of Oyo) and with the metropolis of Ibadan. The religions of the Oyo speakers as a group can also be subjected to a variety of general statements, which this book offers on the basis of fieldwork in Ìgbòho, Kíṣí, Ṣakí, and Ìbàdàn. The argument benefits implicitly from fieldwork in contrasting areas outside the Oyo-Yoruba region—in Ìgèdè-Èkìtì, Abéòkúta, and Kétu.

Oyo North is well over 50 percent Muslim but has a large Christian minority. Indeed, it is chiefly in heavily Islamic contexts that predominantly female possession religions have been studied as expressions of female grievance (e.g., Lewis 1986 [1971]; Lewis, Al-Safi, and Hurreiz 1991; Lambek 1980; Ong 1988). However, this study calls into question a number of generalizations in the literature about the political role of women's spirit possession. With their history of apical participation in the royal state, the Oyo-Yoruba possession religions have come to privilege women in the articulation of the shared interests of extended, rural-based communities of men and women, rich and poor (see also Boddy 1989).

Yoruba Islam, Yoruba Christianity, and the various "traditional" religions impute rival meanings to the shared signs of Yoruba social life. Thus, they have become emblems of distinct forms of community and allegiance in modern Nigeria. Hebdige (1979:17), in a much-quoted phrase, referred to the subaltern invocation of signs shared by the oppressor and the oppressed as the "struggle for possession of the sign," in which the oppressed intentionally *disrupt* hegemonic expectations. However, in the context of Yoruba religious pluralism, it is not clear who is disrupting whose hegemony. Here the point of signification, both religious and political, has been just as much to *send out* the sign—to make it and the meanings imputed to it *familiar* to other interlocutors, to demonstrate that even newly asserted meanings are really a common legacy. This process of *familiarization* involves the deliberate blurring of boundaries between divergent religious identities. Centuries of dialogue and familiarizing rhetoric have transformed not only the local practice of Islam but the symbols and practice of "traditional religion" (èsìn ibílè). Hence, Islam, "traditional religion," and the ideological assertions of the Nigerian state must be studied as a shifting gestalt, within which the possession religions of Oyo North cast wives as exemplars and leaders of a moral order credibly rivaling the national state.

Laitin (1986) argues that, before the nineteenth century, "ancestral cities" like Ọ̀yọ́, Ìwó, and Ìjẹ̀bú-Òde had thrived on the myth of ethnic homogeneity as the basis of political unity. Although interethnic alliance and coresidence during the nineteenth-century wars undermined that principle of political organization, the British restored the "ancestral city" as an important administrative unit and, therefore, the chief emblem of factionalism in the twentieth century. The British made agents of resurrected kings, who in turn recovered their role as foci of Yoruba identity and political action. By the same token, I would add, the ancestral towns tributary to royal city-states, like Oyo's tributaries in Oyo North, also recovered the highly charged loyalty of their sons and daughters. Despite resident populations regularly reaching thirty thousand, such towns in Oyo North are sentimentally called "villages." In this particular region, they attract far more sentiment than the capital city of Oyo. Not only has the colonial reinvention of the "ancestral city" acted as a brake on Muslim/Christian discord, as Laitin argues, but it has authorized and financed a distinct sacred genre of hierarchy, inclusion, and exclusion that crosscuts Muslim and Christian identities.

"Traditional religion" has become a dynamic element of religious change in modern Nigeria, where it plays a key role in the renegotiation of authority and collective identity. Under the Oyo Empire at its late eighteenth-century height, not only Sango possession priests but palace wives, eunuchs, and *ilari* messengers made up the majority of palace delegates and functionaries. These personnel remained central figures at the juncture of British administration and Oyo-Yoruba communal identity. They delivered royal directives and crowned subordinate chiefs. Not only that, they advertised the gendered symbolic constitution of the king's authority and of communal integrity in the "ancestral city."

Throughout Yorubaland, initiates of the *orisa* priesthoods (*olórìṣa*) have always been a small minority of the population. So the fact that most contemporary Yoruba identify themselves as Muslims and Christians is not the reversal of an earlier situation. Instead, it indicates the relatively recent emergence of a *new and distinct type* of religious identity, amid the enduring appeal of the *orisa* in various key political projects. Labor and trade migration have proliferated since the colonial era. In the towns and quarters where these migrants predominate, one is unlikely to find *orisa* shrines. However, *orisa*-worship retains a central place in the towns and quarters that most Yoruba Muslims and Christians consider their ancestral homes. That is not to affirm the standard, and often racist, claim that Christianity and Islam are but superficial elements of African culture and personal identity. On the contrary, the interaction among these religions is a constituting dynamic in Oyo-Yoruba culture, which resists being classified as fixed and bounded.

The postcolonial kings and palaces play an ambiguous role in the administration of the Nigerian state. No longer represented officially on the elected local government councils, as they were before independence, chiefs act as arbiters in local civil cases and oversee the exercise of land rights among emigrants, residents, transient pastoralists, and newcomers. Since farmland is so plentiful in Oyo North, chiefs are called upon to defend their constituents' rights over central residential plots in the town. Because they are metonymic of absentee membership in the patrilineage, rights over such plots are hotly disputed.[1] Both Onígbòho and Alépàtà chiefs of Igboho, among others, hold permanent seats on the local "Grade C" Native Court, which handles civil cases, including divorce, and minor criminal cases throughout the town.[2] The local branch of the police force, ultimately headquartered in Lagos, is officially responsible for all criminal matters. However, whenever possible, people prefer to settle matters without police intervention— through the mediation of chiefs, for example—because police reportedly expect higher bribes and show less commitment to fair solutions.

At least since the colonial era, two neighboring population centers have been considered parts of the town of Igboho—Igboho itself and Igbópẹ̀. Further, a dozen nearby hamlets of Fulani, Ibariba, Tankita, and Jukun peoples acknowledge the authority of the Alepata chief. In keeping with precedents recorded under Indirect Rule, Alepata is still officially recognized as the paramount chief or king (*oba*) of Igboho in its entirety. Subordinate according to these precedents, local chiefs (*ijoye*) reign in a score of quarters or neighborhoods (*àdúgbò*) that make up the town (see figures 2 and 3). Each chief has been chosen among rival candidates born of the patrilineage ruling that quarter. Contrary to the colonial precedent, two of those chiefs rival Alepata in their claims of paramountcy over the town—the Onígbòho and the Ònà-Oníbodè, whose loyalists call them kings (*oba*) too. Beyond those two, the chief of Igbope claims that his village is autonomous. These chiefs often ally themselves with national political parties in exchange for the provision of material services—like road building in their quarters—and support in the factional struggles within the town. Among the chiefs, Alépàtà and Onígbòho alone receive salaries from the state government, an acknowledgment of their official staxtus as the town's most important chiefs. Their salaries, however, are small, and, like other chiefs, they rely on personal earnings and donations from far-flung supporters to fulfill their personal and official obligations. Thus the community's form and livelihood intersect with a cosmopolitan political economy.

For much of this century, Igboho's population has been highly itinerant, but the Age of Abiola has occasioned a particularly intense population outflux. The Nigerian national census of 1963 set Igboho and Igbope's combined resident population at 58,674 and projected the 1981 population as 91,511. By contrast, Agbaje-Williams (1983:161–62) estimates the actual 1983 population at 30,757. Even compensating for the possible political bias in the census figures and for their inclusion of the sparsely populated hamlets around the town, these figures strongly suggest rapid out-migration. Sons and daughters of the town trade and labor in Ibadan, Lagos, Kano, and Cotonou, as well as towns in Mali and Burkina Faso. They contribute money through the town-improvement society, which has in the past built schools, dams, a post office, and a clinic. Emigrants also build houses, their most costly single investment, in the town so they "will not have to go begging for keys when [they] return for ceremonies." These houses, along with graves and shrines, mark and legitimize migrants' enduring place in the town. Such material monuments are the foci of a dispersed and cosmopolitan community. The "ceremonies" centered on these monuments—such as weddings, funerals and their anniversaries, Christmas, *Id el-Kabir* (*Iléyá*) naming ceremonies, and the "washing" of new houses, cars, and businesses—constitute cycles in a community's self-recognition and transformation, a major reason they should not be missed.

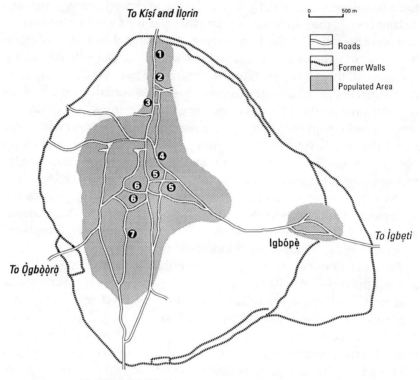

1. Òkè-Lóko; **2.** Ìsàlè Bónní Quarter; **3.** Òkè-Ìgbòho Quarter; **4.** Owódé Market; **5.** Igbó Ọba (Alaafin graves); **6.** Ọba Ago Quarter; **7.** Mọdéké Quarter.

Fig. 2. Map of Igboho, identifying several important quarters. Adapted by the author from Agbaje-Williams (1983:149).

Kings and chiefs are generally regarded as the "heads of [all] the priests" (*olórí àwọn ìwòrò*)—including imams and ministers—in their domains. Hence, both religiously and geographically, kings, village churches and mosques, and *orisa* remain conjoint foci of some of the most important sociopolitical groups in Nigerian civil society—ancestral towns and households. However, there is an emergent dissonance among these foci. The state recognizes no *orisa*-related holiday, as it recognizes Christian and Muslim holidays. Yet various *orisa* in every

Fig. 3. The main road of Igboho. Photograph by the author (1989).

"village," chieftaincy, and lineage remain important. Virtually every Christian and Muslim citizen can name them. Such knowledge is indeed one in a variable cluster of elements *defining* his or her citizenship, since the *orisa* are regularly named in the history of such sociopolitical units. The *orisa* historically associated with the main title in the capital town or village is particularly likely to have an annual festival (*odún*), which in such cases becomes the focus of a "civil religion."[3] In many cases, attendance is reclassified as a dimension of citizenship, rather than as a devotion rivaling Islam and Christianity.

Participation in *orisa* rites can constitute a claim to associated privileges. Aspiring Muslim and Christian titleholders may patronize them. Yet, neither in every "village" nor in every case does such patronage carry an unambiguous effect. For example, female divorcées' patronage of and participation in the *orisa* priesthood may substantiate rights of return increasingly begrudged by their resident male agnates. Resistance to such assertions can take the form of anti-"pagan" discourses. An Igboho man who felt his ancestral property was being usurped by his divorcée aunts (who had also come to act as priestesses of the family goddess) told me that the women are witches (*aje*). Although his verbal attack was private, he was not the only man in the house with that opinion. Moreover, in recent times such suspicions of female *orisa* devotees once reached dangerous dimensions, which we will explore shortly.

Myth and the Moral Authority of "Traditional" Government in Modern Nigeria

Orisa-worship is regularly studied in terms of archaic myths, as though it were a surviving fragment of a previous age. Let us understand it instead amid its modern political, economic, and ideological conditions. Most Yoruba live their lives in the slow but cyclic commute between "village" home and metropolitan "market." The political and economic conditions of "village" life in modern Nigeria are now what overdetermines the ideological role of the possession religions and their Islamic antithesis.

Despite their lack of coercive power, and perhaps because of their marginal role in the Nigerian state, hereditary titles in the "village" are highly coveted. Like the hometown itself, titleholders benefit from a variety of mythic associations and their modern symbolic corollaries. They dress a community's very modern concerns in the royal clothing of "tradition." Costly rituals invest them bodily with the gravity of an extended community's shared past and with graphic images of its future integrity. They represent an orderly, African-controlled world of the past, as contrasted with the immoral and divided world of the post-colonial metropolis, best represented by Lagos. The "village" is also a world of agricultural and uterine production, as opposed to the urban fount of unproductive and laborless exchange, prostitution, and "corruption." For example, most locally resident men and some women raise cassava, yams, corn, guinea corn, and so on, and women process them into consumable or salable forms. Proceeds from the sale of these crops leave Igboho people far poorer than their cocoa-growing neighbors to the south, not to mention the bureaucrats and professional traders in urban areas. Ijebu women up from Ibadan buy these products of rural labor in order to sell them in urban centers—for profits that most Yoruba, encouraged by the national broadcast media, assume are unreasonable.

It is not that all Yoruba at all times regard the city as morally bankrupt. Indeed, virtually every Yoruba town represents the metropolis to a range of smaller, subordinate towns, urging a relativity of scale upon our reading of this moral template. The metropolis is, positively, a source of revenues crucial to the life of the "village." Yet, to obtain those revenues in the metropolis, sons and daughters of the "village" sometimes engage in forms of "corruption" that they would be ashamed for their kinfolk and townspeople to know about. Likewise, the metropolis does not objectively exclude women from financial power, at least not as market women. Rather, the rural image of the metropolis suggests the antisocial nature of urban market women's power and distinguishes it from the moral leadership that priesthood and procreation confer upon wives in the "village." The cumulative effects of urban freedom and anonymity inspire powerful suspicions about the metropolis, which in turn reinforce commitment to the "villages" that most urbanites see only once or twice a year.

Their occasional visits rehearse an *ultimate* commitment to the "village" and its social/moral order. For decades, people plan their retirement to and burial in the "village." Hence, the money that people earn in the city is mobilized as the raw material of which the "village" and, literally, most of its architecture are built. The metropolis is not objectively chaotic, but the ritual occasions that define community in the "village" detail a moral order that the metropolis cannot and does not obey. The Yoruba metropolis abounds with immigrants who have found a certain independence from their home "villages" but usually lack a sense of community with their urban neighbors. The metropolis is *not-home*; it is the market. Therefore, for the people of Oyo North, the metropolis is not always identical with Lagos and Ibadan, though those cities are emblematic. It includes all those distant places where sons and daughters of the "village" go to earn by trade and wage labor, where mutual interest in the market vastly exceeds shared descent as the principle of community.

Postcolonial history is full of warnings not to neglect the ancestral home. Under the First Republic, the Sardauna of Sokoto not only ruled the ranking Hausa emirate and the entire Nigerian Ummah (Islamic community) but called the shots in the federal government as well. In 1966, when Igbo army officers concerned about corruption in the state selected him and high-ranking Hausa army officers for assassination, churches burned and Igbo traders were slaughtered by the tens of thousands in Hausa cities. In December 1969, two hundred thousand Yoruba fled back to Nigeria when Ghana, resentful of Nigerian businesspeople, allowed "aliens" only two weeks either to obtain a residence permit or to quit the country. The lesson for the postcolonial Nigerian was reinforced when Ghanaian residents were expelled from Nigeria in 1983, amid popular allegations that they were responsible for a crime wave. It has become all too clear that migrants must remember their hometown and protect their place there, for the hour may come suddenly when it is their only refuge.

Yet the Nigerian imagination is rich in characters who, in the city, abandon the norms of "village" community and commit themselves to unprincipled acquisition.

Villagers and urbanites alike describe the wealthy compradors of the city as *Alhajis* and *Alhajiyas*—men and women whose pilgrimages to Mecca epitomize their extreme wealth and extravagant consumption. These compradors attracted headlines in the urban press during the 1980s, bearing prurient witness to their theft of ever-larger sums of money from government coffers. In small Oyo-Yoruba towns, the *Alhajis, Alhajiyas*, and ministers are mythologized as mass murderers, who allegedly use people's heads in moneymaking magic (*lùkúdì* and *èdà*)—images of an urban and Islamic Other run amok.[4] I paraphrase the 1988 report of a farmer in Igboho:

> In Ibadan [the capital of modern Oyo State] they recently tore down some buildings. They discovered that most of the rich *Alhajis, Alhajiyas*, and ministers had the dead bodies of people they had used to carry a calabash on their heads and thus make money. These people would die after carrying the calabash and their bodies would be kept. There are special things in the calabash. It is put on the person's head. Incantations are said. The person's name is called. Paper money pours out of the calabash. The victim *cannot see where the money is coming from*. The calabash is stuck to the victim's head, even in death. (emphasis mine)

Like the victim, the villager cannot see where the money is coming from. Not only peasants but contemporary *orisa* priests single out

Muslims disproportionately for accusation, ridicule, and critique. Yet the actions attributed to the enemy reflect an old and familiar thematic core. As they are imagined, *lukudi* and *eda* rites exploit for illegitimate ends the vessel and head motifs of royalist spirit possession, which will be discussed in chapter 5.

By contrast, the just king of the "ancestral city" finds his mythic counterpart in Sango, god of thunder and lightning and often characterized as the god of justice. Nowadays, he is the greatest enemy of thieves and witches. An early king of the Oyo Empire, he is worshiped among nearly every people formerly subject to the empire—the largest and most renowned of the Yoruba kingdoms. As we have seen, his priests are called not only "brides" (*iyawo*) but "horses" (*esin*) of the god. This vocabulary is historically redolent, for Oyo's imported cavalry enabled it to conquer the Yoruba savannahs and establish its empire in the first place. Through his initiation in the Sango cult, the king of Oyo embodies the history and spirit of empire. He becomes "Sango himself" on earth (Alaafin Adeyemi III, personal communication, 17 October 1988). Sango is said to "mount" (*gun*) his sacred horses when he descends to earth, evoking an integrated symbolic complex in which horsemanship, spirit possession, and sexual penetration are homologous. Mimicking the character of profane wives, even Sango's *male* possession priests wear women's coiffures, cosmetics, jewelry, and clothing. Hence, in the complex of modern Oyo royalism generally, wives are the paradigmatic delegates of political and religious power, or *àṣẹ*.

Other *orisa* cults as well, along with their own nexus of wifely symbols, define the character of subject chiefs' authority and the moral order of extended "village" communities. For example, the tutelary goddess of several chieftaincies in Igboho is Yemoja, goddess of the River Ògùn. Festivals of Yemoja and other female *orisa* regularly index possession with another exclusively female sign—carrying loads, especially of water, on the head.[5] Hence, possession priestesses and supplicants of the river goddesses Osun and Yemoja, for example, make a ritual display of bearing calabashes or pots of water on their heads when they manifest the presence of the goddesses, convey the goddesses' sacred power to and from the palace, and regulate it on behalf of the royalist community. The priestesses' action itself is a metaphor for *containing* the substance of divinity in their heads (Matory 1986:92; see also

Apter 1992:97ff.). These rites link female and wifely conduct to a potent nostalgia, to the memory of an indigenous empire, to an era when the Oyo Yoruba were, politically as well as religiously, the center of their own world.

Myth and the Moral Authority of the Bourgeoisie

Since the latter half of the colonial era, a rival ideological complex, with its own attendant myths and ritual practices, has progressively over-shadowed and marginalized Oyo royalism, often by recodifying royal-ist signs. Islam is one of its most prominent emblems and Muslims among its privileged representatives. Reversing the policy of the previ-ous thirty years, the British began in the 1930s to scale back their com-mitment to royal supremacy in Oyo Province. By 1951 they had made provisions for Western-educated and commercial indigenous elites to assume increasing power through elected town councils and regional legislatures (Dudley 1982:45). Independence signaled not only the dis-placement of the British government from command of the Nigerian state but also the definitive marginalization of Oyo-Yoruba kings and chiefs at the hands of a disproportionately non-Oyo bourgeoisie. Its most prominent members originated from the less centralized Ijebu and Egba kingdoms.

Oyo royalist chauvinism therefore faced a variety of popular chal-lenges. The claims of the non-Oyo bourgeoisie to authority in Yoruba-land and the largely Yoruba Western Region were based, naturally, not on the recollection of Oyo royal grandeur but on the coexisting and rival understanding that the mythic father of all the "Yoruba" and neighboring dynasties, Odùduà, had founded the world at Ilé-Ifè, a city-state that Oyo never ruled.[6] Based on the testimony of Oyo royal bards (arókin) and written by a forefather of the British-educated Yoruba bourgeoisie, Johnson's highly influential *History of the Yorubas* (1921) says that Odudua was a princely immigrant from Mecca, a brother to Hausa royalty, and originally a Muslim.

By the dawn of independence, Odudua would also become the bour-geois emblem of Yoruba unity.[7] In 1948, the late Ijebu-Yoruba leader Obafemi Awolowo (one of modern Nigeria's founding fathers and the most famous Yoruba among them) named the precursor to the region's preeminent political party Ẹgbẹ́ Ọmọ Odùduà—"the Association of Odudua's Children." Although Awolowo appropriated a particular royalist myth to consolidate Western Region under his party's control, the Oyo king reigning at the time contemptuously labeled Awolowo and his allies "sons of commoners" (ọmọ tálákà) and chose to ally him-self instead with the commitedly royalist political party of the North. He had misjudged the mythic and material power of his enemy; in the end, Awolowo had him deposed (see Atanda 1970:226–27; Matory 1991:64–67).

Thus, Oyo North found itself triply alienated. First, the region was already distant from the federal and regional capitals (Lagos and Ibadan). The 1934 demotion of the Oyo royal capital as an administra-tive center had begun its isolation within the Nigerian state. Second, the alienation of Oyo hereditary authorities from the reigning political party in the 1960s closed a major conduit of popular influence and state largesse. Thus, only in the past few years has Oyo North known the benefits of paved feeder roads, and it still lacks telephones and piped water. Third, the investment of local people in the prestige of their royal institutions had been inversely proportional to their access to Western-style education. Because of the Oyo palace's restrictions on mission influence and Alaafin Ladugbolu's resentment of the emerging bourgeoisie, Oyo Yoruba had fallen far behind various southern Yoruba groups in the educational, financial, and managerial quali-fications to assume command of the postcolonial state and, in 1972, the heights of the economy, when other groups benefited disproportion-ately from the policy of "Nigerianisation."[8]

These forms of exclusion have affected women more negatively than men. They marginalized a sphere in which women are the foremost delegates of sacred and political power. Moreover, in an effort to for-malize chieftaincy succession principles, British agents assembled elders to make "chieftaincy declarations," codifying patrilineal ideo-logical pronouncements that had previously been subject to more flexi-ble negotiation. Matrilateral succession had not previously been so rigidly excluded. Indeed, both the Ọnà-Oníbodè chief in Ìgbòho and the Iba of Kíṣí claim authority on the grounds of being matrilateral kin to the Oyo royal dynasty. Newly codified and rigidified agnatic princi-ples carried great consequence in the town of Igboho during the explosive dispute over succession to the Onigboho sectional chieftaincy title in the 1950s. Formalized injunctions against matrilateral inheritance and succession yielded two consequences for the worshipers of the river goddess Yemoja in Igboho and for *orisa*-worshipers generally.

Devotion to an *orisa* was often inherited matrilaterally. So, first, the new rules undermined the legitimacy of the priesthood as a family-based social and political organization. Women who had remained with the patrilineage to care for the family *orisa* sometimes founded large matrilateral segments. Hence, second, priestesses found their sons and grandsons disfranchised, excluded not only from office but, by analogy, from the inheritance of material property. In the 1952–54 dispute over succession to the Onigboho throne, the Muslim son of a Yemoja priestess competed against a Christian candidate. The former had the support of the Oyo palace.

The rhetoric opposing the Muslim candidate was explicitly and coterminously antimatrilateral, anti-"pagan," and against the will of the Oyo palace. All of his opponents hammered away, during various meetings and inquiries, at his lack of an agnatic link to Onigboho House. In the Native Court inquiry of 17 March 1954, testimony linked the wider set of issues in a highly prejudicial manner. According to the court record, "an Onigboho quarter tax-payer . . . maintained that Adeshina [the Muslim candidate] was in the female line of descent from an Onigboho through his grand-mother and had better claims to the title of Igi-Subu [quarter chief and head of the *orisa*-worshipers]." The witness continued: "The tax-payers insist on Afolabi and do not want Igboho to become a second Irawo."[9] Adeṣina's grandmother Olomide had been an *arumi*, or possession priestess, of the Onigboho family goddess Yemoja. She bore Adesina's father, who married an official of the Sango priesthood. Adesina's father and mother, along with all of Olomide's children, lived in Oke-Igboho, the quarter directly under the Onigboho chief. Contrary to the critic's suggestions, his mother does not appear to have been of Igiṣubú House. It is unclear whether matrilateral succession to the Igisubu throne was considered a correct practice then. What this critic intended was apparently a side-long attack against *orisa*-worship, along with its implications of binding women to their natal patrilineages. The reference to Ìràwọ̀ probably alludes to the fact that the paramount chief of Irawo is the regional head priest of the goddess Òrìṣà Oko, many of whose priestesses are said to be former witches (aje). In this 1952–54 succession dispute, Oyo's preferred candidate lost, but his opponent would be installed by two of the Oyo king's wives, a eunuch and an *ilari* messenger.[10]

In view of Laitin's observations of mutual tolerance between Muslims and Christians, it will come as no surprise that the Muslim and Christian religious identities of the candidates were secondary in the immediate conflict. Yet neither was a self-identified *orisa*-worshiper—affirming that an emergent anti-"paganism" had become a factor in both direct and indirect forms of exclusion. This was a dispute, coded in religious terms, over the political rights of female agnates, priestesses, and their male children in the lineage (see Matory 1991: 240–56).[11]

Although the postcolonial state bureaucracy is predominantly Christian, a Muslim-dominated military has dictated policy during most of the years since independence. Regional and national governments make costly public gestures to forestall discontent among other Muslims. For example, the national government heavily subsidizes the hajj for all Nigerian pilgrims. On the other hand, federal and regional governments conspicuously ignore *orisa*-worshipers and other "traditionalists." Although it was premised on the suppression of Oyo royalty and its female religious personnel, the bourgeois accession to the heights of the state entailed not only appropriations of royalist myths but transformations of royalist ritual. One movement sponsored by members of this emergent bourgeoisie blended Muslim and "traditionalist" signs in a popular usurpation of both royalist and wifely authority in the "villages" of southwestern Nigeria.

Crisis and the Convergence of Signs: The Atinga Witch-Finding Movement

In 1951—soon after the foundation of Awolowo's "Association of Odudua's Children" in 1948 and shortly before the Onigboho chieftaincy dispute of 1952–54—a foreign movement to eliminate "witchcraft" (aje) entered Yorubaland with the sponsorship of the new indigenous bourgeoisie and attracted vast popular support. By combining signs highly redolent of royalist ritual—like blood sacrifice and spirit possession—with signs of Islam, it *familiarized* itself across various religious boundaries. Like *zār* and *bori* elsewhere, it spread far beyond its origins and found resonances amid local politico-religious tensions. It might be read as a ritual manifestation of the impending bourgeois revolution known as "independence," embedded with its leadership's sense of colonial power and the religiously hybrid constitution of the New Oyo Empire.[12]

British restrictions on the ritual conduct of kings—especially their sponsorship of witch-controlling cults like Oro—reinforced the sense in the 1950s that uncontrolled witchcraft had proliferated. This sense dovetailed with increasing divorce rates, as well as the growth of capitalist-derived economic inequalities and consequent tensions in the patrilineal house. Naturally, the solution came with the sponsorship of those ready to displace the royalist-colonialist alliance in the post-colonial hegemony—bourgeois Yoruba men and particularly the Muslims among them. Morton-Williams (1956:333) describes the sponsors of the Àtíngà witch-finding movement as "wealthy and influential men. . . . Some of them, indeed, were chiefs whose offices had once commanded ritual sanctions, but had been made secular under the [British] Protectorate; others were secular office holders. . . . The rest were men who had achieved status through utilizing wealth obtained in commerce." Perhaps the only document written by the movement's Yoruba supporters that appears in the colonial archives is a letter from two *Muslim* representatives of the Ilutoro Society of Iseyin, Oyo North, which praises the witch-finders' success and begs the administration not to outlaw Atinga.[13]

The Atinga witch-finding movement had originated in southern Gold Coast (now Ghana) in the 1940s under the name of Tigere, a spirit that possessed its devotees and enabled them to detect witches. Those who confessed upon accusation could be cured, whereas those who professed innocence underwent an ordeal (Morton-Williams 1956:315). The movement reached Dahomey (now the People's Republic of Benin) in 1947 and by 1950, with the permission of the Oyo king, had entered Ibadan and the other Oyo-Yoruba towns of Ìgànná, Òkèihò, Ìseyìn, and Ìjìó to detect witches. Atinga officials prepared an altar in the host town, using animal blood to consecrate it and to prepare protective kola nuts. Blood-fed altars were important in virtually all the *orisa* cults, making Atinga's claims of efficacy locally convincing. Like *orisa* posses-sion priests, those possessed by the witch-detecting spirit were called its "wives."

Although the movement originated outside the centers of West African Islam, Atinga's eastward permutations revealed important Hausa and Islamic influences. For example, Atinga's name in Dahomey was the Hausa word for kola nut—*goro*. The site of the ordeal was "a small square clearing made just outside the area of settlement, looking in position and form rather like a Mohammedan praying ground" (ibid.:316). Although the reporter did not pursue the emic grounds of his description, the badge of Atinga-protected persons—a disk-shaped chalk mark in the middle of the forehead—consonantly recalls another image of Muslim devotion. Pious Hausa and Yoruba Muslims take pride in the appearance of dust and a circular lesion on their foreheads, which proves the regularity and intensity of their pressing their heads to the ground in prayer. Prohibitions against adultery, theft, murder, and witchcraft address the shared concerns of scriptural Islam and Yoruba possession religions, while suggesting a petit bourgeois Islamic solution—the absolute demobilization of women.

Under the hot sun, an accused woman had to sit still for hours on the "praying ground." Her innocence could be proved only by means of an oracle, whereby a hen's throat was slashed and the bird released to run until it died. Only if the bird died on its back—in the least mobile of positions—was the woman acquitted. This posture suggests a reversal of the excessive female mobility that many Yoruba blamed on the liber-al divorce laws instituted by the British and on the lapse of earlier royal controls over wives and witches.

Atinga is not to be dismissed as the non-Muslim conduct of soi-dis-ant Muslims. It lies along a continuum of divinatory, "magical," and astrological practices that have followed Islam throughout its expan-sion (see Lewis 1986 [1971]; Lewis, Al-Safi, and Hurreiz 1991). No more and no less than any other local practice does the Yoruba synthesis deserve to be studied in its peculiarity. The point is that the persuasive-ness of Atinga lay in its blurring of the symbolic boundaries between Islam and "traditional religion," in which it achieved such success part-ly by identifying itself as foreign and *beyond* entrenched local cate-gories. It successfully *familiarized* antagonistic Muslim, male-hegemonic, and bourgeois assertions to audiences in the "village" and the "ancestral city."

Most of Atinga's victims were individual women. All were ordered to bring forth for destruction their "calabashes."[14] The calabash was assumed to contain the substance of her witchcraft. But calabashes are also the most common icon of the predominantly female *orisa* cults among the Oyo Yoruba—like Yemoja, Òrìṣà Oko, and Òrìṣà Ńlá (Ọbàtálá). Indeed, in the cases that Morton-Williams details, what women brought forth were precisely their *orisa* cult objects, which the witch-detectors would then destroy (1956:322ff.). Shrines for women's deceased twin offspring "were destroyed with particular zeal." In attacks on collective shrines, none of the possession cults appears to have been exempt, whereas four cults that are almost entirely male and nonpossession-related were exempt—Gèlèdé, Egúngún, Orò, and Ògún.[15]

This movement was explicitly intent on suppressing female powers widely considered destructive (*aje*), for which objective it enjoyed widespread approval. However, before they were stopped, Atinga's agents had exploited this popular imprimatur to justify attacks on women *orisa* worshipers, collective *orisa* shrines, and an Ogboni lodge, to the outrage of at least one king (ibid.:325).[16] The degree to which this bourgeois-sponsored movement might have become directly hostile to kingship itself will never be known. What is clear is that its *familiarizing* rhetoric concealed an adversarial posture toward witchcraft uncharacteristic of contemporary royal ideals, and a posture directly hostile to the feminine capacities that long made wives central icons and agents of Oyo royalism.[17]

On the eve of Atinga's penetration into Oyo town, the British enforced legislation outlawing it, suppressing the movement entirely by the mid-1950s. It never reached Igboho. But the class of Muslim and Christian businessmen that, through Atinga, usurped and transformed royal responsibilities and challenged British policy in the 1950s has progressively taken over the thrones of the postcolonial era, never suppressing but sometimes neglecting the possession cults. Yet priestesses successfully justify their increasingly autonomous ritual assertions in the name of the mythic king Sango, his mother Yemoja, his wives Osun and Oya, and through a potent recollection of imperial grandeur.

Whereas the Nigerian state and its religious allies have deofficial-ized the possession religions, they lie at the heart of many Oyo Yoru-ba's conception of "traditional government" and the "village" home. Virtually all members of the extended "village" community share the profound concerns about health, fertility, and safety from witchcraft that the *orisa* cults are "traditionally" responsible for managing on behalf of worldly and divine royalty. These concerns are the axis of a rival government with powerful precedents in two hundred years of empire and thirty of Indirect Rule.

Possession rituals in the "village" manifest and valorize an economi-cally marginal but ideologically potent politico-religious order, one closely identified with a "past" Oyo Empire and radically opposed to the symbolically "present" and symbolically chaotic space of Muslim sovereignty. They fertilize through the historically charged metaphor of "mounting," which *displays and mobilizes* "wives," unlike an Islam that recommends veiling and seclusion as ideal. Not only that, the roy-alist possession religions represent wives as the paradigmatic vessels of divinity, as exemplars of ritual political competence, and as regulators of Oyo-Yoruba society's supreme value—childbearing. They confront the radically patrilineal ideology shared by world Islam and the late-colonial formulation of Oyo-Yoruba inheritance. Despite the condition-al hegemony of royalist and feminine tropes of authority in Oyo-North "villages," these communities are internally divided. The Oyo palace has been the ultimate arbiter of contemporary conflicts in Oyo North, and the gendered symbolic terms of Oyo hegemony have been the idiom of the debate.

Gender and the "Clash of Knowledge"

The structure of regional administration, hierarchy among chiefs, and the politics of religious identity have been hotly contested in Oyo North ever since the departure of the Oyo royal dynasty for its final home, far to the south. Igboho businessmen and educated elites recount the town's history in yearly court battles over which chieftaincy title is supreme. They dwell on a distant past and frequently quote Johnson's *History of the Yorubas* with aplomb and creativity. The arrival and departing gestures of the Oyo dynasty in Igboho remain the central reference point of narrative arguments. Stuck between the interstices of legal points are details whose fullness at first seems intended simply to create an impression of authority through sheer quantity of data. The fact that those details continue to inspire such popular fascination outside court, however, hints at their qualitative importance as well.

The town of Igboho has existed at least since the sixteenth century and was long central in the political economy of the Oyo Empire. Hence, even more than most Yoruba cities, Igboho has generated multiple and contradictory accounts of its history, often in the service of intergenerational political rivalries. The narration of history by men and in male-controlled forums reveals not only the bases of conflict but also the *shared understandings of the constitution of hereditary authority*. These narratives guide us to the salient themes, concerns, and controversies that arise—presumably with modified emphases and outcomes—in the rites of the predominantly female possession religions. The most contrary assertions among bourgeois historians and male authorities in Igboho often invoke, as common terms, signs of Oyo power closely related to the religious practices they publicly dismiss as outmoded. Even partisan efforts to resist and undermine Oyo royal authority find their voice in these terms.

Conflicts among various male-run chieftaincies are debated with reference to mutually contradictory histories of the town, in each of which arise seemingly extraneous and, on second thought, revealing details about gender and the Oyo-Yoruba political charter. During the period of my research—spanning the 1980s—prominent Igboho men recounted and revised the town's histories in yearly court battles over which chieftaincy title is supreme—the Onígbòho, the Ọ̀nà-Oníbodè, or the Alépàtà.

The dispute hinges explicitly on who founded Igboho and thereby earned the right of sovereignty. Some say that Igboho was founded by the king of Oyo after Nupe (Tapa) armies ransacked the previous Oyo capital. Therefore, the Oyo king has the right to indicate which chieftaincy is locally sovereign. Others say that the first Onigboho had already lived there by the time the refugee Oyo dynasty arrived. Therefore, Onigboho is sovereign. Beyond dispute is the fact that four Oyo kings ruled from Igboho, approximately from 1555 to 1610 (Smith 1965:74). Nineteenth-century testimony from the Oyo palace bards affirms that the Ona-Onibode chief was sent there to rule in the dynasty's name after the palace returned to its earlier capital (Johnson 1921:166). Twentieth-century Oyo kings, on the other hand, have endorsed the supremacy of the Alepata.[18]

The beneficiaries of Oyo's rule recall the exile of the dynasty in Igboho as an era of recovery and vast prosperity. They set Oyo's historical themes of politics and gender transformation at the heart of the local political charter. Authorities in the Oyo capital have reported that the second Oyo monarch who reigned in Igboho, Orompoto, was a woman (Smith 1965:68), but Muslim and Christian men in Igboho agree in supposing that a woman could not have been king. The female Orompoto must have turned into a man before assuming the throne. One school headmaster and brother of the founder of the independent African Cherubim and Seraphim Church reported:

> Alaafin Egungunoju founded Oyo Igboho. When he died, there was no heir apparent. His eldest daughter was Ajuwọn Olode. People wondered where they would get a successor. Ajuwon said, "Don't worry." On the day of her installation she was dancing in and out. People discovered she had turned male. "Orompoto" (meaning "something soft") became her name. A woman who turns into a male must be a softhearted man.

A Muslim primary schoolteacher amended the tale significantly:

> Egungunoju was the first Alaafin in Igboho. Egungunoju's child was a female. No sons. She was to rule but this is against Yoruba tradition. She proposed, instead of shifting the throne to another family, to change her sex. The female Orompoto changed herself miraculously into a male *and stood naked before the kingmakers to prove it*. Orompoto became Alaafin. Her son Ajiboyede took the throne after [Orompoto's] death. (emphasis mine)

Whatever Orompoto's pedigree, according to this account a penis was the sine qua non of Orompoto's sovereignty.

Up until the time of Orompoto, by all agreement, no woman had ever assumed the throne, and no woman has done so since. As we have seen, Orompoto introduced cavalry into the Oyo military, a factor rich in implications for both gender and politics. Orompoto's successor, who also reigned in Igboho, is remembered as the first Oyo king to impose castration as a condition of service upon the ranking male official of the palace (see Johnson 1921:163).

When the palace abandoned the Igboho capital in order to return to its original seat, many chiefs resisted the move, as it uprooted a lively commercial, political, and cultural center. Whereas the political centralism and prosperity of Igboho under the Oyo dynasty are rendered in metaphors associating horsemanship with extraordinary gender transformations, the departure of the dynasty and the subsequent political disorder, with some symbolic consistency, yield sexual disjunctures and bizarre sexual mismatches. In a 1982 public inquiry over the current chieftaincy disputes, a female elder of Ona-Onibode House dictated:

> After the departure of Alaafin [Oyo king] Abipa there was a bad and notorous [sic] incident in the town so that everybody in the town was not happy. The incident was that *dogs were meeting* [i.e., having sex with] *goats, cocks were cohabiting ducks, etc*. It was this time that Oba [paramount ruler— sic] Ona-Onibode sent a message to Alaafin on the incident and the then Alaafin sent one of his servants bearing [the title] AARE to Oba Ona-Onibode to be leading the Ayabas [Oyo royal wives] to perform the sacrifice on the tomb of four Alaafins who dies [sic] in Oyo Igboho. (signed by Mojere Asabi—representative of the Alayabas, in Aderele 1982:163)

According to this account, the disorder created by the Oyo dynasty's departure was not only political but sexual. Not only did the local political hierarchy lose its head, but the Oyo king abandoned hundreds of his and his predecessors' wives. Mojere Asabi tells us that this improper politico-sexual order was repaired with the arrival of the Àáre, an *ilari* who led the royal wives in the worship of the kings' graves. As late as 1965, the descendant of this delegate appears to have cross-dressed in order to lead this annual procession (Aderele 1982; see also Smith 1965:60).[19]

All Igboho people acknowledge that the Alaafin once ruled from Igboho, but defenders of Onigboho paramountcy deny that the Alaafin founded the town and that he subordinated the town's founder to the delegates he appointed. One legal correspondence submitted on behalf of the reigning Onigboho characterized the imposition of Alepata's sovereignty as "political rape" (Aderele 1982:163). A reigning Onigboho and an elder of Onigboho House together dictated the following history to a Yoruba scribe:

The Pre-Alaafin's Era

Tondi—a renowned hunter and founder of Oke Igboho migrate[d] from Eruwa to settle at a place known as Iju Sanya for hunting purposes after a chieftanc[y] tussle at Eruwa.

Iju Sanya was then a rocky place with large holes in the rocks in which animals and big snakes used to inhabit and people dreaded the place and avoided going there for fear of the animals and snake.

Shortly after Tondi settled there passers-by used to hear the sounds of his guns and used to see smokes of fire emanating from the rocky bush. Then the passer[s]-by started to wonder who was the strange hunter living in "Igbo-Iho" (Bush or forest with rocky holes). . . . After sometime more people joined Tondi to live there and the place later became known as "Oke-Igboho" coined from "OKE-IGBO IHO."

This was how TONDI founded and permanently settled at OKE-IGBO-HO now shortened to "IGBOHO." (Afọlabi and Babalọla 1972:1)

Oral accounts consistent with this legend imply that Tondi himself was alive and living on the nearby and now-sacred Osanyinta Hill when the refugee Alaafin arrived looking for shelter. Rival accounts suggest that Tondi arrived after the Oyo dynasty and rested atop the hill. When Alaafin called him to pay obeisance, according to these rival accounts, the hunter on the hill claimed that an ulcer (*egbò*) on his leg prevented him from coming. Alaafin exclaimed, "*Elégbò wo ni mo pè tí kò wá dá mi lóhùn?* ("What kind of ulcerated person is this who cannot come when I call?"). The question was shortened to "*Elégbò wo,*" which then evolved into "Onígbòho." Alepata partisans hereby deny the literal meaning of "Onigboho"—"the Owner of Igboho." Malicious humor and tonal rhyming in the tale are intended to stifle reflection on the unlikelihood of their etymology.

The sequence of the two dynasties' arrival will forever remain uncertain in what one colonial officer described as the local "clash of knowledge."[20] Stories of origin in this town vary so systematically and obviously with the political interest of the raconteur that the search for a true version avails little. Still, a review of common themes in this etymological discourse on sovereignty reveals a common, hegemonic logic.

Onigboho partisans' *igbó ihò* etymology is, on the grounds of its tonal pattern, an even less likely original form of "Igboho" than "Elégbò wo" is of "Onígbòho." Yet the fact that Tondi was a hunter replicates a common theme among town-founding stories in those many parts of Yorubaland never subject to Oyo, and especially those identifying their origins with the hunter and warrior god Ogun, such as Ire-Ekiti. That Tondi settled and commanded a place full of holes, themselves filled with dangerous animals, recalls the old mythic image of powerful mortals who disappear into pots in the ground and thereby become gods (see, e.g., Epega 1931:23). Able to contain dangerous beings in these rock holes, Tondi is like Sango, who, according to one story, trapped a man-eating leopard inside a mortar (Jones 1988:22). Subsequent generations of Oyo-Yoruba kings would contain *orisa* and other powers (*oògùn*) in pots and in holes under their houses and courtyards (*ojú òrìṣà* and *aya ilé*). Royals are immobile because others come to them and run errands for them. The image of a local monarch sitting on a hill and awaiting the arrival of another monarch suggests the former's superiority, unless his immobility can be attributed to an incapacitating flaw, such as Onigboho's ulcer.

To prove their claim of sovereignty, Onigboho partisans have played on hegemonic structural logic at the root of Oyo imperial claims:

old	:	young ::[a]
provider	:	dependent ::[b]
central	:	peripheral ::[c]
sedentary	:	mobile ::[d]
Sango	:	Ogun ::[e]
crowned kings	:	hunters ::[f]
Oyo dynasty	:	subject dynasties

This chart represents that logic as a set of proportions, which may be read as "old is to young as provider is to dependent" (proportion *a*), "provider is to dependent as the central is to the peripheral" (proportion *b*), and so on. This diagram represents the logical relationship between any given pair of terms—for example, "young : old"—as equivalent to the relationship between any subsequent pair, and vice versa.

In order to deny Onigboho's subjection, Onigboho partisans implicitly affirm what is obvious to those immersed in the "commonsense" patterns of Yoruba myth and legend—proportions *a, b, c, e,* and *f*. However, at the level of proportion *d*, something subversive happens in the tale of the Onigboho partisans. It might be represented as follows:

old	:	young ::[a]
provider	:	dependent ::[b]
central	:	peripheral ::[c]
sedentary	:	mobile ::[d]
Ogun	:	Sango ::[e]
hunters	:	crowned kings ::[f]
subject dynasties	:	Oyo dynasty

The inversion of proportion d is meant to escape notice amid the symbolic "rhyming" of resonant metaphors in the rest of the tale's imagery. Moreover, the hunter becomes credible as an old, providing, central, and sedentary figure because a word that everyone identifies with the Onigboho—that is, "Igboho"—includes the hint of a word that is associated both with hunters and with the containment of power: "*ihò*" ("hole" or "lair"). Ogun and the hunter's power usually abide in noncontaining objects like spears, knives, and guns. Through poetic license, the authors of this legend have invented the hunter's powers of containment and made him, in the very vocabulary of Oyo hegemony, a suitable king. The "clash of knowledge" reveals a harmony of logical themes. Sovereignty and resistance are registered in a common repertoire of gendered themes: transsexualism, cross-dressing, castration, sexual intercourse, marriage, horsemanship, rape, vessels, and containment. Even more than in the Oyo capital, these are the uncontested substance of political history in Igboho. Yet their diverse articulations yield equally diverse resolutions of Igboho's contemporary political disorder.

The "clash of knowledge" is sometimes about whether women should participate at all in the politics of the town. But its discourse is often self-contradictory, revealing precisely where in the town's politics women's action is inextricable from the political life of the "village." As we shall see, the enemies of women's political participation also *familiarize* their misogyny with explicit reference to the tropes of wifely delegation in Oyo. The disposition of wives and their powers of containment are central determinants of political success and failure for both men and women.

Women are indeed excluded from elected office and hereditary chieftaincy in Igboho. Even less often in Oyo North than elsewhere in Yorubaland do women run for office in local government. One woman who ran in Igboho was warned by her pastor, "If you run, you will win, but you will die on the third day." So, she withdrew her candidacy. There are no women on the council and none in the town-improvement society, which determines, as effectively as Tammany, who will run. Since the Onigboho House chieftaincy dispute of the early 1950s, women have lost their minor foothold among the chiefly offices of that house as well. The single chiefly office reserved for a woman was among the kingmakers at that time. However, it has now been vacant for several decades.

Whereas the imperial order once delegated a central role to wives in the state, the modern processes of exclusion are justified by perverse references to Oyo history—rendered richly in the leitmotifs of Oyo royal ritual. A particularly bitter Baptist and member of the Ìfélódùn town-improvement society (whose wife had divorced him) explained why women have no place in Ifelodun or in the town's electoral politics:

> Women are not allowed to attend Ifelodun because their political under-standing is not developed. Among the Yoruba, whenever there is a discussion over the town or sacrifice for the town, consideration of a land dispute, or a planning decision, women are never allowed to attend. They are unreliable. Here is a story: Once there was a war between Alaafin [king of Oyo] and Aláké [the senior king of Abeokuta]. In those days, victory took months. Alake had a commandant with a type of magic in a *koto calabash* from which he would take water and bathe himself. Then he would get on his hands and knees on four *mortars*. That way he would become an elephant and go to the war front and fight invincibly. . . .
>
> Alaafin made a deal with the commandant's wife that he would *marry* her if she would reveal the secret of the commandant's power. The commandant performed his magic. When he went to the war front his wife destroyed the juju. He realized that something had happened at home. He rushed back and found only a bit of water, which he used to change back into a human before, finally, he died.
>
> The woman went to Alaafin to be married. He took her in, and on the seventh day Alaafin invited everyone in the town to Akesan market, in front of the palace, telling them he would marry her. Alaafin offered her fine food and courtesy, but refused sex. He just told her every day how soon the important day would come. Alaafin sent the guards to bring her out. He said, "You married your husband, you bore children for him. All the good things he did for you, and you would have me marry you so that you can betray me the same way? Never!!!" Then he had his messenger cut off her *head*. (emphasis mine)

Despite the political program immediately justified by it, this tale is laced with the iconic motifs of politico-religious processes from which no one, in truth, has succeeded at fully excluding women. Calabashes, mortars, marriage, and women's heads are elements of a metaphor-based technology whereby husbandly powers take control over vessel-like wifely heads. The duplicity of the Abeokuta commandant's wife is, significantly, both *sexual* and *political*, and it warrants the removal of her *head*. This testimony affirms royal men's dependency on wives but foregrounds the threat posed by the nonfixity of women's loyalties.[21] Hence, despite the silencing of women in local government politics and administration, they are blamed for the intractability of conflicts among the men of the town. This Ifelodun member concludes, "The trouble in Igboho is caused mainly by the daughters of the house [àwọn ọmọ ọṣú]." Like the Atinga movement, the tale evokes men's unsuccessful aspirations to control women's powers of containment. "Mounting" and its paradigmatically female objects remain key symbols in the constitution of sociopolitical order in Igboho. Although women are excluded from the electoral government, women's power is as undeniable as that of hereditary government, which remains a primary locus of wifely authority.

Gender and Religion as Tandem Factional Principles

The politics of religious alliance conceals a gendered cultural subtext in Igboho. The Sango/Ogun contrast illuminates a broader and tension-fraught contrast between two sets of religions in the town, and alliances among them reflect the duality of gendered political styles. Not unlike the predominant forms of orisa-worship in Igboho, the most popular Christian church here—Cherubim and Seraphim—attributes a prominent role to women's spirit possession. Moreover, not only are relations among local Christians and orisa-worshipers now generally congenial, but Christians and orisa-worshipers have developed similar organizations in response to their perception of a Muslim threat.

Like Oyo North at large, the town of Igboho is predominantly Muslim with a large Christian minority. Division in the Muslim community prompted the building of two rival Friday mosques here—the "Central Mosque" and the "General Mosque." The Muslim communities of most Oyo-Yoruba towns demonstrate their unity by sharing *one* Friday mosque. Churches are more numerous and constitutionally diverse. There are two Baptist churches, a Celestial Church of Christ (another independent), and several smaller churches. The largest Christian congregation and edifice in the town belong to an offshoot of the independent African Cherubim and Seraphim Church.

Muslim dominance in the national state has created a unity of interests among Oyo-Yoruba Christians, *orisa*-worshipers, and women generally. Northern predominance in the postcolonial military and in the national population of voters has given rise to a sense among Yoruba that Hausa and, therefore, Muslims disproportionately control the distribution of national resources. Although colonial records document considerable antagonism between Christians and *orisa*-worshipers, relations between them nowadays are remarkably congenial. Some Oyo-Yoruba Muslims appear to draw encouragement from Muslims' national dominance to antagonize *orisa*-worshipers. The churches have one ecumenical council, in response to a perceived threat from the Muslim majority, while the worshipers of diverse *orisa* from all over Oyo North also have a union that meets regularly and is constitutionally headed by the Igisubu quarter chief. The present Igisubu is Muslim. His personal prerogatives are highly limited. Typical of male chieftaincies in this region, his office authorizes women to act on its behalf. Two of his Sango-worshiping kinswomen, who also maintain the palace Sango shrine, speak for him in the union.

It is not clear when the Igisubu became the chief of all the *orisa*-worshipers, but early colonial records identify the office as such. However, there is no evidence that the office had carried any especially religious portfolio in the Age of Sango, nor that it had any privileged relationship to the Oyo palace. According to the earliest archival records, this chieftaincy had ruled over a town to the northwest of Igboho. After its destruction by Ibariba armies some centuries ago, the town's citizens fled and settled their own new quarter in Igboho.[22]

In the 1980s, the officeholder identified himself to me specifically as the chief over all the Sango-worshipers from Kisi in the north to Iseyin in the south—that is, throughout Oyo North. At the very least, it is clear that his is the central Sango shrine in Igboho, though secessionist Igbope denies his authority over it. The Sango priests, in turn, form the ranking *orisa* cult in the town. Their festivals occur in every quarter and are the largest; they predominate among the priests at festivals of Yemoja, Ọ̀rìṣà Oko, and Ọbàtálá. Hence, in August 1988, the Igisubu officially hosted the major annual regional meeting of Olórìṣà Parapọ̀ ("the Union of *Orisa*-Worshipers"), which convened about 150 representatives from all the major *orisa* priesthoods of Ìgbòho, Kíṣí, and Ṣèpètèrí. Conspicuously absent were representatives of Ogun and the divinatory Ifa priesthoods, which are exclusively male.

The only predominantly male priesthood well represented at the gathering was that of the Egungun masquerade, which manifests a slightly hybrid notion of gender and divine communion. Although its priests are not understood to be possessed by the divine entity, the small number of women who participate are among its ranking priests. Moreover, male priests salute the sacred masquerade not with the usual male gesture of submission (*dọbálẹ̀*) but with the female gesture (*yíkàá*), and, according to Johnson (1921:30), Egungun's chief priest in Oyo was partially castrated. Consider also Drewal's suggestion (1992:185) that the cloth mask of Egungun is like a female in relation to the male wearer it "contains."[23] Most Yoruba deny that there is any person, especially not a *man*, inside the mask. Hence, one might hypothesize that the *ancestral spirit* thought to occupy the mask is structurally male or, more likely, *husbandly* in relation to its earthly vehicle. I have not had an opportunity to pose this question to Egungun priests. Nonetheless, the Egungun cult is clearly imbedded in the Oyo-Yoruba hierarchy and ideology of "mounting" and gender transformation. Yet an anomaly flags the need for further research: Egungun's sizable annual festival in Igboho has absorbed the small festival of Ogun.[24] The compatibility of the two festivals may reflect a shared sense of the impossibility that males could literally be "mounted." Yet, unlike the Ogun-worshipers in the town (who are found among not only blacksmiths but hunters and transport workers), the Egungun-worshipers have found a common cause with the predominantly female possession priesthoods.

The union among these "traditionalist" cults is not primordial. Most are still attached to particular chiefly houses, which are said to "own" them. They still perform important roles in the coronation of sectional authorities, and thus in the reproduction of identity in the quarter and

the lineage. However, the *orisa*-worshipers as a group have now institutionalized a shared identity and leadership in response to a shared
enemy. The Union of *Orisa*-Worshipers demonstrates the new relative
autonomy of the priesthoods from local sectional chieftaincies.

In a sense, the form of that autonomy recapitulates the centripetal
action of Oyo imperialism: Sango is its leading figure. However, the
local Sango priesthood has been detached institutionally from the Oyo
palace. Possession priests no longer go there for the final phase of their
initiations as their predecessors once did. Perhaps even *because* of its
relative autonomy from the palace, the Sango priests and their new
empire transcend the factionalism of town chieftaincy and electoral
politics, enacting an order of power and knowledge with universal
appeal.

There is no more prominent a context of ecumenical and cross-fac-
tional cooperation than the festivals of the possession religions. (The
Sabbath gathering of either major mosque or of the Cherubim and
Seraphim Church draws a larger crowd, but, in each case, it is religiously segregated. The Ifelodun town-improvement society draws attendance from all quarters, but in much smaller numbers than does a
Sango festival.) Nor is there any more prominent a sphere of women's
leadership in the "village." In the annual round of festivals, thousands
of women and perhaps scores of men—representing all quarters, all
ages, and all religions—convene under the leadership of women, transvestite men, and their mighty but invisible husband. Amid the collective disarray of chieftaincy in Igboho, the leadership of the Sango
priesthood is the ultimate representative of the hegemonic principle of
royal sovereignty and efficacy. The proof of royal authority is marriage,
and the function of marriage is reproduction.

No other institution in the "village," including the government clinic,
possesses the authority of the possession religions to manage effective
symbols in the joint fecundation of wives and reproduction of the
household. What gives the seemingly unambiguous appearance of a
"sex-linked religious pluralism" (Lewis 1986 [1971]:100) is not men's
disinterest but wives' *leadership* in the pursuit of these values. Muslim
and Christian women form the majority of supplicants at public *orisa*
festivals. Their headlong involvement reflects the strong incentive behind their leadership—anxiety. Whereas their marriage and fertility are

the material proof of community health, their barrenness is above all proof of their personal failure. Yet, where other means have failed, husbands and affines share an investment in the success of these women's "pagan" endeavor to conceive children. Thus wives lead in a circumvention of Islamic dominance in the national state and challenge the very notion of mutually exclusive religious identities, while their sacred gestures of obeisance bring life to a rival politico-religious order.

Conclusion

Modern Igboho has taken form amid a new Age of Ogun, of which the renowned nonroyal businessman M. K. O. Abiola is richly emblematic. Though the ancestral city and town depend economically on the modern metropolis, Igboho and its counterparts are symbolically opposed to it. They represent a "village" home within what seems a chaotic national and regional political economy, where Islam rules. Despite challenges, Sango's kingdom and its gendered logic still exercise a powerful gravity at the margins of the Nigerian state, canonizing the wordly leadership of the wife.

It will come as no surprise that provincial Oyo takes gendered imperial themes of "mounting," containment, and especially gender transformation to even greater extremes than does the imperial palace. Igboho's geographical position had shielded it from Ibadan's influence during the nineteenth century and the financial wealth of the metropolis in the twentieth. Moreover, for at least sixty years, the town's many factions have been engaged in the competitive pursuit of Oyo's sanction—through appeals to district officers, succession struggles, court battles, and official inquiries. Although the local logic of community and hierarchy is centered upon metaphors of the female biography, it defines a set of options for men as well. As we have seen, kings and husbands are made effective and productive only by the proper disposition of their wives' heads.

What is qualitatively new about the state political hierarchy of postcolonial Igboho are efforts of the local petite bourgeoisie not to erase the trope of "mounting" that defined political order in the Age of Sango and the Oyo Renaissance but to literalize its sexual coordinates. Igboho's petit bourgeois men have systematically excluded women from electoral politics in the present era. In explanation, oral historians have revised the local Oyo charter, monumentalizing the image of *disloyal* wives to the detriment of the many loyal ones who made Oyo royal sovereignty possible. In a complementary formulation, male Christian and Muslim raconteurs have literalized the sexual character of the central figure in Oyo Igboho—Orompoto. By the latter revision of the Oyo charter, no woman could possibly have ruled as Alaafin. The kingmakers gave their approval only when Orompoto showed them his penis.

In chapter 6, we will consider how the possession cults in the Age of Abiola continue to mobilize royalist logic in priestly hierarchies and healing techniques highly empowering to certain women. First, however, we must explore the source of the operative metaphors, which is not female biology but the emergent social forms of modern rural wifeliness, motherliness, and daily female gender-crossing. We will see how common women in the Age of Abiola become husbands.

Chapter 4

A Ritual Biography

The possession priestesses of Igboho have been born, they have married, they have borne and reared children, and they have grown old according to the changing laws of two ages—the Oyo Renaissance and the Age of Abiola. These women's forms of consent and resistance have transformed the hegemonic models of ritual conduct and political expression for members of both sexes. There is a long precedent for the statistical and moral norm in Oyo North that a woman goes to live with her husband and his parents after marriage. People also tend to attach great importance to the natal patrilineage in the negotiation of social identity, rights, and privileges. However, the degree of enforcement of these principles and their weight relative to other principles of residence, identity, and cooperation have been anything but stable since the advent of the colony. Genealogies, colonial chieftaincy declarations, and a long record of chieftaincy disputes reveal the progressive ascendancy of agnatic over cognatic rights, resulting in the coincident marginalization of matrilateral kin, women, and *orisa*-worshipers from the dynastic houses of Oyo North.

Each quarter (*adugbo*) is the home of several "houses" (*ilé*) or compounds (*agbolé*). Such a house is called by the name of its founder, of its foremost chieftaincy title, or of an important bit of local geography. For example, the Yemoja-worshiping compound in Oke-Igboho quarter is called *Ilé Onígbòho*, or "The House of the Onigboho." Although some compounds in Oyo North include multiple lineages (see Eades 1980:48), the house ideally hosts members of an agnatic lineage (*ìdílé*) or of several sublineages that are assumed to be related ultimately through the same man.[1] Hence, the denial that any particular subgroup or individual is lineally related to the founder of the house is tantamount to a denial of its effective membership in the house—that is, of its right to furnish candidates for its chieftaincy. As we have seen, the denial of an agnatic link was used to devastating effect in Onigboho House during the succession dispute in the 1950s. Unrelated clients may live in a compound, but such cases are rare in Igboho.

Living with one's husband and his parents (i.e., viri-patrilocal post-marital residence) is one of the strongest defining features of the patri-lineage in Igboho. Married couples in the town almost always live in part of the husband's father's natal compound, although men and women identify strongly with their natal patrilineage. Igboho kinship terminology is cognatic, and marriage to any relative, lineal or cognatic, is forbidden.[2] Competing claims over usufruct, residence, and the inher-itance of titles and property are now subject to judgment according to a clear hierarchy of authorizing principles: maleness, agnatic descent, cognatic descent, religious affiliation, coresidence, and friendship, not to mention reputation, wealth, and divinatory authorization. Moreover, though records reveal an increase in the determining force of maleness and agnatic descent in the negotiation of identity and privilege in Oyo North, the resident population that must daily negotiate its position with reference to these principles has grown increasingly female.

Chieftaincy titles now tend to devolve exclusively within the patri-lineage that forms the core of the compound. *Orisa* priestly titles are a different matter. Certain offices in the worship of each *orisa* "belong" to particular patrilineages, but, in recent history, the larger boundaries of the residential "house" or of the cognatic group have increasingly defined the real limit of *orisa* title inheritance. We meet a complex situa-tion in Onigboho House, which contains two or three traceable sublin-eages, all presumed to be related to the lineage founder, Tondi. Three sublineages appear on the 1951 chieftaincy declaration of Onigboho House: Oyèbọ́ọ́dé, Òtú, and Agánnà (or Aláàtípó). The 1952–54 chief-taincy dispute, however, raised the possibility that Otu and Oyeboode are really branches of the same sublineage.[3] What remains clear, though, is that Oyeboode sublineage/branch and its cognatic kin have monopolized the Yemoja priesthood in the house. However, anyone vaguely related to a compound may return from another compound to seek the help of the *orisa* of his or her "fathers," as long as the god retains a viable priesthood. Even if a diviner sends a woman to solicit help from a particular unfamiliar *orisa*, it is presumed that some genealogical link connects her to a house worshiping that god (see Bascom 1969b [1944]:43). Women are especially common among supplicants with both explicit and implicit genealogical links to the house.

Houses, such as Ilé Onígbòho, are rooted in a particular residential geography, but they branch out beyond that geography. Men and women depart temporarily to labor, trade, or wed in distant places—be it for two weeks at the farm or a decade in Burkina Faso, or a few decades in one's husband's house. People may also depart more or less permanently to take up residence with affines or with spouse and children alone. Yet agnates retain variable rights of return, whose modification and clarification were the objects of copious litigation and lobbying under the British colony. It seems clear enough that male agnates are welcome to return and take up residence in the house, but Igboho's resident men currently opine that the rights of female agnates and matrilateral kin to land and titles are minimal. One evangelical Christian son of Oyeboode line declared that his sisters had better not even consider coming back to take a single chair from their father's house, much less try to live in the house. Yet, in their favor in this struggle for place, women and matrilateral kin command the potent symbolism of the *orisa* and the ancestral pedigree thereof. The sense of "the house," then, is as manipulable as the discursive uses of its core metonyms— the land, the "fathers," and the *orisa*. A variety of convincing but adversarial meanings may occupy them. Against their nephews' moral convictions, the elderly widows and divorcées who move into their natal patrilineal house must mobilize the historical, poetic, and ritual precedents of their own interpretive assertions to justify their return.

The physical house is inhabited by more wives of agnates, daughters, and children of daughters than by sons of the house. Although many young wives travel, some also remain under the authority of mothers-in-law while their husbands pursue work and trade abroad. Grandchildren are often sent back to stay with their grandmothers, that they may not forget their ancestral "home." Many of them thereby learn and remember their grandmothers' religion as well. The limits of genealogical memory also encourage a certain residential flexibility. The memory of precise kinship links in quotidian settings is short, undoubtedly allowing a wide range of personnel to occupy the patrilineal home without scrutiny. It is only when resources are limited or vital interests endangered that litigants unsheath the knowledge of cognatic links and proclaim the ultimately patrilineal principles of contemporary inheritance.

Women's Livelihood in the "House"

Ideals recently clarified—in the face of competing demands for the throne—fully endorse the coresidence of a father, his sons, their sons, and their wives, as well as their male and unmarried female children. Men are ideally and commonly polygamous. They "take" additional wives when, they say, their money is sufficient to wed and support them. Although men and women everywhere in Yorubaland generally express the expectation that husbands furnish the main livelihood of the family, women are expected to work and earn. The quality of children's clothing, nutrition, and education tends to reflect disproportionately the size of their mothers' income, especially in polygamous situations. Most men residing in Igboho cultivate the land, and many teach secondary school, hunt, or conduct a trade as well. Virtually all Igboho women identify themselves professionally as "traders" (oníṣòwò). Ideally, upon marriage, a woman's husband supplies the initial capital for a trade venture, from which the profits will belong entirely to her.[4] Although some resident women sell agricultural products and small manufactures, the most common commercial endeavor is the small-scale preparation of cassava meal (gààrí), corn-starch pudding (ẹ̀kọ), and hot meals. However, few find the capital or the market locally to earn at significantly remunerative levels. Neither within Igboho nor in the parts of its trade diaspora already studied does the stereotype of the independently wealthy market woman find many examples (see Eades 1975:39).

There are, however, exceptions. For example, Titilayọ (a pseudonym) of Onigboho House lives in the town, where she sold concrete during the oil boom and still runs a small bar, with which she modestly assists a network of her sisters, wives, and children. Another exception is a Muslim trader from Oke-Igboho who had apparently earned enough abroad to begin constructing a house on the land of her natal patrilineage. The work on it stalled some years ago, and the skeleton stands among half a dozen neighboring houses built and owned by sons of the quarter. Neither she nor her children live nearby. The disincentive for the completion of this house may not be simply financial. Women's investment options and priorities, like the norms of their residence, tend to be different from men's. In a patrilineal society, women face a different set of obstacles to converting metropolitan profits into wealth-in-people and security of social place. Pecuniary wealth is but one prerequisite to authority and security in Oyo-Yoruba society. What mitigates even wealthy women's power is their increasing disfranchisement from or structural subordination in a variety of central social institutions—the patrilineage, the chieftaincy, local government, and the town-improvement society. In chapter 5, we will consider the sacred context of Titilayo's rare success.

Women's Organization

Despite financial poverty, common rural women possess social options for power and enjoyment outside the patrilineage. Women organize themselves in a variety of elective ways. Groups of friends of the same sex often form clubs or associations (ẹgbẹ́). They attend one another's "ceremonies" and significant rites of passage as a group and, like houses, ideally wear the same outfit and contribute food and labor for the occasion. Egbe may be based on friendship, religion, life stage, and/or profession. For example, in a large church, all the married women belong to one of a limited number of clubs that collectively render service or contributions to the church. Religious and nonreligious egbe tend to be gender-segregated.[5] Virtually the only exceptions are the ẹgbẹ́ Ṣàngó—the association of Sango priests and the Union of Orisa-Worshipers.

Women who trade are also likely to cooperate socially and economically with all or some of the other women in the market. Women may guard one another's stalls when one woman must be absent. Clubs made up of the sellers of particular goods may buy them in bulk to save money and then sell their lots separately. Major markets in metropolitan Yorubaland have general market-sellers' associations with elected female leaders. Igboho has but a small marketplace, where large numbers of buyers and sellers convene only once every four days. Market women there establish special relationships with itinerant merchants, especially Ijebu women whose trucks convey Oyo-North produce to the cities. Traders believe that such regular business contacts diminish the likelihood of their being cheated. Both market women and nonmarket women participate in rotating savings clubs known as *èsúsú*. Each member of such a club contributes a fixed amount of money, say, monthly, and the total monthly sum is given to each member in turn. Participants may collect out of turn if an emergency arises—such as an unexpected illness, ceremony, or legal expense.

By far the most important social group of the elderly women of Onigboho House is the Yemoja priesthood, whose relation to the patrilineage is silently being transformed. It brings numbers of these women together on the market day (every four days) from various parts of the house, the quarter, and the town. It brings together even greater numbers during the annual festival. For half of the year, the Sango priests of the town—most of them women—participate in a weekly round of sacrifice, celebration, and feasting. During the rest of the year, they cooperate financially and socially, as other *egbe* do. Women are prominent in the leadership of the large Cherubim and Seraphim and the small Celestial independent African churches. However, neither the mosques nor the Baptist churches attended by the balance of the town population allow women any such status.

Despite the pleasure and importance of other associations, no affiliation is as compulsory for Yoruba women as marriage. They might not trade profitably, participate in savings clubs, or join any given religious group, but virtually all women marry. Moreover, an overwhelming array of female status transformations and achievements in religion, commerce, and government are defined by metaphoric and metonymic references to marital and reproductive status.

Women's Lives

Women's and men's participation in the lineage is a matter not simply of heredity but of ritual design, and that design is the *source* of the metaphors that structure personhood and authority in the possession religions. Any report of that design must take account of the struggle for the possession and familiarization of the female sign among modern village actors with diverse interests and moral dispositions. The diverse meanings they impute to women's bodies and statuses carry a number of effects with which we are here concerned. First, they constrain and motivate women's action. Second, they continually add new dimensions to the hegemonic model of royal and priestly authority. What follows is an outline of women's ritual lives. These are the conditions of women's entry and the metaphoric source of both women's and men's status attainments in the possession religions.

Birth

Before a child is born, she kneels and chooses her "head" (*orí*) in heaven (*òrun*—literally, "the sky"). That "head" or her choice of it is linked to an ancestor. The "head" comprises a person's intelligence, competence, personal limitations, and capacity to defend herself. Although symbolized by the physical head (*orí òde*), this spiritual, or "inner," head (*orí inú*) is distinct from it. The "inner head" is considered a person's most important *orisa*. It is made in heaven by the divine potter Àjàlá.

If a female child is born soon after the death of a grandmother, she is likely to be named "Yétúndé" or any of several other names that also mean "Mother Returns." Some children behave in special ways when they are born—for example, crying excessively or expressing antipathy toward warm water. Such behaviors may be interpreted as signs of a calling by the *orisa*, whereupon the child will be initiated. Children born in answer to a woman's appeal to an *orisa* also belong to that god. Many of the children who die within the first years of life are believed to be *àbíkú*, children "born to die," only to be reborn and to die again. Priests may perform rituals to correct the improper cycling of these child spirits through the world.

On the "seventh" day—that is, six days after the birth—a girl undergoes what is known in English as "the naming ceremony." In Yoruba, it is called *ikó ọmọ jáde*—"the carrying outdoors of the child." The same condiments that are assembled for weddings, the ceremonial liberation of apprentices (*fírídòm*), and the assumption of some chieftaincy titles are each inserted into the infant's mouth amid prayers for long life (as bitter kola is inserted), for a sweet life (honey or candy), for the avoidance of others' anger (kola nut), for the preservation of her life (salt and alcohol), for her reproductive fertility (alligator pepper), and so on (see Appendix V).

Whereas in the 1930s Oyo-Yoruba women were subject to clitoridectomy just before marriage (Fadipe 1970:79f.), female babies in Igboho now have their clitorises (ọba inú ayé—literally, "the king inside the world") knicked or removed in infancy (see Verger 1970:144; H. J. Drewal 1989:235–60). Clitoridectomy alludes to various premises of female role prescription in Oyo-Yoruba society. Whereas many Igboho men and women believe the operation prevents promiscuity, one Yemoja priestess explained the need for the operation in more graphic yet more perplexing terms: if the adult woman's intact clitoris hit the head of her child as it passed through the birth canal, the child would die.

Spirit possession and marriage symbolism together suggest the emptying of female bodily vessels and their refilling with the signs of a will, inner "head" (ori), or god belonging to the palace or the patrilineage. The children born to the patrilineage ideally share with patrilineal ancestors aspects of identity akin to the "head," whose further significance will emerge in due course. Hence, the juxtaposition of the maternal "king" (the clitoris) with the vessel of the child's patrilineal identity (in the child's physical head) seems to symbolize a social rather than a physical death. Conceived in lust rather than the ritually sanctioned marriage, the ọmọ àlè, or "bastard," is born without a legitimate claim to any social identity or privilege in the Oyo-Yoruba "village."

That this operation is now performed on infants suggests a new urgency in the demand to desensualize the girl. It also suggests a hurry to extract from her any identity independent of potential wifeliness. Visually, a clitoris assimilates the phallic sign of perfect belonging in the natal patrilineage, and it is extricated immediately. On the other hand, it represents something belonging to the girl alone—that is, erotic pleasure.

Girlhood

A girl's sexual conduct is the object of candid and serious attention across the spectrum of Yoruba religions, investing her with and depriving her of various capacities and opportunities. During the simultaneous blessing of her son's new house and a major annual sacrifice, a priestess prayed for her teenage granddaughter:

> My child who is looking for a husband, [only]
>   sexually irresponsible young men are around.
> Let them not fuck indiscriminately.
> The child who is by my side and who is going to school,
> May she not have a bad husband.[6]

The priestess is conscious of the options for a schooled young woman with a prosperous father like her son and knows that indiscriminate childbearing is the least desirable among them. Addressed to Yemoja, the prayer is meant to be heard by the gathered priests and the girl outside the shrine room as well.

In a variety of contexts, religious acumen relies on freedom from worldly sexuality. For example, virginity (*ibálé*—literally, "meeting [her] at home") is associated with special spiritual gifts. Some Igboho people attribute clairvoyance—including the specific ability to detect thieves—to virgins. A virgin is allowed to carry the goddess's statue to the river during the Yemoja festival in Oke-Igboho. As we shall see, *orisa* rites regularly center on the ritual regulation of such junior females' "heads" and wombs. This prayer invokes Yemoja in a characteristic way, giving force to worldly acts of redirection and control.

One of the most important ritual duties of priestesses is also the secular duty of most rural children of both sexes. However, by adolescence, boys and girls understand the highly gender-coded sense of that duty. As four- and five-year-olds, both girls and boys learn to carry water on their heads. They are given a small bowl of water to carry back from the river. Graceless, they have spilled half of it by the time they reach home. As they grow older, they manage larger and larger containers without spillage. However, as soon as their arms grow strong enough to manage full buckets, older boys refuse to carry water on their heads. They think the gesture unmanly. Among these village children, the girls are also the most likely to hover near enough to learn their grandmothers' religion, and they are the only ones who will "carry water" as a sacred duty.

Most girls assume they will marry and bear children in their early twenties. They may marry men locally or choose a man, preferably from the town, who lives abroad. Even if he is previously acquainted with a girl, a proper suitor makes his marriage proposal to her elder siblings or, through an intermediary, to the girl's father. Her mother is then left to discuss the matter with her. Her preference is important, but, among rural girls, the parents' recommendations and vetoes are decisive in the choice of a husband. Parents generally prefer a man from the local community who has proven himself, through education or enterprise, to be an able provider.

Most agree in regarding childbearing as the indispensable fulfillment of marriage, whatever its auxiliary emotional or financial conditions. Therefore, some potential husbands insist on premarital pregnancy lest they inadvertently marry a barren woman (àgòn). Many believe that a girl who has undergone frequent abortions may become infertile, and that fathers sometimes put infertility "medicines" on their daughters to prevent premarital pregnancy and then prove unable to remove them. Some girls get pregnant by men who refuse, in the end, to marry them. The man and his family generally do not, however, fail to claim the ultimate custody of the child.

Marriage, according to every Yoruba elder, not only demonstrates respect for the woman and honors the child with "legitimacy" but creates a relationship between two families. Hence, the prerequisite gifts in cash and kind are called ìdáná—"the creation of affines." Before a man and a woman marry, the two families investigate each other's history for evidence of hereditary flaws. If the families approve of each other, they arrange to meet, eat, and chat together. During a sequence of subsequent meetings, the husband and his family present a series of gifts—of alcohol, nonalcoholic beverages, livestock, yams, and other foods with which the bride's family will entertain the numerous guests expected at the wedding. The husband must also present ceremonial gifts of kola nuts, bitter kola, salt, honey, alligator pepper, and so on— each representing desirable qualities of the future marriage, such as longevity, sweetness, and fertility. From the groom, the wife herself will receive clothing, pocketbooks, shoes, an umbrella, and a watch, depending on his means. Christian brides receive a Bible.

The payment of bridewealth in particular legalizes the relation of the bride's children to the husband and his lineage. In the case of premarital pregnancy, a man may recognize the child as his own; but he is equally able to deny recognition. On the other hand, according to a Yoruba proverb, "One does not ask a married woman where she brought her pregnancy from" (*Wọ́n kìí bi abilékọ ibi tí ó ti gbé oyún wá*); that is, marriage, and therefore the payment of bridewealth, create the legal assumption that all the children recently and subsequently born belong to the husband and his lineage.

The symbolism of this payment displaces reproductive concerns onto the head, providing a crucial symbolic link between women's reproduction and women's consciousness, as well as the tandem control of the two in the possession religions. Not only is the cure of female barrenness the foremost demand addressed in those religions, but that cure, like priestly initiation, centers on the head. Over time, Igboho husbands have paid ever-increasing cash sums as bridewealth. The total bridewealth averaged between ₦500 and ₦1000 in Igboho at the end of 1988, well in excess of a village farmer's annual earnings.[7] In this respect, Igboho contrasts with a variety of non-Oyo-Yoruba groups for whom the presentation of cash is but a pro forma affair. In some towns, the cash is promptly returned on the grounds that no sum of money is sufficient to buy one's daughter. However, in those towns, gifts of a much greater pecuniary value are not only gladly accepted but demanded. In Igboho and elsewhere, a woman's in-laws may use jocular or serious references to bridewealth to check her insubordination. Yet, as we will see, the very cephalic symbolism applied in appropriating women's reproductive capacities becomes, in the possession religions, a means of emancipation from affinal authority.

On an evening after all the gift giving has been completed, the bride visits all the rooms of her father's house, soliciting the blessings and prayers of her parents, her senior agnates, and her nonkin guardians. They pray most of all for her fertility, but for other benefits as well, which the bride herself will tearfully articulate as she sings the *ẹkún iyàwó*, or "weeping of the bride." Oyo-North brides compose this nuptial chant based on conventional, but no less heartfelt, themes: longing for the parents' company, fear of slander by parents-in-law and abuse by co-wives in her husband's house, luck in childbearing, and the desire for the protection of her own ancestors (see Faniyi 1975).

Friends of the bride and the wives of her agnates lead her to the house of the groom's family. This "carrying of the bride" (ìgbéyàwó) gives its name *pars pro toto* to the entire wedding (see figure 4). The groom must absent himself before she arrives. Instead of meeting him at her destination, she will meet the other wives of the house, who bring out an enamel bowl containing cool water, a kola nut, and some coins. They pour the water over the bride's feet or use it to wash her feet, amid prayers that her tenure in the house will be cool, peaceful, and prosperous. In former times, calabashes were broken at weddings to insure the bride's fecundity:

> On the route by which the wife will enter the house, one must place a *broken calabash*. The tradition is in order for the wife to step on this calabash with her foot and break it into many pieces. The reason is that the Yoruba believe that the number of pieces that the calabash has broken into is the number of children that the wife will deliver. That is why the people of the husband's house will have searched for a calabash that is so brittle that, if stepped upon, it will break into countless pieces. (Daramọla and Jeje 1975 [1967]:39— translation and emphasis mine)[8]

The husband's momentary absence bespeaks the primary importance henceforth of her relations to the "wives of the house" (obìnrin ilé) and identifies the parties with whom she must try the hardest to keep the peace. The presence of kola nut suggests not only the hospitality of those receiving the bride but the avoidance of their anger (see Appendix V). A similar ritual washing of the feet is performed for kings taking the throne and for women supplicants during Yemoja festivals. The bride's friends demand small monetary gifts of the groom's kinsmen before allowing her to enter. They thereby ritualize the claim of financial support that the wife herself will exact from her male and female affines forever after. Such ritual claims are reenacted by wives, to the chagrin of husbands, at virtually every "ceremony" the affinal house undertakes. The prayer most commonly heard from everyone she encounters on her wedding night is Ẹ̀ẹ́ pọn ọkùnrin; ẹ̀ẹ́ pọn obìnrin— "You all will [give birth to and] carry on your back both males and females."

Married Life

Although some Igboho couples marry monogamously by the license and authority of the Nigerian state, most Muslim, Christian, and *orisa-*

Fig. 4. The wedding (*ìgbéyàwó*) of a Muslim bride. Photograph by the author (1989).

worshiping marriages are "customary" and allow polygyny. However, none of them fails to include bridewealth, without which the real raison d'être of the marriage—childbearing—cannot legitimately be fulfilled. That raison d'être subsequently defines not only the success and endurance of most marriages but the parents' social status in the eyes of most people who interact with them.

Husbands are ideally superior to and financially responsible for their wives—a strong ideological principle despite the existence of numerous empirical exceptions. Most Yoruba attach similar levels of value to male and female children and to male- and female-coded professions. Yoruba women, considered as a lot, are famously assertive, both physically and verbally. However, there are central social institutions in which "self" is neither the idiom nor the instrument of successful action, and where the collectivist idioms of action depend on *hollowing out* the wifely agent and nullifying her subjectivity.

Far stronger than the ideology of male superiority to the female is the ideology of senior's superiority to junior, which contributes to the practice and the specific form of gender inequality in this society. Respect for the elderly and the hierarchical superiority of senior siblings, regardless of sex, are perhaps the most consistent principles of Yoruba social conduct. It is significant, then, that husbands are generally older than their wives, and especially so among rural dwellers and the less educated. Men's average age upon the first marriage is higher than women's, and the average gap increases systematically in the context of polygyny. Yet women of all classes tend to prefer marriage to men not only older but better educated and more prosperous than themselves. Hence, despite exceptions, marriages tend to be socioeconomically unequal partnerships. Moreover, viri-patrilocal marriage sets the wife at an initial disadvantage, with respect to knowledge and political clout, in her new residential home.

Whether or not the marriage is officially polygynous, wedding ritual dramatizes a new wife's relationship not just with her husband but with his agnates and all of their wives. The "carrying of the bride" specifically underlines the importance of relations with other *women* of the house, to whom she must thereafter show humility, servility, and generosity. The elder daughters and wives of the affinal house—especially the groom's sisters and mother—can fill her life with grief and drudgery. A wife may live in the diaspora with her husband, live in Igboho with him, or remain in Igboho with their children and his agnates. Even at a distance, her mother-in-law and female affines exercise the leverage either to ease or to undermine her relationship with her husband.

Entry into the affinal house places a woman within a cooperative hierarchy of wives of the house and often subjects them to exploitation by its daughters. Fadipe (1970:85–86) reports that, some days after the wedding, the bride is first drafted ceremonially to sweep and carry water for a range of her husband's kin, in exchange for which they give her small gifts. Thereafter, she shares cleaning, cooking, and child-care duties with the other wives of the house and is subject to the sometimes unceremonious authority of her female affines, senior co-wives, and senior wives of her husband's agnates. She must defer to all those affines born before she married into the household. In turn, she possesses authority over any woman who marries into the house after her. Such hierarchical arrangements are the precondition of much female

cooperation, which, in economically livelier environments than the village, liberates senior women disproportionately to engage in remunerative endeavors.

Clearly, this hierarchy and even the ideologically central place of
men in it are not coded as the superiority of one *biological* sex to another. Yoruba kinship terminology expresses ideological grounds suc-
cinctly. Upon marriage, a woman becomes a wife (*ìyàwó*) not only to the
man she marries (*ọkọ gidi*) but to all of that man's male and female
agnates and to the women who married him and his agnates before her
arrival. Conversely, not only the man she married but all his agnates
are classified as her husbands (*ọkọ*). Female affines senior to her *ọkọ gidi*
may be called *ìyáọkọ* (husband's mother), which is also a subset among
her husbands, possessing equal authority over her. Wives who married
in before her are classified as her *ìyálé*—"mothers of the house." In principle, her husbands and *iyale* all outrank her in the affinal household. A
wife's cooperation is obviously not a fait accompli. It depends on her
personality, her sense of decorum, her alternative options for social and
financial support, the security of her relationship with her *ọkọ gidi*, their
possession of a distinct living space, and her evaluation of the threats
her superiors can bring to bear in the short or long term. Especially in
her relations with the elder women of the house, not all of those threats
are visible. Senior women are often suspected of witchcraft (*aje*), whereby they can, among other things, undermine their co-wives' fertility.

All other things being equal, a woman ranks low in the affinal house
until she bears a child. Until then, she is addressed by all her affines
simply as *iyawo*—"bride," or "wife [junior to the speaker]." Any delay
in conception subjects her to pity, contempt, or even suspicion. Hence,
women and their allies go to great lengths, ritually and medically, to
ensure their fertility. The birth of a child earns her a position of great
respect. If her first child is named, say, Tunde, junior members of the
house and junior nonkin will honor her with the title *Ìyá Túndé*—
"Mother of Túndé"—although senior members and wives of the house
may, and her *ọkọ gidi* does, exercise the privilege of calling her *iyawo*
indefinitely. If she does not bear enough children to satisfy her husbands (especially her female husbands) and if the wife has not cultivated good relations with them, they will urge their brother and son to
take other wives, a prospect that most contemporary wives find dis-

tasteful. Motherhood does not convey any rights in affinal lineage property, except as a representative of her children's interests in their natal lineage. Nor does it, by itself, deprive her of rights in her own natal lineage.

Later in life, she may come to be known for some commercial or professional competency, for which she will be called, say, Ìyá Aláta ("Mother [or Female Seller] of Pepper"), Ìyá Ẹléja ("Mother [or Female Seller] of Fish"), Ìyá Onírun ("Mother [or Dresser] of Hair"), and so on. Such titles in Igboho are associated disproportionately with religious rather than commercial competencies per se—Ìyá Ṣàngó, Ìyá Yemoja, Ìyá Aládúrà. Nonetheless, most Igboho women identify strongly with the role of "trader." That is their official profession, no matter how little they earn from their market stall of plastic containers, pan of cassava flour, or tray of sundries.

As a pillar of their education, many girls and a few boys peddle their mothers' hot bean curds (ọlẹ̀lẹ̀) or corn-starch pudding (ẹ̀kọ) from head-borne trays. Thus, even more than men, Oyo-Yoruba women grow up thinking about money and its role in defining them as self-responsible people, making rural women's dependency upon remittances from the metropolis all the more poignant. Some of the women now residing in Igboho conducted a small trade in northern Ghana before they and their husbands were expelled at the end of 1969. Others have remained in Igboho, shifting continually among laborious food preparation, soap making, sundry selling, and bar tending. By and large, women's very residence in Igboho is the measure of their failure in or withdrawal from profitable areas of trade. Here, and in much of Igboho's diaspora as well, what English speakers call "petty trading" is less a livelihood than a historically conditioned sense of self, ever exchanging one limited option for another. It is the *multiplicity* rather than the *profitability* of these options that makes the lives of Oyo-North women so rich.

Many believe that after a few births, the husband's level of attention and affection naturally declines. The man no longer needs to compete with other suitors; she is worthless to another man, he reasons. Now in competition with his girlfriends and other wives, *she* must work to maintain her *husband*'s devotion. Hence, a woman whose husband remains affectionate in the long term is suspected of "cooking" (sè) him (O. E. Fatoye-Matory, personal communication, 18 January 1993).

Through procedures associated, again, with pots, the *wife* must actively and sometimes ritually maintain her marriage. Various elaborate ritual strategies are attributed to the wives of a faithful and generous husband.[9]

There is an increasingly dominant sense in Yorubaland—perhaps less believed there than in Europe since the Crusades and the Inquisition—that a person belongs to one religion and one only. Just as widely spoken (and equally often disobeyed) is the supposition that a bride must assume her husband's religion, just as any ward assumes the religion of his or her guardian. The reality of women's devotion in Igboho is much more fluid. Women asked to recount the circumstances of their own "conversions" from one Christian denomination to another sometimes credit their husbands but, like other categories of convert, more often speak of independent incentives, such as a solution to health problems (especially infertility) or the inheritance of religious obligations from their parents. Consequently, many women declare religious affiliations different from their husbands'. The subtle truth is that wives *participate* in the activities of their husbands' religious groups just as in his other associations, or *egbe*. Although they participate in their husbands' religions, the support women endeavor to lend to events in their fathers' households regularly involves them in alternative devotions. Under the banner of filial loyalty, women might even neglect to follow the religion of the *current* majority in the natal house. Wives who periodically return home from their husbands' compounds are often the chief conservators of the lineage *orisa* tradition. Women's piety toward the ancestral *orisa* may follow material motives as well. Barrenness, affliction by *àbíkú* ("children born to die"), and a range of persistent personal afflictions often find resolution in *orisa*-worship, and the *orisa* of the natal house is the first order of appeal.

On the other hand, many women do declare themselves converted from the worship of their mother's and father's gods to new devotions. The conversion stories of elderly first-generation Christians are a virtual genre in their own right, emphasizing the unconditional leap of faith from one religion to another. Yet the public convention of categorical self-declaration often conceals a sequence of conditional appeals to the healers and to the beliefs of other religions.

Women's marital and reproductive status directly affects their standing in every local religious organization. Menstruation compromises the participation of women of childbearing age—the characteristic *wives*—in *orisa*, *Aládúrà* Christian, and Muslim rites. Among the few secluded Muslim women in Igboho, married women of childbearing age are naturally the most common.[10] However, the labor of most wives is far too important for many households to demand women's seclusion. Although both secluded Muslim women and *orisa* possession priestesses are relatively few in the general population, they are highly public and influential representatives of rival politico-religious orders in Oyo-Yoruba life. The sartorial iconography of the secluded Muslim woman—with her full-body, black *jelubábà* veil—contrasts diametrically with the image of the village woman sculpted and enshrined foremost on Sango and Yemoja altars. In *orisa* shrine sculpture, women kneel to offer service and sacrifice, carry head loads, and/or tie a baby to their back to free the hands and facilitate easy transport. The woman remains the paradigmatic image of married wifeliness not only in the *orisa* religions but across the Yoruba religious spectrum. In popularity, that paradigm has reigned over the alternative but increasingly popular images sanctioned by the Near Eastern traditions. The Sango and Yemoja priesthoods *sacralize* wifely mobility, activity, and labor, albeit in submission to husbandly and divine forces. Unlike the paradigmatic Yoruba woman, the exemplary Muslim Yoruba woman (that is, the secluded *eléhàá*) is both laborless and immobile in her submission.

In Igboho, a woman's most frequent and arduous duty is to carry water. Fadipe's reports that Oyo-North nuptial ritual requires brides to fetch water for a wide circle of the husband's kin recommends water carrying as an emblematic duty of wifeliness (see Fadipe 1970:85). An *elehaa*, or secluded Muslim woman, is in principle exempt from that duty—a fact that greatly inspired my female Christian research assistant. To her, purdah seems a species of leisure, in which the husband commits himself to providing a range of lesser services as well—like shopping and fetching firewood. The research assistant sharply contrasted the *elehaa*'s experience with her own subjection to affines' onerous demands on her labor and household food, which her husband's mother, aunts, and cousins conceive to be her husband's and therefore their own property.

Orisa iconography, by contrast, makes a virtue of women's paradigmatic labor. For the priestesses of Yemoja, bearing water on the head becomes a display of prowess and control, a means of incorporating divine power, and a metaphor of the goddess's power to fill the uterine vessel. In the shared and extant values of the Yoruba majority, women's heads and their capacity in symbolic and material labor must be paid for. Local Islamic authorities, on the other hand, condemn any payment of bridewealth, or "money for the bride's head." If *orisa* rites objectify women's "heads" and submit them to the symbolic media of market exchange, then local Muslim ideals literally shroud these erstwhile key symbols of female social and political efficacy, surely with ambiguous consequences.

Although they are indispensable to the sociopolitical units that define their role as wifeliness, most Yoruba women are far more affectively committed to their role as mothers. Conversely, most Yoruba men and women are far more devoted to their biological mothers than to their wives. The mother-son bond tends to be affectively strong and, as such, constitutes a gravity that is highly threatening to the lineal order of authority in patrilineage and kingdom. A woman possesses her most guaranteed authority, sense of achievement, and sense of belonging—in short, her foremost wealth-in-people—among her children. She invests the lion's share of her hope and resources in their health, education, and enterprise, necessarily in currency of the sort that she can manage independently of the institutions that exclude her: money. During the 1980s, many men's commercial transport vehicles bore the huge inscription *Ọla Iya*—"Wealth from Mother"—to honor their major investor. Given the forms of their subjection in the patrilineage, women became exemplary investors in the market and in their sons' independence from lineage hierarchies. Even at the inauguration of what promised to be the mightiest and most inclusive institution in Yoruba life—the Nigerian nation-state—some women sensed either the inevitability of exclusion or the advantage of autonomy; perhaps the one necessitated the other. Months after Nigerian national independence, Mabogunje (1961:16) wrote, "Market-women find political agitation for national independence difficult to interpret in the reality of their world. They want to trade; no one has stopped them. Their most profitable trade, even when the profit does not amount to much, has been with the whitemen."

This incongruity between some women's interests and the collective endeavors of their male countrymen resonates with others that have branded women as antisocial, hoarding, and dangerously selfish— hence the association of witchcraft (*aje*) with the market. Although the Oyo Yoruba have long recognized the existence of witchcraft and actively sought to control it ritually, our understanding of its present meaning must reflect recent and present circumstances like the ones Mabogunje observed. Indeed, many believe that the witches have multiplied and grown more powerful in the Age of Abiola.

In several senses, the witch is a further historically conditioned transformation of the wife. First, women's reason for marrying is to become mothers, according to which role the witches are known in daily discourse. So closely are they identified with motherhood and the control of reproductive processes that they are literally called "our mothers" (*àwọn ìyáà wa*). Indeed, no one who wishes to avoid their wrath speaks the name *aje* openly. Second, colonial legislation made a woman's money and its "secretive" accumulation optional conditions of freedom from potentially oppressive domestic situations. Third, viripatrilocal marriage makes her children's education and enterprise far more attractive objects of investment than, say, the construction of houses on patrilineal land.

Indeed, women's recent judicial and popular disfranchisement from the natal patrilineage has decreased the attractiveness of the latter option and of other investments in the patrilineal order as well. Women's investment in the transport vehicles that carry their driver sons and every other migrant to the metropolis is evocative on many levels. It escapes the choice between investment in natal and affinal patrilineage. Instead, it finances and profits from the metropolitan order rivaling "village" patriliny and royalism generally. Appropriately, its most visible vehicles are the mobile altars of Ogun. Hence, the conduct of "our mothers"—that is, of the wives who have escaped or transcended patrilineal control—reveals not selfishness and anomie but some of the fundamental politico-religious forms of the dominant metropolitan order.

Yet Mabogunje's 1961 account of market women's political opinions illustrates continued reservations about women within that metropolitan order. The interior spaces of Ogun's modern altars are inscribed

with sons' ambivalence toward their wives and potential wives in particular. The decals omnipresent in Nigerian taxis and *dáñfó* (commercial
vans) report, "A beautiful woman never stays with one man" and *Owo
lobirin mo*—"Money is what women know."[11]

Divorce

Yoruba rates of legal divorce are high by African standards, a fact
that Peter Lloyd (1968) correlates with the high degree to which Yoruba
women retain rights of residence and inheritance in their natal kin
groups.[12] However, in Igboho, the degree to which women retain those
rights is not sufficiently fixed to explain other dependent variables like
the divorce rate. Many Igboho residents complain that divorce rates are
increasing or that they are higher than they should be—this at the same
time that women's rights of return in Igboho are being questioned. We
have no overall statistics on divorce in Igboho, but residents' anecdotal
observations suggest a notable concentration of divorcées in Onigboho
House, many of them actively associated with the Yemoja priesthood.

Religion is a factor in both divorce and rights of return. There is
some indication that predominantly Muslim Yoruba towns have higher
divorce rates than predominantly Christian ones. However, there is
disagreement over whether these two religions affect the likelihood of
divorce within any given town. Whereas Lloyd denies any effect, the
Okedijis report that among residents of central Ibadan Muslims are
much more prone than the members of other religions to divorce,
owing to the frequency among them of polygynous marriage, with its
implications of male financial neglect and co-wife friction, and domination by the mother-in-law in Muslim households (Lloyd 1968:78;
Okediji and Okediji 1966:160).

These authors present little data on *orisa*-worshipers as such. Yet, in
the possession priesthoods associated closely with one house or
another, the primary caretakers of shrines are female agnates who
return periodically or permanently to their father's house, be it under
conditions of visitation, divorce, or widowhood. To the degree that
other residents favor the cultivation of the family *orisa* and have no
conflicting interest in the residential space and other prerogatives these
women appropriate, such residents also welcome the return of certain

daughters of the house, or ọmọ ọṣú. The ọmọ ọṣú has a variety of reasons to return to her father's house. Particularly if her children have migrated away from her affinal house, she might expect to find a warmer community and greater material support in her natal house. If she has divorced a husband in the trade diaspora, she is even more likely to seek the community of kin at home.

Divorce is nearly always initiated by the wife. In the context of legal polygyny, a man has relatively little incentive to pursue formal divorce, for he can simply neglect a wife he dislikes and cultivate other relationships. In order to divorce, a woman must see that her estranged husband is compensated according to "Native Law and Custom" little changed since the Oyo Renaissance. In many cases, a husband may demand compensation for a range of gifts, services, and loans to the wife and her family. Sufficiently prosperous women are able to compensate the estranged husband themselves. Others must rely on the cooperation, liquidity, and goodwill of their natal families, who received the bridewealth in the first place. However, most women rely on the prospective husband to repay the bridewealth. This fact elicits various explanations and moral valuations.

Some attribute it to women's gold digging. Countless legends and anecdotes report that women abandon humble men when richer ones come along. Data from Ibadan in the 1960s suggest that most women divorce after they have begun a sexual relationship with a new partner (Lloyd 1968:70). Moreover, most divorcées say they not only prefer to but do marry men richer than their previous husbands (Okediji and Okediji 1966:157–58). However, such declarations are directly connected to women's hopeful if uncertain inference that a man who (1) buys them gifts during premarital trysts and (2) promises to refund the bridewealth on her behalf *must* be richer than the estranged husband. Even if we are able to compensate for optimistic distortion, we must be cautious about extending empirical data from Ibadan's resident population to Oyo North or its diaspora, especially in light of the various sociological, economic, and political contrasts already established between them.

Although we have no systematic data on divorce rates in Igboho, it is clear that marriage into the rural patrilineage is fraught with its own qualitatively and quantitatively different oppressions and nonfinancial difficulties, in the light of which we must contextualize rural divorce and the financial concerns that rural women too undoubtedly feel. In Ibadan, women who anticipate the generosity of apparently wealthy husbands are frequently disappointed, and, in general, financial neglect is these urban women's foremost explanation for seeking divorce. In the context of rural poverty and husbands' out-migration, rural women's disappointment and deprivation must be even greater. After financial neglect, co-wife hostility and mother-in-law problems are the most prominent reasons Ibadan women give for divorce (Okediji and Okediji 1966:155–56). In Igboho, where viri-patrilocal marriage is all the more standard, these problems likely occur to a correspondingly greater degree.

Divorce is not always as formal or clear an event as the American and British term for it suggests. Among middle-class North Americans, the term "divorce" denotes a specific and instantaneous change of legal status declarable only by constituted authorities of the state. In Yoruba society, by contrast, many women are moved by personal grievances to quit the husband's home for indeterminate periods. A woman may feel so financially neglected or so aggrieved by the arrival of a second wife that she moves out. She and her husband may still communicate or have sex intermittently, or they may not. The Yoruba term for divorce—kíkò—specifically denotes "refusal" and "desertion." It therefore applies to various degrees of estrangement, the most extreme of which occurs only at the moment when a woman has found a new partner and decides to legalize her union with him. Such progressive estrangement is more normal than the case that colonial officials and twentieth-century critics of divorce generally describe, in which women simply leave one man because they have found a richer one.

Ultimately, the presence of minor children is the foremost among many factors determining the form and longevity of a given union. "Native Law and Custom" clearly stipulates that children belong to their natal patrilineage and that the father's house has preeminent rights of custody over children above five to seven years of age. However, women estranged from urban marriages frequently retain de facto custody of older children as well, especially when the father lives away from his mother and from female agnates willing to take care of the child. If the couple or the wife and their children have lived in the rural patrilineal compound, the husband's mother and female agnates may be quite assertive about retaining custody of the children following divorce or separation. Thus her affines' rights of child custody provide a strong incentive for an Igboho wife to remain in or near her husband's home.

Amid various degrees of the husband's estrangement or geographical absence from her personal abode—and many husbands have left to find work—the wife is likely to remain in active contact with her children's agnates. The female-directed marital rites (*igbeyawo*) and the dicta of pontificating elders alike remind us that contact with one's husband's *kin* is at least half the definition of a marriage. A wife and her children serve senior members of the resident lineage and are likely to receive varying degrees of material support from both sons and daughters of the house. When support is inadequate, a wife may leave, but, if there is any doubt about the woman's willingness to remain in contact, her children must stay. Senior women possess not only the legal but, in young women's understanding, the mystical means of enforcing their authority.

Tales recounted among *orisa*-worshipers also report the frequent flight of women, usually on account of the husband's betrayal of a promise. The goddess Yemoja herself fled from her husband for that reason.[13] Just as the *orisa* shrines represent women ideally bearing large breasts, large abdomens, and pots on head and in hand, *orisa*-worshipers' tales of women's flight invariably involve the dropping, breaking, bursting, and spilling of pots, heads, breasts, and abdomens. When they leave, mythical women take not only their pots but their children, a version of events still evident elsewhere in Yorubaland but unusual in Igboho. Oke-Igboho, however, is the home of a much-discussed exception.

Dotage

After menopause, women enter a new phase of both reproductive and social life. They have reached the heights of the patrilineal order and are, at once, beyond its restrictions on the movement of wives. Hence, an elderly woman possesses multiple options. However, she must circumvent new ideological and material constraints. Around them, she negotiates the social place and meaning of her seniority.

Because of the marital age gap, the husbands (ọkọ gidi), particularly of junior wives, are likely to be dead, and elderly women's children have usually left the rural town to labor or conduct trade. Ideally, these women continue living with the affinal lineage. All other things being equal, they are subject to disapproval if they leave it for good. However, in the absence of their children, they may prefer the company of their natal kin and childhood age-mates.

Also ideally, a woman's children support her in old age. Widows generally possess few rights of inheritance over their deceased husband's property. Any properties she held as her children's guardian eventually come under the control of adult sons and daughters. The moveable property women inherited years earlier from their fathers and mothers is generally limited in value and durability. When their children have migrated away from their natal agnatic home, mothers may receive remittances from the metropolis but, in practice, also depend on resident affines with few resources and sometimes little commitment to their well-being.

Widows of particularly affluent and monogamous marriages may retain control over the house in the metropolis or in the viri-patrilocal hometown that the couple shared in life. The average elderly Igboho woman is not so secure, financially or socially. Hence, the ideal is for her to live either among her children residing in the town or with a son and his spouses in the metropolis, assuming he has the dwelling space and economic means to accommodate her. Or she may reside with various children in turn. Among her children and their wives, she enjoys incomparable authority and comfort. Some women who have lived abroad for years prefer to continue trading there until they die, despite their children's invitations to join them wherever they are. Nevertheless, elderly women's residence in the village entails, ipso facto, various degrees of separation from their prosperous offspring.

Their next best option is often to dwell in the bungalows erected by their emigrant brothers, male cousins, and, occasionally, sons over the foundations of their fathers' leveled laterite compounds. Prosperous resident sisters may lend support to less prosperous ones, and their resident grandchildren provide both joy and important material services, like fetching water. To a degree, however, elderly women always depend on the welcome of their male agnates. That welcome may come only grudgingly. The inheritance rights of women and matrilateral kin were angrily challenged in the Onigboho House succession dispute of 1952–54, and in 1988–89 I heard resident men explicitly deny adult female agnates' rights of residence.

That denial has not only legal roots in the 1950s but diffuse and enduring foundations of an economic, moral, and mystical nature. First, some resident men seem to covet the choice residential spaces that these women sometimes occupy. Second, the moral quality of all women who return to the natal house is colored by a disrespect for divorcées, who are particularly likely to make such a return. Christian men are especially prone to refer to them privately with expletives like *dálémoṣú* (a pejorative word for daughters who return to *live* in the house) and even *aṣẹ́wó* (prostitute). Third, both the denial of adult daughters' residential rights and the hesitation to enforce it arise partly from the fear of powers often considered inherent in these women's age and sisterly cooperation.

Yet the very qualities of age, unmarriedness, and reproductive emptiness that suggest witchcraft to some are part of what qualifies elderly women for the apical positions in the possession priesthoods. A dimension of the homology between sexual intercourse and spiritual mounting is that one excludes the other. Consequently, periods of *orisa* ceremony regularly require sexual abstinence. For the same reason, only "bloodless," or postmenopausal, women can make ritual pottery for the *orisa* (G. Beier 1980:48). Postmenopausal women are regularly abstinent, free of menstruation, and sufficiently knowledgeable to direct all the necessary rites. Hence, the aegis of their "fathers' religion" allows many women to return to the house from which advocates of the modern patriliny have sought so assiduously to exile them. Sanctioned by its association with the ancestors in the rural space consigned to them in the nation-state, *orisa* religion redefines the return of daughters as the arrival of *wives* of the family god.

As a precondition of an untroubled death, many elderly women are expected to pass on secretly guarded truths or substances. For example, witches cannot die until they have either confessed their acts of murder or vomited up the substance of their witchcraft and passed it on to a younger woman. Similarly, *orisa* possession priestesses must pass on the substance implanted in their heads during initiation. They cannot be buried until a suitable recipient for this head-stuff is found.

Death

Whereas the living can negotiate and narrate the meaning of their lives, they leave others to make meaning of their deaths. Symbolic interpretations of death reveal, by negation, the symbolic constitution of life. For example, the spirits of *abiku* children—"born to die"—circulate repeatedly between heaven (*orun*) and the wombs of their mothers, between the freedom and formless "play" of the other world and, on the other hand, the socialized containment of wombs and their own earthly bodies. They may die in infancy, in childhood, or even on their wedding day, but, unless ritual specialists harness them within the world (*ayé*), they will repeatedly join their heavenly "playmates."[14]

People might be devoured at any time by the witches, who are also called "the world" (*aye*). According to folk etymology, they are "mothers [who] eat" (*ìyá jẹ*) (Prince 1961:797). They envelop life force not passively and productively but actively and destructively. They are the opposite of fertile wives. They must have killed at least one person in order to become witches (Abimbola, personal communication, 12 October 1990). Their deadly acts of forcible containment may take a number of forms. For example, they may devour others' "blood" or block others' wombs. The following paraphrases the testimony of a Christian obstetric nurse in Igboho's public clinic:

> The nursing assistants sent a pregnant girl to my house because they were not sure of the extent of her dilation. I put on my gloves, looked and saw the child with its two hands pressed to the sides of its head. I sent the girl back to the clinic. I do not like family members to hang around. They can come around at intervals. The maternal grandmother of the girl in labor was hanging around, so I sent her away. The girl was in labor for a long time. She finally delivered successfully. But do you know why she was delayed? The grandmother died later at home. She confessed to the pregnant girl's sister that she was using her hands to hold up the baby's delivery because she wanted to kill the girl. It was the grandmother's turn [as a witch] to contribute someone to her *egbe* [i.e., to contribute someone for her cabal to eat]. It's normally a member of the witch's family who is contributed. Since I sent her away, she could not monitor when the girl was being told to push or not. So she could not know when to hold the child back. She could not success-

fully kill the girl. So her *egbe* killed her. That is why I send the family away from the delivery area. Yes, I do believe in witches.

Stories of witches' destructive effects on fertility, pregnancy, and childbirth are particularly common, but a witch can kill anyone whom she envies or who has offended her. She may do so herself or by the proxy of a "sister" who lives closer to the intended victim. Indeed, her "sisters" are all around us—hence their name *aye*, or "the world."

The "inner head" (*orí inú*) guides us and protects us through this adversarial world as best it can. Like pots, some are well molded and fired, whereas others are flawed. Some people believe that the prenatal choice of an "inner head" is inextricably wrapped up in the process of reincarnation. Euba's informants report that "each individual has his or her personal head as the reincarnation of a particular ancestor" (Euba 1985:7). Bascom's informants say that "every living person is a reincarnation, in most cases of an ancestor in the patrilineal clan." In their view, the "head" is chosen by this reincarnated patrilineal ancestor (*ęlędàá*) (Bascom 1956:409; 1969a:117). Thus, the influence and the return of the dead are what animates the living. Except when the bodily vessel is emptied by death or filled by another being during possession, the ancestors continuously affect our consciousness, identity, and safety—from within our very bodies.

According to orthodoxy, Muslims must be buried on the day they die. However, the reunion of numerous friends and relatives at burial ceremonies is so important that some families of all religions delay burial for months, allowing them time to notify everyone and raise sufficient funds to entertain them honorably. A simple or poorly attended funeral shames both the deceased and her children, as it implies their poverty and social unimportance. The Ifelodun town-improvement society has tried on several occasions to curb competitive funerary entertainment. Local petit bourgeois accuse their townsmen of using funerary display to conceal their protracted neglect of old people's feeding and medical care. I am unable to determine the objective degree of filial neglect in Igboho, but lavish spending on funerals clearly has not stopped.

Igboho people of all religions entertain guests on the day of the burial ("the first day"), two days later ("the third day"), six days later ("the seventh day"), and thirty-nine days later ("the fortieth day"). Other entertainments commemorate the burial after one year and then annually as often as the offspring of the deceased can afford it. Egungun masquerades perform on each of these days at "traditionalist" funerals. Wives of the house prepare increasingly copious meals for the guests after the "first day." They sing the panegyrics of the dead woman and her patrilineage and, as at every ceremony in their affinal house, demand monetary gifts from their male and female husbands.

On the "first day," an *orisa*-worshiper is buried with her clothes on backwards. A chicken of the same sex as the deceased is killed and its blood sprinkled on the corpse. This sacrificial fowl is called by some *adìẹ ìrànà* ("the chicken that buys the road"), by others *adìẹ ìràlẹ̀* ("the chicken that buys the earth, or dirt"), and by still others *adìẹ ìbọrí* ("the chicken used to worship the inner head [of the deceased]"). Manifest in this collective indecision over the function of the sacrifice is the sequential worship and dismissal of the dead. The dead must go away for a time, but the nourishment of her head seems to be premised on the expectation of the return of some of her inner stuff to this world.

All people who do not die obscene deaths—as in motor accidents— promptly go to "heaven" (*orun*) for a time. At "traditionalist" funerals, they are dismissed on the "first day" through the breaking of calabashes over the filled grave. Good people go to "good heaven" (*ọ̀run rere*), whereas bad people go to "the heaven of potsherds," suggesting that they will never reincarnate. The words of Oyo's King Aole remind us of the difference between calabashes and ceramics. To finalize the curse that condemned tens of thousands of his disloyal subjects to enslavement on three continents, Aole declared, "A *broken calabash* can be mended, but not a *broken dish*; so let my words be—irrevocable." The deaths of good people and properly cultivated spirits are, like the breaking of calabashes, *revocable*. Calabashes are instruments of not only dismissal but fertility, as we have seen in archaic wedding ceremonies, and of the earthly reinstatement of the dead. In some towns, pieces of broken calabash are used in a small meal for the grandchildren of the deceased, apparently miming her reincarnation. This food symbolism evokes parallel events in kings' and witches' embodiment of the substance of their predecessors' power. Kings eat the ritually pre-

pared hearts of their predecessors, while witches swallow their predecessors' witchcraft substance.

Ritually unmediated manifestations of the dead in the world are
frightening. Nonetheless, tales about them illustrate ritually structured
understandings of Oyo-Yoruba personhood. The àkúdàáyà tales are literally deconstructions of the living, social person and reverse reels of
her composition in the world. *Akudaaya* are dead people who appear in
foreign towns, in the bush, on the farm, or otherwise outside *containing*
social forms. As if alive, dead people present themselves to their living
townsmen or kinsmen away from home. They communicate memo-
rable messages or send word to kinsmen back home. Only when the
unfortunate traveler returns does he or she discover the real source of
the message. Perceptive friends and kinsmen often endeavor to conceal
the truth lest the messenger become too upset. Pots and head-borne
containers regularly appear in descriptions of female *akudaaya*. For
example, one young Christian man told me:

> My grandmother died while my brother and I were at the farm. We saw a
> *kowéè* bird. It uttered its first cry but not its second. That meant something
> bad had happened. We were eating when *grandmother appeared with her gath-*
> *ering baskets [apèrè] on her head.* She declined when we called her to eat with
> us. She had already eaten. She had come to collect indigo leaves at the farm.
> When we wanted to leave, we invited her to join us. She told us to go on
> because she was not finished. As we approached the house, people greeted
> us with Ẹ pèlẹ́ ti màmá ["I'm sorry about your grandmother"] and Ẹ kú ọ̀rọ̀
> ènìọ̀n ["I greet you on the occasion of your loss"]. When we reached the
> house, we met people crying. They said grandmother was dead. (emphasis
> mine)

A Muslim told me:

> My brother's wife gave birth to a child. I bought a lot of things [to contribute
> to the naming ceremony] because my senior brother could not [afford to].
> Early the next morning, I went to his house to greet them. On the way, I met
> the mother of the child on the veranda outside *carrying a bowl [abọ́] on her*
> *head.* She said she was going to collect herbal medicine [àgbo] from someone
> for the baby. She thanked me for my part in the naming ceremony. I asked
> her where my senior brother was. "Inside the house," she said. As I entered,
> the people started crying immediately. They said that just then the woman
> had died.

The woman had said she had diarrhea (inú ẹ̀ ń rùn). She had taken medicine. She said she was feeling better and wanted to rest. The people left to conduct the morning Islamic prayer (*kírùn*). When they returned, the woman prayed (*gbàdúrà*) for them and thanked them for their assistance on the previous night. She said she was completely well. After thanking them, she died. Maybe her tough junior wife poisoned her. (emphasis mine)

Women's mythical departure from the affinal home and from the world is associated with the spilling of pots, the outflux of inner fluids, confession, vomiting, the surgical removal of head-stuff, the emptiness of head-borne containers, and the breaking of calabashes (see figure 5). Yet, ritually mediated, these departures are associated with eventual return, through reincarnation, digestion, or religious initiation. Thus, much Oyo-Yoruba lore represents people as vessels of inherited objects and substances that, like the "inner head," instill consciousness, social identity, and competence. Many of these substances and objects cycle intergenerationally between heaven (*orun*) and the world (*aye*), the bush (*igbó*) and the town (*ìlú*), the metropolis and the village, the dead and the living. The axes and scale of such containment and flow are highly variable (Matory 1986). We will see how this structure of personal existence and transformation, so characteristic of patrilineal descent, is used in particular to substantiate sacred lineages that transcend the patrilineage. Such transformation is inevitable in Oyo-Yoruba social life, for the only vessel that never surrenders its contents and therefore never dies is the universe itself, which some regard as a calabash whose halves are never separated (Ojo 1966:196).

Before she dies, many a woman expresses a preference as to the location of her grave. If too few of her sons live in her affinal home, she is likely to request burial in her natal compound. Only an infinitesimal Christian minority chooses the church graveyard. It may take years after his death for the estate of a prosperous man to be settled. In theory, most of his property is divided into equal portions according to the number of women by whom he fathered children. In turn, the children of each woman divide up their part among themselves. However, the eldest child of the father is likely to receive a superior portion, and, within each matrifocal family (*ọmọ ìyá*), the eldest is likely to receive a superior portion, for the eldest sibling ideally has special responsibili-

Fig. 5. *Egungun* worshiper's grave on the first day of the funeral. Note the broken calabashes. Photograph by the author (1988).

ties in support of the burial and in support of his or her junior siblings. A man's house and furniture remain, in a sense, collective property, but, as we have noted, women's right of return is in dispute. A man's male descendants are likely to share his land among themselves, while females inherit moveable property, such as money, of which there is seldom a large sum. A man's agnates may lay claim to important properties, especially if the deceased has left only minor children. The agnates are supposed to use those properties for the benefit of the man's children. However, the mothers of those children are often skeptical of that supposition. Although inheritance disputes are common, a prosperous man is likely to have too many children and agnates for anyone to inherit enough to guarantee any individual beneficiary's continuing prosperity. Chiefly and priestly titles seldom devolve directly to one's children. Many chiefly titles rotate among sublineages, and priestly titles devolve to those interested, drafted, or called by the oracle. Only "medicines" (oògùn) are likely to devolve to one child with rights of access undivided.

Women's bequests tend to be settled much more simply. Women have fewer children, and those children's material interests tend to be less adversarial than those of a father's collective offspring. Furthermore, a woman's heritable resources are likely to be small. Women's chieftaincy titles in Igboho are now few but their priestly titles numerous. The devolution of the latter follows complex routes, but, even in the absence of successors to a given priestly title, a woman's daughters and granddaughters are numerically prominent among the caretakers of the altars that women leave behind. These altars are constructed as the "bodies" and "heads" of a higher-order personality, in which the deceased and her inner being are imbedded.

Women's lives are not, conceptually, confined to their visible bodily and social lives. Their identities live on in the graves, altars, heads, and bodies of their descendants and junior consanguineal kin. Like those of abiku, women's identities cycle through various worldly bodies. Ritual intervenes to keep that cycling regular and orderly. However, some claim to possess the ritual technology to undermine the proper cycling of feminine life for their own or their clients' benefit.

In the service of such claims, some men and far more women are murdered. The most famous series of ritual killings of women has occurred in the neighboring capital of the non-Yoruba Igbira. Yet such killings are familiar in Yorubaland. Between 1969 and 1970, by accounts heard throughout Igboho, a Muslim woman in Igboho fell victim to such rites. She was kidnapped and dismembered, and her remains were found in a tree trunk. What the three culprits did with her excised "private parts" and breasts is not known with certainty. However, it is widely assumed that they performed lukudi magic.[15]

Such practices are horrendous and unacceptable to the vast majority of Yoruba. Yet they find precedents in the iconography of orisa-worship

and in the nuptial practices of all Oyo-Yoruba religious groups, where-
in various female body parts are marked out as metonymically significant in fertility and therefore metaphorically significant in the appropriation and cycling of social, political, and spiritual power. *Lukudi* and
the similar *eda* moneymaking magic occupy a nightmarish space in the
national imagination far out of proportion to their actual incidence.
They not only tap an extant and widespread symbolism but vividly
symbolize the sense that acquisitive strategies in the mercantile capitalist state cannibalize normal forms of collective and personal life.

Conclusion

A woman's existential cycle of birth, maidenhood, marriage, childbearing, dotage, death, and reincarnation is mediated by various images of
containment and kindred ritual operations, which structure and
defend her progress through an adversarial world. A woman may invest herself and her material resources in any of a range of social projects. Particularly if she is educated or has children and friends well
placed in the metropolis, she possesses symbolic options far beyond
those implicit in the reproduction of the village patrilineage. Yet
despite its juridical premise of wifely subordination, this project
attracts many women, who regard "traditional" marriage as indispensable to the realization of their own desiderata and obligations.

This ritual biography charts the normative course of some women's
empowerment. In marriage, the patrilineage appropriates her productive and reproductive labor, officially displacing her authorship of her
most important achievement—her children. However, the "bride"
matures into a "mother" (*iya* and *iyale*) and a "husband" (*oko* and *iyako*)
with authority over her co-wives, her children, her daughters-in-law,
and her agnates' wives. This status progression is among the dividends
that encourage women's initial forbearance of "bridely" submission,
and these are the local terms of what Kandiyoti (1988:286 n) calls "the
patriarchal bargain"—the "set of rules and scripts regulating gender
relations, to which both genders accommodate and acquiesce, yet
which may nonetheless be contested, redefined, and renegotiated."
Given the history of women's participation in the Oyo-Yoruba state
and the sexual complexity of the "husband" category, one would not

describe the Oyo Yoruba as "patriarchal" without numerous quali-
fications. Oyo-Yoruba royalism and patriliny are based not on the systematic superiority of men over women but on the *contextual* superiority of husbands over wives and fathers over children. However, fathers'
jural authority is offset by strong bonds of affection between mothers
and children. Moreover, not all husbands are men; all women are husbands to certain other women. We must also modify Kandiyoti's sense
of the "bargain" as women's capitulation to a monolithic male privilege
and authority. In Oyo-Yoruba society, the royalist "patriarchal bargain" is motivated strongly by the historical *vulnerability* of prominent
male authorities (see chapter 1) and the objective dependence of the
patrilineage upon women's reproductive capacities.

Nevertheless, Kandiyoti's assessment of the Asian and North African cases she details aptly captures the nature of the sacred bargain of
which women's lives in the patrilineage have been such a rich metaphoric source: "The cyclical nature of women's power in the household
and their anticipation of inheriting the authority of senior women
encourages a thorough internalization of this form of patriarchy by the
women themselves" (ibid.:279). Yet the realities of divorce, sons' emi-
gration, and rural poverty, on the one hand, and the rationalization of
patriliny, on the other, have undermined the corporate patrilineage's
material commitment to its senior daughters. Thus we grasp the modern character of senior women's stereotypical disgruntlement and suspicions about their mystical destructiveness.

In the remaining chapters, we will see an exclusively female possession priesthood engaged minutely in patriarchal bargaining amid
social changes in Igboho, as well as the implications of that bargaining
for the self-conception of male and female participants in this village-
centered community. Finally, we will see how the metaphoric uses of
the female life cycle in the imperial Sango cult transform enormous
fissures in the royalist community into instruments of healing and principles of a new hierarchy.

Chapter 5

Engendering Power:
The Mythic and Iconic Foundations
of Priestly Action

Local Islam and the possession religions sanctify rival visions of world-ly hierarchy and social inclusion. Yet each form of devotion is rich in the symbolic influence of the other, each trained by Oyo-Yoruba actors' sense of their own possibilities and limitations in a cosmopolitan soci-ety. The village is one geographical pole in the itinerant biographies of Igboho citizens and one ideological pole in the negotiation of the social and moral constitution of collective life. That pole is internally complex and divided. Almost exclusively female in its membership, the Yemoja priesthood articulates, more than any other major local priesthood, the political possibilities elderly women recognize in their lives. Although configured prominently in gendered terms, those possibilities do not govern the lives of women alone. They crosscut sex and display gender as a profoundly variable element of personal action and identity.

The relationship between Igboho's Yemoja-worshipers and Sango-worshipers nowadays seems natural. The concept of èsìn ìbílẹ̀ ("tradi-tional religion") has embraced them equally during an era of Muslim and Christian dominance in the national state. The possession religions in particular are brought together by the aspirations of village women and the common constraints on their lives. However, "traditionalists" represent a wide range of ritual formulations and hereditary dynasties. In the past, Sango-worship and Yemoja-worship, for example, have expressed *opposing* political interests. Sango represents an empire whose authority the sons and daughters of Yemoja have resisted legal-ly, ritually, and, at times, violently. Yet their priesthoods share not only common personnel but a common conceptual focus: the containment of power (àṣẹ) and the direction of its flow. In similar ways, they also draw upon the power of a shared enemy in modern Nigeria—Islam.

Islam and the Making of "Traditional Religion"

Both Yemoja and Sango have been informed substantially by Islam. Oyo North is well over 50 percent Muslim. Here Islam and "traditional religion" have interacted for centuries. According to a Yoruba proverb,

> Ifa [the divination cult] is as old as life
> Islam is as old as life
> It was at noon day that Christianity came in.[1]

Indeed, journalists and Christian leaders of the late nineteenth century emphasized Islam's harmony with "African" society (see Gbadamọsi 1978:144, 198–201). The constructive participation of Muslims in the Oyo kingdom is documented as far back as the dynasty's exile in Igboho. Then, significantly, a Muslim *marriage expert* ("Baba-Yigi") counseled the king (Johnson 1921:164). Hence theirs is not an interaction between primordial and discrete elements but an old and mutually constituting dialogue. This proverb calls to mind historically specific battle lines, in a colonial age of Christian dominance (not to mention resistance to African polygyny and church leadership). The lines have shifted substantially in a postcolonial age of Muslim dominance, recontextualizing an ancient interaction and adding a further layer to the political contrast that has given importance to the possession religions at least since the Age of Sango.

From the tenth to the sixteenth centuries, Islam spread southward from the Maghreb through a succession of Sahelian and savannah polities. Among them, Oyo's northern neighbor Nupe had a Muslim ruler by the close of the eighteenth century. Non-Yoruba Muslim clerics were probably present in Igboho—then the Oyo capital—before the last decade of the sixteenth century, but Yoruba conversions were not documented until 1775 (Ryan 1978:105–8, 137 n.; Smith 1965:74). Among the Yoruba kingdoms, the Oyo Empire long hosted the largest concentration of Muslims—including Arabs and Hausa. Before 1840, Igboho hosted a Muslim quarter called Molaba or Molawa, populated by approximately 350 persons, according to Gbadamosi's estimate.

Conventional narrations suggest that Islam sweeps away the African religions in its path—if not immediately, then in progressive stages (e.g., Gbadamosi 1978; Parrinder 1972; Fisher 1973; Trimingham

1968; Levtzion 1968). However, orisa-worship has not disappeared. Indeed, it has expanded to other parts of Nigeria, the People's Republic of Benin, and the Americas amid the simultaneous expansion of Islam and Christianity. Nevertheless, a nominal identity conceals a phenomenal difference: the practice and meaning of orisa-worship are not what they were four centuries ago.

The native-born missionary Moulero speculated long ago that the orisa-worshiping Yoruba (or Nàgó) acquired the concept of a high god from Muslims (1925:4, cited in Verger 1970:506). Even if the high-god concept predated the arrival of Islam, some of Verger's mid-twentieth-century informants clearly understood their own worship of the orisa by contrast to Muslims' and missionaries' worship of the high god (Ọlọ́run or Olódùmarè). "Traditionalists" had bounded their own devotion according to a local division of religious labor in which Islam and Christianity were among the defining elements.

Still, the influence of "traditionalists" and Muslims on each other's ritual practices is extensive. For example, the convergence of Islamic and orisa-worshipers' calendars receives special attention in the possession cults' ritual schedule. Whereas the Yoruba week has four days, the Muslim week has seven. Every twenty-eight days, when the day of the Yoruba week consecrated to Sango coincides with the Muslim sabbath, Sango- and Yemoja-worshipers conduct a special celebration called Jímọ̀ Olóyin—"Sweet Friday." Some terms and concepts central to orisa-worship derive from Arabic and Hausa—such as common terms for "secret," "spirit being," and "sacrifice."[2] Most Arabic loan words in Yoruba probably entered before the nineteenth century, only after which Islam itself became widespread (Gbadamosi 1978:208). Hence they disclose a history of ideological and political interaction with the bearers of Islamic concepts from other ethnic groups. For example, saraa ("sacrifice" for orisa-worshipers) apparently entered Yoruba through the mediation of non-Muslim Hausa, who describe annual offerings to the ancestors with the Arabic-derived term sadaka (Gilliland 1986:38).[3] Johnson's Oyo sources identify Ifa divination as a Nupe invention (Johnson 1921:32–33). On the other hand, Ifa verses recorded by Abimbola identify the original Muslims as the sons or slaves of Ọ̀rúnmìlà, the god of Ifa divination (see Abimbola 1973:57; Ryan 1978:85–87, 97 n). Yoruba Ifa diviners (babaláwo) inscribe divinatory signatures in sawdust on sacred boards (ọpọ́n'fá) similar to the writing boards used by Hausa teachers of Arabic and the Koran.

Although the Ifa verse Òtua méjì has been interpreted as prescribing the client's conversion to Islam, it encodes a profound antagonism toward that faith, representing Muslims as thieves and extravagant wastrels (Gbadamosi 1978:93; Ryan 1978:85–89; also Idowu 1963:100). These stereotypes foreshadow the horrific imagery of lukudi (money-making magic) in modern Yoruba mythology. Instead of consulting Ifa, members of the possession cults generally use cowry-shell divination, during which Sango and Yemoja priests in Igboho are heard chanting barika ("Congratulations!") and even La illah illalah (Arabic for "There is no god but the God") when certain divinatory signatures appear.[4]

"Traditional" religion participates in a cosmopolitan dialogue on power and social order. By integrating various artifacts of Sudanic Islam, "traditional religion" encodes the history of an interregional political economy and taps what, to the orisa priests, are the sacred instrumentalities of their ethnic neighbors' power. It recontextualizes the images, paraphernalia, ritual cycles, and concepts of Sudanic Islam amid distinctive canons of value and hierarchy. In the metropolises to the south and along the highways, the god of war and iron, Ogun, focused a cosmopolitan vision of Western technology and its appropriation during and after the oil boom of the 1970s, not to mention the nineteenth century, when the importation of European guns and iron fueled a military and commercial revolution. In the royalist domain of Oyo, on the other hand, Sango, Yemoja, and other gods identified as "Nupe" embody visions of a cosmopolitan and orderly world centered on ancestral city and village.

In a predominantly Muslim town, in an ideally patrilineal society, and in a Muslim-ruled country, it would be difficult to think of a more provocative ritual statement than one in which women ritual experts exercise control over not only their own and other priestesses' bodies but the polysemic process of fertilization and social reproduction itself. It may come as a surprise, then, that Sango himself is a Muslim (see Idowu 1963:92, 100–101; Frobenius 1968:210). In Yoruba, even his main natural manifestation is known by an Arabic-derived word: àrá, or "thunder," comes from the Arabic word ra'd (Gbadamosi 1978:208).

The sense of irony is not lost to *orisa*-worshipers, who alternately affirm through their panegyrics and deny with their reasoning that Sango is Muslim. Today, he embodies the irony of the modern Muslim or Christian king and the Muslim Igisubu, chief of Igboho's Sango-worshipers.

However, manifest in the words and bodies of Oyo-North women, Sango also transforms that irony. Islam is recognized even in the most central and secretive rites of Sango-worship. Concluding portions of the initiation for his possession priests involve nude bathing in the river, a rite remarkably parallel to the Nupe celebration of the Islamic New Year, Muharram, in which nude and seminude ablutions occur at the river. The Nupe rite includes play with lit torches and bonfires (Nadel 1954:244–45). Likewise, fire is among Sango's most prominent emblems, further suggesting a Nupe and Islamic inspiration behind this ritual bricolage. And Sango is not the only possessing god invoked in this way. Some tales say that Sango's mother, Yemoja, and the god of smallpox, Sonponnon, are Nupe and Muslim.[5] Like that of similar tales about Odudua—founder of the Yoruba race and bourgeois emblem of Yoruba unity—the enduring importance of these narratives reflects, among other things, (1) the importance of trade relations with Islamic states to the north—Bornu, Kano, and Nupe—which created much of Oyo's wealth and supplied Oyo with the equestrian means to conquer southward; (2) the esteem in which the British held Islam; and (3) Muslim power in postcolonial government.

Embracing Power:
The Poetics of Contestation in the Possession Religions

The new axes of politico-religious rivalry were quite evident in Igboho by the late 1980s. Sango- and Yemoja-worshipers in the town confided privately that they disliked the Muslims. Nonetheless, since public funds had been used in the construction of the General Mosque, the entire town of Igboho was invited to its official opening in 1989. The Sango-worshipers attended as a group. A poet (*eléwì*) visiting from Ibadan prefaced his recitation of praise poetry (*ewì*) for Allah with an enthusiastic plea for his audience to stop attending *orisa* festivals. In the background, young local men cried *Allahu akhbar!*—"God is great!" This inhospitable call for Muslim separation might have gone over better in metropolitan Ibadan than in royalist Igboho, where the *orisa* remain éminences grises behind the chieftaincy and a public focus of Muslim and Christian women's pursuit of fertility. Not surprisingly, such antagonistic expressions came from someone with no aspirations to local hereditary office and were endorsed largely by young men. These young men were below the age of both access to chieftaincy titles and concern about the fertility of wives.

Orisa-worshipers make their most vivid rejoinder through the public *ritual* display of female sacred capacity on the bodies of women and male transvestites. *Orisa* festivals are also the occasion of *verbal* articulations just as potent as the allegories and exhortations we have heard from Muslim and Christian men. Women follow the canons of their own art and a pan-Yoruba tradition of women's collective self-expression.[6] *Orisa* possession priestesses have composed the critical and didactic songs that the mainly female supplicants and revelers repeat.

On the occasion of the 1988 festival of the river goddess Yemoja in Oyo town, the Muslim and Christian women and children who made up the majority of the audience sang of women's main desideratum and, against the hegemonist aspirations of the exclusively male Muslim clergy, apportioned credit to a female *orisa*:

> Water is our religion;
> In our house, when we have successfully given birth,
> The Imam may not conduct the naming ceremony.[7]

Another song challenges the very grounds of Muslim and Christian identity:

> We ourselves will practice Yemoja;
> The Owners of Faith [Christians] practice Faith;
> We ourselves will practice Yemoja.[8]

In the past, the "Owners of Yemoja" (*Oníyemọja*) were specifically the few priestly initiates, whereas the "Owners of Faith" are all those who profess to be Christians. Yet this song draws a parallel between the two identities, submitting both to a transformation. On the one hand, it might suggest that, rather than *being* something, Christians are just people who *do* or *practice* something. Christianity is a temporary conduct rather than a fixed identity. On the other hand, it might suggest that all who seek Yemoja's help assume an identity with the cult. Such is the compromise involved in *sending out* the sign. The persuader too is transformed by her predication. In either case, Muslim, Christian, and "traditionalist" women have declared their unity under a single sacred purpose and the logic of "mounting."

The *oríkì*, or panegyrics, of the gods that "mount" are assembled, revised, and sung almost exclusively by priestly *women* (see Barber 1990). Recorded in Igboho in 1988, Sango's panegyrics (*Ṣàngó pípè*) specify his Muslim "practice":

> When Sango was living in Sálúù he was a Muslim
>   [literally, when he was *doing* Islam],
> Who ate *dog's head* with pounded yam,
> And ate *pig's head* for breakfast during Ramadan. . . .
> One who "fasts" during Ramadan . . .
> . . . one who carries balls of pounded yam to eat under his clothes
>   [during the Ramadan fast]. (emphasis mine)[9]

This image of Sango not only declares Sango a Muslim but ridicules Islamic practice. Many peoples ridicule their neighbors by reference to the latter's eating habits, but this iconivorous meal draws contrary modes of symbolic production into Sango's imperial vortex. These panegyrics use Islam to signify qualities typically associated with the *orisa*—foreignness, brazenness, audacious disregard for social rules, and disrespect for the cult's enemies (see Matory 1986:30–33; Barber 1981). Sango not only breaks the Ramadan fast but does so by eating highly forbidden foods. He is both crafty and fearsome enough to violate Islamic law, and no one dares challenge him. This burlesque submits Islamic rites scripturally intent on submission, abnegation, and spiritual cleanliness not only to mockery but to a culturally imperialist reinterpretation. The norms of sacrifice to Sango specifically require the presentation of the victim's *head* to the god. Images of both sexual penetration and its international homologue—eating—inform the meaning of spirit possession by Sango.[10] Not only does he eat heads, but he "mounts" the female and feminized *heads* of his possession priests.

A further order of belief about the head informs the drama of sacrifice and possession alluded to in Sango's panegyrics. Before the ram sacrifice that accompanies a Sango initiation, the ram's head is touched to the heads of the initiand and other possession priests, apparently identifying victim with sacrifier (Hubert and Mauss 1964). The subsequent decapitation thus appears to sever the head of the novice (*iyawo*, literally, "bride" or "wife") by proxy. The proxy is then placed on Sango's altar for him—digestively and sexually—to eat. Much as worldly husbands purchase the "heads" of their brides with bridewealth (*owó orí ìyàwó*—literally, "money for the head of the bride"), Sango demands the "head" of his new bride. The rite, like the richly polysemic poetry of his panegyrics, suggests Sango's audacious power to extract the personnel of the patrilineage, and of other religions, in order to recruit them into his own order of royal affinity. The followers of Islam are no less vulnerable than those of Ogun—the nonpossessing god of war and iron—whose favorite food, alluded to in Sango's panegyrics, is dog!

Possession cults are not necessarily just palliatives for suffering or silenced women. They can privilege priestesses in the articulation of concerns far beyond the personal and the female—among female supplicants, the men who depend on their fertility, chiefs and kings, farmers, Christians, and "village"-centered communities generally, not to mention an expanding number of the alienated in the cities of the New World. In Oyo North, their rites are a privileged site of symbolic production, where they articulate a key and perhaps hegemonic vocabulary of "village" consent and resistance to the major institutions of Yoruba sociopolitical life.

The religious conflict in Igboho is cognate with a tension between gendered leaderships, between residential spaces, and between communal orientations. It is not, however, a conflict between primordially discrete religions classifiable as "local" and "world" or "high-god" and "pagan." As we saw in chapter 3, the religions of the Yoruba have reformulated each other in often idiosyncratic ways, dependent on a history of political and economic factors. In Oyo North the clearest sectarian battle lines are between the possession religions (of Sango, Yemoja, Osun, Oya, and, arguably, independent [*Aladura*] Christianity) and the nonpossession religions (Islam, mission Christianity, Ifa, and, among the Oyo Yoruba, Ogun). Whereas women are symbolically central in the former, they are expressly marginalized in the latter. This contrast provides an obvious hypothesis for researchers concerned about women's action at religious, cultural, and historical junctures in other societies as well.

Although a negotiated peace between Yoruba Christians and Muslims may be evident (see Laitin 1986), contests over the control of lineage resources and the constitution of civic order are regularly articulated in other religious terms. Such contests are ritualized in the opposed iconographies of female self-presentation in Islam and the possession religions: the veil versus the head-borne pot. Although young and metropolitan Muslim men and the beneficiaries of radical patriliny denounce it, rural women of all the religions argue the virtue of female sacred authority in sacred songs and poetry. Migrants who retire to the "village," who seek moral validation through title taking, who escape the violence of the metropolis, or who seek healing and fertility from the possessing *orisa* affirm an Oyo-Yoruba royalist construction from which the female link is difficult to remove. The great husband (*oko*) Sango is a god of empire with economic and political links reaching not only Mecca but the heavenly origins of the human race. For his worshipers, he represents an experience no less cosmopolitan than Allah: Sango simply rules from a different capital, one much closer to the food producers and wives of Oyo North.

Amid divisions in the Muslim community and the generally shifting nature of Yoruba religious identity, not only Sango-worshipers but Yemoja-worshipers possess the means to appropriate and send out signs, to assert a confidently totalizing vision of the locally centered world. Sango altars sit in the reception rooms of the official head chief of Igboho (*Alepata*) and of the chiefly descendant of one of Oyo's *ilari* (*Aare*), although these men are Christian and Muslim, respectively. Only under the Alepata's auspices does the divided Muslim community of the town gather together periodically as a whole. Once a year, Muslims allied with both Friday mosques leave the town and gather in a large clearing. While they face Mecca, they also face the Christian head chief, who has donated the ram they will sacrifice for 'Īd El-Kabir. The irony is not lost to perspicacious *orisa*-worshipers, who know that the ram is also Sango's sacred animal and food of choice. The panegyrics of the river goddess Yemoja appear to "signify" doubly on this Islamic rite. Giving the lie to female marginality and powerlessness, they assert the goddess's ability to master both Sango and Islam:

My mother kills people, [but] we call her a woman.
Mighty water of endless expanse is the home of Yemoja,
    who eats *two rams* in the river.[11]

Possession and Its Icons

The inclusion of women in the royalist order is a given, but several questions remain. How does an assertion that empowers a goddess and her priestesses arise out of a royalist order based on wifely submission? What kind of woman is Yemoja? What makes her devouring anger congenial to the women of Igboho and exemplary to the communities that support her priesthood? Although I have mentioned various elements of possession symbolism in discussing the history of Oyo royalism, it is worth drawing them together before we detail the conditions of Yemoja's extraordinarily assertive force. Sango and Yemoja have the two largest possession priesthoods in the town of Igboho. They both lend wide publicity to a shared iconography of power (*ase*) and its regulation. Heads, stones, calabashes, mortars, and pots form a circuit of images manipulated in the appropriation and delegation of power in contemporary possession rites (see Matory 1986). They stand in direct visual contrast to the guns and anvils that represent Ogun among the Oyo Yoruba (see figures 6 and 7). The concept of "mounting" (*gigun*) likens the priest (*elegun*) to a royal charger (*esin*) and to a royal wife (*ayaba*), making the possessed priest the most dramatic and visually evocative image of a past sexual-political order with which Igboho's oral historians and lawyers unfavorably compare every subsequent epoch. Just as pots and calabashes represent the hierarchical orderliness and fertility of the patrilineal marriage, they are used to mime and incite the action of god upon priest, to call the imperial sexual-political order into contemporary action. For example, vessels filled with river water are placed on the heads of Yemoja priestesses in order to induce possession. Since Sango is the god of fire and lightning, a vessel containing burning coals may be placed on the head of his medium. The ritual juxtaposition of the head with vessels full of the god's divine emblems demonstrates, for public view, an interested socioanatomical conception: heads are containers that potentially host a variety of beings, who may change places at ritually induced moments. Political-

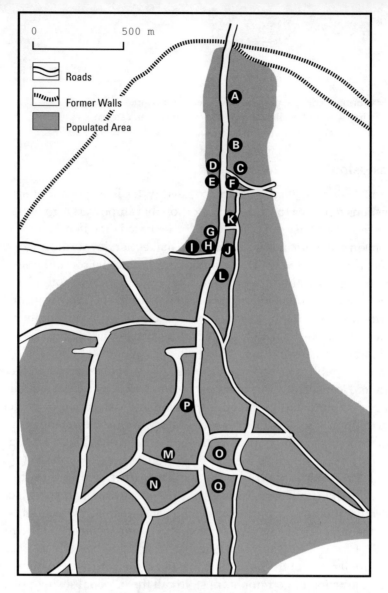

A. Yemọja calabash of the deceased Ọlaniiwọn; **B.** The *Jagun Ṣàngó's* house; **C.** The *Arumi* Adewọyin's Yemọja calabash in Alhaji Sule's house (see figure 10); **D.** A riverine Yemọja shrine; **E.** Sango shrine of the *mọ́gbà* in Arókè Ṣágun Ẹ̀hìnkè House (see figure 11); **F.** Blacksmith's Ògún shrine in a smithy; **G.** Two Yemọja calabashes in the Onígbòho palace (see figure 8); **H.** Olówó Bar; **I.** *Arumi* Olomide's grave; **J.** Yemọja calabash in Madam Ọladunni's house; **K.** Yemọja calabash in the house of a female *ẹlẹ́gùn Ṣàngó*; **L.** Sango altar in the house of the *ẹlẹ́gùn Ṣàngó* of Onigboho's Yemọja priesthood; **M.** Sango altar in the Alépàtà's palace; **N.** Yemọja altar in the Oníkòmọ's palace; **O.** The *ìgbàlè*, or Egungun shrine (see figure 12); **P.** Sango altar in Ààrẹ's house; **O.** Ogun shrine in the house of the hunters (see figure 7).

Fig. 6. Map of Igboho showing the locations of various shrines discussed in this work.

Fig. 7. The Ogun shrine of an Igboho hunter. It includes rifles, anvil stones, and an animal skin. Photograph by the author (1989).

ly useful forms of consciousness and action may be induced by a sacred and symbolic but nonetheless technological process. Not only that, but particular heads are replaceable as vessels of any given being. Patriliny and viri-patrilocal marriage make women the primary exemplars and objects of this cephalic changing.

The physical head is regarded as the site not only of personal consciousness but of participation in kin groups and their shared dispositions. For the Yoruba, the "head" (*ori*) comprises a person's intelligence, competence, personal limitations, and capacity to defend herself or himself (see Bascom 1969a:116; Abimbola 1976:113–14). The "head" is distinct from but is symbolized by the physical head, which may be called "the outer head" (orí òde). The invisible "head," by contrast, may be specified as the "inner head" (orí inú). The latter is also widely regarded as chosen by or inherited from deceased agnates and as the content of reincarnation (Bascom 1969a:117, 409; 1956:409). Abimbola, on the other hand, regards the "head" as the "symbol of free choice," emphasizing that a person's prenatal selection of his or her head is unmediated, nonhereditary, and freely made (1976:113; personal communication, 19 October 1990). In either case, the irreducible element of intelligence and competency is given origins outside the person. Spirit possession, as the displacement or invasion of the head, is proof of what is implicit in this image of the "inner head": the junior, subordinate, and wifely self is hollow. Such wifely hollowness is both the premise and the product of Oyo-Yoruba politico-religious hierarchy.

That heads are vessels is the fundamental logic of these cults' iconography. Mythically, people's heads are said to have been molded and fired in heaven by the divine Àjàlá Amònkòkò—"Ajala the Potter."[12] Those with permanent interests in the project of control and delegation—such as kings and priestesses—own altars on which pots, calabashes, and mortars represent, in a fixed frame, what possession rites depict in action: the filling of human heads and the replacement of their contents with the consciousness and authority of the sacred and superordinate. The contents of these vessels elaborately diagram the character of the god—indeed subjecting him or her to ritual manipulation— with cowries, conch shells, river stones, and thunder axes (èdùn àrá).

Indeed, while they potentiate effective hierarchies, heads and other ritual vessels also represent resistance to hierarchies and the renegotiation of one's place in them. The word for "skull" in Yoruba (akotorí) compares it to a calabash known as koto—the same kind that regularly represents Yemoja in Oyo-North shrines and contained the Abeokuta commandant's war medicine, according to the misogynistic cautionary tale told by members of Igboho's town-improvement society. As we have seen, the calabash of the commandant was an instrument of his struggle against the Oyo king. His wife's head was the sine qua non of her own failed efforts to trade upward in marriage, as well as the Oyo king's own means of foiling her effort.

Gender and the Iconography of Resistance

In the absence of their prosperous children and amid the hegemony of "mounting" in the royalist village, how have elderly priestesses achieved not only relevance but considerable authority? Our answer derives from one prominent case—the Yemoja priesthood of Onigboho House, which differs sociologically from the Sango priesthood in various ways. First, all of the Yemoja priestesses of the House are post-menopausal and postmarital, whereas the Sango possession priests range from young to middle-aged. Second, whereas there are many male Sango priests, the Yemoja priesthood in the town is exclusively female, except for the executive participation of the chiefs of the two Yemoja-worshiping houses. Being made up of not only female but mainly matrilateral kin of Onigboho House, the Yemoja Onigboho priestesses are under special threat by the new patriliny. Third, Yemoja-worship is more clearly identified with a single local lineage than is Sango-worship. The latter belonged to an empire, with which it is still prestigiously identified. Yemoja belongs to a house embattled by the consequences of Oyo imperialism. Her priesthood organizes its multiplex projects of resistance in rich tropes of not only vessels and brideliness but motherhood and husbandliness as well. Despite the Yemoja priesthood's appearance of gender segregation, its rites, vocabulary, and iconography reveal that gender is as protean as other axes of political power and resistance. Political resistance in the village transforms the very biological and symbolic coordinates of gender.

Motherhood vs. "Mounting"

In important ways, "mounting" arose as an Oyo strategy *against* the social and political implications of motherhood. As we have seen, the mother of the Oyo king himself was killed upon his accession to the throne, in order to eliminate her as a crosscurrent of authority over the king and the dynasty. At the same time, the king was inserted into a unitary and lineal axis of descent and power. He ate the heart of the preceding king and was submitted to the same initiation that the Sango possession priests underwent. It is very likely that the techniques of his initiation appropriated and masculinized the "blood" symbolism of which uterine reproduction is, as we shall see in the next chapter, an exemplary source.

The authority of Yemoja is represented in images implicitly oppositional to Oyo and its wifely emblems. First, she is featured in *flight* from her husband. Second, that flight displays her transition from the primary role of *wife* and *delegate* to that of *mother* and *source* of others' power. Third, in her panegyrics she claims the powers of Ògún. Most Yemoja myths identify her husband as Ogun or a historical character identified with him; most commonly identified is the Òkèrè of Ṣakí, a town founded, according to myth, by *orisa* Ogun.[13] Its uncrowned rulers conducted repeated raids against Oyo's northern domains during the nineteenth-century Age of Ogun. Although some tales from elsewhere identify Yemoja as a trader, the tale recounted by the head Yemoja priestess in Igboho mentions no such theme. What the head priestess Adewọyin highlights is the community's condemnation of Yemoja's divorce and the power that children's loyalty to their mother brings. She is explicitly the power source of Ṣàngó and Òrìṣà Ńlá (Ọbàtálá), who is, among other things, the lord of the womb:

> God created Yemoja, who had no father or mother. No one sired her except the rivers and the water. . . . She had come from Igboho. Everybody who saw her was afraid. When they discovered that she had no mother and father, they refused to marry her. . . .
>
> Finally, she married the chief of the town of Saki—Okere. She related her taboos to him, and he related his to her. He had a room that she must not enter. She agreed. She told Okere that even if they happened to fight, he must not make any unkind remark about her breasts. Despite her warning, he insulted her breasts. So she packed her calabash of belongings and set out for the river. . . .
>
> When she arrived at the River Ògùn,[14] everyone had gathered to condemn her for leaving. So she stopped. Most of her *orisa* children abandoned her. . . . Sango, however, supported and stayed with his mother, just as the Sango-worshipers have stayed with us. The troublemakers denounced her. Of the five children she gave birth to, only two stayed with her. . . .
>
> She called the two loyal children and gave them *ase* [politico-religious power]. She said, "You two here—Orisa Nla and Sango—whenever you call my name, I will help you. War came, and you did not run." . . . The hostile crowd converged upon her, but when they reached the river, all they found were the breasts of Yemoja at the River Ogun. They did not find Yemoja herself.

Two of the raconteur's companions quickly added a widespread explanation of the river's origin: "It was there, where she lay down and vanished, that water started coming out of the small pots (*orù*)." That pot is specifically of the type mothers use to dispense children's medicine. Panegyrics for Yemoja and other female *orisa* throughout Yorubaland also compare their breasts specifically to this type of pot. The tale poignantly recasts the lot of the women of Oke-Igboho. It furnishes the images of wifely resistance and narrates key constituents of female power—vessels, vessel-like body parts, and the loyalty of children. It also structures the idiom of resistance by the Onigboho dynasty, matrilateral kin, and excluded sublineages generally.

Yemoja and the Chieftaincy

At least since the middle of the early twentieth-century Oyo Renaissance, the reader will recall, the Onigboho dynasty has claimed primordial sovereignty in the town. This claim defies the state-recognized sovereignty of the Alepata, who has enjoyed the direct support of the Oyo kings at every stage of the conflict. Although Alepata and the other recognized Oyo representative in the town, Aare, have Sango shrines in the reception halls of their palaces, they appear to have made no direct appeal to the *orisa* cults as grounds for their authority. Indeed, the Oyo palace has ceased to play the material role it once played in the initiation of Oyo-North priests, thus abbreviating the priesthood's functions in political delegation. By contrast, both of the local chiefs challenging Alepata and the Oyo king's joint authority underline their own sacred imprimaturs.

The late Onigboho Jeremiah Afolabi claimed that he was head of all of Igboho's *orisa* cults, including those of Yemoja and Sango, as proof of his seniority and exclusive sovereignty in the town. Addressed to a commission of inquiry on the local "chieftaincy tussle," one legal correspondence from 1982 reported:

> The Onigboho is the Chief celebrant of all the festivals in Igboho and [they]
> are performed for him namely
>   1. Egungun   (2) Yemoja
>   3. Sango   (4) Osanyinta
>   5. Abenugboro

> The High Priests of these "good [i.e., gods]" still hold consultations with and obtain the approval of the Onigboho before celebrations (including propitiations) can begin. . . . The Alepata, Ona-Onibode and Aare merely hold watches during these events. (Aderele 1982:234; see also 180, 222)[15]

King Jeremiah had been the first Christian Onigboho.[16] Although he was probably convinced of the legal weight of this claim, it was sentiments against matrilateral kinship and the "pagan" priesthoods it structures that finally carried him to the throne. The heavily matrilateral priestly branch of the family, Oyeboode, suffered as a result of his victory.

The irony is this: Whereas the Oyo dynasty has long delegated power to and through women, Onigboho House and Igboho generally have distinguished themselves primarily by their contemporary *exclusion* of women from important political processes. Nevertheless, the priestesses of Yemoja have been privileged by the most recent strategy of opposition to Oyo. Through their role in that opposition, they are guaranteed a forum and an attentive audience for their own sacred recitations of history, which, though amended continually, are taken to be primordial repositories of efficacious truth (òótọ́).

The Oriki

Oriki are oral poems that are believed to invoke the essence of a being, class, place, or thing in word, metaphor, rhythm, and melody. For the sake of readability, I translate the term *oriki* as "panegyrics," despite the English term's suggestion of eulogy or praise. *Oriki*, however, may contain normatively positive, negative, or neutral passages. Moreover, *oriki* are neither narrative nor descriptive but, in Yoruba belief, *effective*: they "name" things. Hence, in her magnum opus on *oriki*, Barber (1991:75) states: "The subject's latent qualities are activated and enhanced. . . . The *oba* [town sovereign] is most fully an *oba* when he is enhanced by the royal *oriki*. . . . The dead, addressed by their *oriki*, can be called to the world of the living." Anyone who has seen one person "naming" another with *oriki* has seen the involuntary physical transformation of the addressee's face, body, and gestures, which Barber sums up as "afflatus." She adds that panegyrics "are crucial in making the relationships, human and spiritual, that constitute the Yoruba world" (ibid.:2). They "name" those relationships into their fullest being. The panegyrics recited by Yemoja priestesses in Oke-Igboho "name" the relations among the goddess, the Onigboho chief, Onigboho House, and the larger polity.

In the "Name" of Motherhood

These panegyrics "name" the resistance of the house to Oyo in terms of Yemoja's protective and threatening motherhood. They repeatedly address Yemoja as "Mother" and "Our Mother." Indeed, all members of Onigboho House are classified as ọmọYemọja—"the children of Yemoja." To her mighty motherhood, Sango is as an infant (verse 8):

> Òpéèpèé Yemọja, who has the back to carry Sango
> [pòn means "to carry (a baby) on one's back"].

> Òpéèpèé Yemọja ti réhìn pọn Ṣàngó sí.

Yemoja is the goddess of the River Ogun, which is supposed to origi-nate near Igboho. Thus, the chorus of her *oriki* endlessly reports:

> The river is her homestead.

> Ààrin ilé l'ódò.

Through a highly parsimonious metaphor, the Onigboho is warned that if he does not wish for Sango (god of thunder, lightning, and fire) to burn down his house, he must rely on and pay due respect to the river goddess:

> The *Arsonist*-Who-Won't-Deny-It [Sango] became the landowner in Kòso.
>   . . .
> (70)   The son of the *houseowner would not like his house to burn.*
>   . . .
> *Akunlé*-má-ṣèrú di onílè ni Kòso.
>   . . .
> (70)   Ọmọ *onílé tó nílé kò níí fẹ́ kí ilée rẹ̀ ó jó.*
>   . . . (emphasis mine)

Only "water" (verse 6) can extinguish Sango's fire. So great is Yemoja's power that no one can restrain her movement or harm her children, rep-resented by the fish, of which the goddess—whose name is often inter-preted locally as Yèyé-ọmọ-ẹja ("mother of fishes")—is the mother:

(60)   I will never [dare to try] to dam the mighty river of endless expanse, which carries away fish traps.

(60)   Èmi ò jé sé alagbalúbú odò tí ń gbé ìgèrè lọ.

She can equally defend her "children" in Onigboho House. Ever a military threat to Oyo's northern domain during the nineteenth century, Yemoja's mythic ex-husband Okere becomes a metonym of Yemoja's own martial power and of her capacity to resist Oyo royal sovereignty. She is Òkèrè òkun—"The Chief of Saki in the Sea" (verse 58).

These assertions of her protective motherly and martial powers coincide with assertions of her internal control of the house. In a passage describing various gods and kings as the owners of the lands where they turned into gods (verses 62–72), Yemoja appears:

My mother [Yemoja] became the landlord in Oke-Igboho.

Ìyáà mi di onílẹ̀ l'Ókè-Ìgbòho.

As the parent of the houseowner (verse 70), she is the mother of Onigboho himself. Hence, the chorus Ààrin ilé lódò can be understood in a second way: "The center of the house is the river." The river is the center of Onigboho House and its source of not only autonomy, power, and safety but internal order.

Her motherly authority and competency have two dimensions. The quality of Yemoja's presence in river water suggests the first. Verse 74 describes the goddess as "bean pudding in the water" (ọ̀lẹ̀lẹ̀ lómi), apparently likening her to the murky fluid that remains in the pot after steaming the pudding. Its specific symbolic value seems to derive from the near-homonym ọlẹ̀, which means "fetus," the foremost gift attributed to Yemoja's healing powers (see Bascom 1969a:130, 318–19). Verse 52 identifies Yemoja's motherhood with nourishment:

The receiver of the *crown* of childbearing women, who has breasts of honey.

Olówó gbadé abíamọ ọlọ́mú oyin. (emphasis mine)

Hers is a kingdom of a sort that Igboho has not known recently, one ruled by the "owners of breasts."

Although her oriki generally begin with a pacific image, her eating habits quickly reveal a second dimension of her motherhood:

(1)   The drenching water under the leaves,
       Eats in the house, eats in the river, wife of the king Okere.
       One who listens to our complaints,
       My mother kills [but] we call her a woman.

(1)   Omi rẹrẹ lábẹ́ ewé,
       Jẹ nílé, jẹ lódò, ayaba Ọ̀kẹ̀rẹ̀.
       Eléti ìgbáàròyé,
       Ìyáà mi ń pa, a lóbìnrin ni. (emphasis mine)

A Yoruba proverb reports of witches, "If death in the house cannot kill you, death outside the house cannot kill you either." Like the witches, Yemoja can be a powerful internal enemy when riled. However great her power to kill outside enemies, she is even more capable of killing those who live in her midst. With the same power that enables her to answer our complaints, she can also kill us. Subsequent verses warn that unnamed enemies will be eaten by Yemoja as if by the insect called *ìtalẹ̀*, whose invisible but painful nocturnal bloodsucking also resembles the behavior of the witches.

       My spectacularly fierce mother who eats people in the manner of
            the stinging caterpillar.
(20)   The center of the house is the river.
       When *Mother is eating them*, they all think it is the stinging caterpil-
            lar that is eating [them].
       The center of the house is the river.
       They will take up their sleeping mat, and shake their clothes.
       Water-Stops-My-Weeping [Yemoja], they will think the stinging
            caterpillar is eating them.

       Ìyáà mi òrorò ajẹ ni-bíí-ìtalẹ̀.
(20)   Ààrin ilé lódò.
       Bí Ìyá bá ń jẹ wọ́n, wọ́n ó ṣebí ìtalẹ̀ ló ń jẹ.
       Ààrin ilé lódò.
       Wọ́n á máa ká ẹní, wọ́n á máa gbọn aṣọ.
       Omìíránlẹ́kún, wọ́n ṣebí ìtalẹ́ ló ń jẹ wọ́n. (emphasis mine)

We have seen that the word "mother" (*iya*) is a common euphemism for "witch" (*aje*). Both mythology and a popular etymology for *aje* stress the theme of their eating.[17] The object of this oblique threat of bewitching is unclear. It may be either the enemies of Onigboho House or Yemoja's own children, for "witches" *do* attack their children.

In the "Name" of Mounting

When King Jeremiah was still alive, recitations of Yemoja's *oriki* in Onigboho House included prayers for him and passages of his personal *oriki*. The transitional passages and most of Jeremiah's panegyrics are clearly more recently composed than the major part of Yemoja's. Hence, they reflect the current politico-religious hegemony, recent political history, and an intricate negotiation of cooperation and hierarchy between the throne and the priesthood. These passages redress the exclusion of matrilines prominently in the idiom of "mounting." At a 1983 gathering in the palace, the recitation concluded with the prayers and the panegyrics of the king. The transition between sections took the form of a warning and a prayer:

> (90)   Greetings! [archaically]
>   If you have (a) head(s), hold it/them in your hands [i.e., be careful].
>   [You] Sea, who hear our complaints,
>   *The head that I entrusted you to plait, don't unravel it on me.*
>   Magical finger ring that can kill twenty [people], that can kill thirty,[18]
> (95)   Eats in the house, eats in the river, wife of Okere.

> (90)   O kú o!
>   Elérí kó fọwọ́ mú erí.
>   Òkun elétí ìgbáàròyé,
>   *Orí ti mo fún ọ̀ dì má bá mi tú[u].*
>   Aluwó tó ń pogún, tó ń pọgbọ̀n,
> (95)   Jẹ nílé, jẹ lódò, ayaba Òkèrè. (emphasis mine)

In verse 90, a new soloist has begun a direct address to the king. As the singing priestesses grab their heads, the head of the group receives an ambiguous order (in verse 91): it may be his own head or everyone's head that he is being advised to hold onto. *Elérí* may mean "someone with a head" or the "leader of a group," the latter usage suggesting that ownership of others' heads constitutes leadership. Hence, verse 91 recalls the tenuousness of the Onigboho's hold over both his own and others' heads, the uncertainty of both his self-control and his leadership. After calling on Yemoja, who hears her children's complaints, the priestesses ask Yemoja not to unravel the project of head control in which the priestesses themselves, with the help of the goddess, are engaged—that is, the cornrowing of the head or heads. Cornrowing is associated generally with the neatness and decorousness of young-adult village women, but in the politico-religious context it is associated with men's readiness for spirit possession. The only Oyo-Yoruba men who wear braids are possession priests.

The image of hands (*ọwọ́*) grabbing the head suggests the maintenance of self-control. The hands are associated in many verbal formulas with self-willed doing as opposed to, for example, being "mounted."[19] The threat that requires the defensive action of the hands follows—a knocking down by Yemoja's hand. Again it is difficult to tell if it threatens Yemoja's children or their enemies. Yemoja's magically prepared hand (verse 94) can cause her victims to lose their balance, lose consciousness, fall over, or die. Yemoja and other *orisa* that "mount" (*gun*) people fill the heads of the possessed and cause those heads to swell (*wú*), independently of and sometimes contrary to their will. For inexperienced possession personnel, possession begins precisely with physical collapse, paralysis, dizziness, frightening disorientation, or periods resembling madness. Such unpleasant manifestations usually follow the resistance of "called" persons to Yemoja's will. The Onigboho has been warned of the possibility and told implicitly that he must, of his own volition—that is, with his own hands—keep his head in the right position. Otherwise, he may be slapped down or deprived entirely of self-control.

Amid our uncertainty over whose head or heads are being held, the image of hands on heads also recalls the duty of Onigboho in Yemoja priestly initiations. The Onigboho reigning when a new *arumi* (Yemoja possession priestess) is prepared must "lay hands on the head of the initiand" (*Onígbòho máa ń gbé ọwọ́ wọn lé ìyàwó lórí*). The Onigboho's role is an exercise of authority over the possession priestess—the placing of his byline, *ase* (politico-religious power), and personal volition on her head. As long as he lives, the possession priestesses are said to "carry water for him" (*rumi fún-un*). Yet his empowerment or possible drowning by "Water" is conditional upon the degree of his conformity to Yemoja's volition. His conformity also gives him and Yemoja the *ase* to command their subjects. The action of the priestesses (like singing panegyrics), in turn, builds up both chief and goddess. On the other hand, with the support of the goddess, the priestesses chant the conditions of their support for the chief. Hence, the Onigboho's part in the

Yemoja initiation does not simply subordinate the priestesses; they too are empowered by the Onigboho's authorization.

When Afolabi is addressed directly in the recitation, he is thanked for continuing his father's religious observances. This gratitude appears to acknowledge the reality that his noncooperation is imaginable nowadays:

> (97)   Afolabi, thank you, son of Alaatipo.
> Greetings to you who wake to honor your father.
> Your forefathers are the ones who strengthen your hand [i.e., assist you].

> (97)   Afọlábí ọṣé, ọmọ Aláàtípó.
> O kú o, ajísáajo bàbáà rẹ.
> Àwọn bàbáà rẹ náà ni oníràn lọ́wọ́ọ̀ rẹ.

The recitation admonishes Afolabi that his "fore*fathers*," or ancestors, are the source of his personal worldly efficacy. Then his authority is re-"named" not only outside the patrilineal convention but at far greater length. He is reminded of his matrilateral ancestry and the feminine constituents of his authority:

> (100)   Afolabi, child of Fọlasinyẹn (his mother),
> Jeremiah (Afolabi's first name), child of Ọtẹ (his mother's father),
> They held a conference and fixed it, child of Yédé (his mother's mother).

> (100)   Afọlábí, ọmọ Fọlásinyẹn,
> Jeremiah, ọmọ Ọ̀tẹ̀,
> Wọ́n pé súúrú, wọ́n dì í, ọmọ Yédé.

The name of Afolabi's maternal grandmother suggests that she—Yede being the short form of Yétúndé ("Mother Returns")—is herself the reincarnation of one of her elder kinswomen. The singers imply that it is his matrilateral pedigree that enabled him to win the title despite residing all the way over in Gold Coast (now Ghana):

> (112)   Afolabi, child of Abẹnugbọ́rọ́ [the hill god of the quarter], Jeremiah, child of Ote [his mother's father],
> From Wale-wale [a town where Afolabi lived in Gold Coast] you brought the title home, child of Yede [his maternal grandmother].

Éébùkí [a poetic distortion of Jeremiah's personal praise name
Áíbùkí], God has approved of our plans.

(112)   Afọlábí ọmọ Abẹnugbọ́rọ́, Jeremiah, ọmọ Òtẹ̀
Wàlà-wálá lo ti mú oyè wálé, ọmọ Yédé.
Éébùkí, Ọlọ́run rí sọ́rọ̀ wa.

Indeed, his *wife's father* was the diviner who approved his candidacy,
causing his opponents considerable suspicion about the reliability of
the reading.[20]

Subsequent images underline the Onigboho and all hereditary
authorities' intimate and emblematic relations to *wives*:

Each and every elder,
(105)   They said that Jeremiah would have this honor [i.e., had won the
chieftaincy].
Jeremiah, who was never crooked [that is, has never wavered from
the elders' expectations],
Afolabi, child of Alaatipo [eponym of Afolabi's royal line], Àdìgún
Èrán [Afolabi's personal *oriki*] became *the one bathing among the
king's wives.*

Àwọn àgbà kan àgbà kan,
(105)   Àwọn ní Jeremiah lọ́wọ̀ yìí.
Jeremiah tí kò wọ́ rárá,
Afọlábí ọmọ Aláatípó, Àdìgún Èrán, di ẹnití ń wẹ̀ láàrin ayaba.
(emphasis mine)

It is suggested that the elders' continuing approval of Afolabi follows
from his continuing humility among his wives. He stands naked in
their midst, a sign not only of intimacy but of subordination and loss of
former identity. Recall that an initiand in the Sango priesthood must
also bathe nude before the priests. The occasion of the Onigboho's
behavior is saliently associated with Yemoja, for he bathes in water.

Verse 107 clarifies the identity of the ideological nemesis against
which this virtual royal matrilineage is "named" into existence and
salience. His description as *ọmọ Aláàtípó* identifies him with the eponym of the royal sublineage that won in 1952–54 on the basis of sentiments against both "paganism" and matrilateral inheritance. Against
that fact, the Oníyemọja (Yemoja-worshipers), and Oníṣàngó (Sango-
worshipers) of the house boldly claim responsibility for putting Afolabi
on the throne. Afolabi is reminded that he is the instrument of those

singing the *oriki*, an instrument specifically resembling the *ajere* to which the Oyo king himself is assimilated (Babayemi 1982:24).[21] *Ajere* is a roasting pot, a clay vessel perforated with many holes to allow the inward passage of flames and the outward passage of liquids that further fuel the flame. Onigboho's comparison to a similar object is significant:

> *Sifter*, father of the *sifter*, Jeremiah,
>   father of Sẹgi [his daughter],
> *Sifter*, father [or male user] of the *sifter*.

(110)   You *sifter*, Adigun, as we have been doing to you, so the sifter does
        to yam flour in Igboho.
        Onigboho, you are greater than all the [other] kings who have ever
        reigned.

> *Kọ̀nkọ̀sọ̀* bàbá *kọ̀nkọ̀sọ̀*, Jeremiah, bàbá Sẹ̀gi,
> *Kọ̀nkọ̀sọ̀*, bàbá *kọ̀nkọ̀sọ̀*.

(110)   *Kọ̀nkọ̀sọ̀*, Àdìgún, bíi a ń tí ń ṣe ọ́ ló ń ṣe èlùbọ́ ni Ìgbòho.
        Onígbòho, o pọ̀ ju gbogbo ọba tí ń tí ń jẹ lọ. (emphasis mine)

The composers and singers of the panegyrics, Afolabi's female kin, claim here to use the Onigboho for their own purpose—a purpose like the sifting of yam flour. He is the temporary container of consecrated substances, which eventually devolve to the priestesses. Indeed, among the Ohori Yoruba, possession priests wear the *kọ̀nkọ̀sọ̀* sieve as a hat (Drewal 1977:47).[22] A further fact demonstrates the integrity of this play of words and images: the word *konkoso* may be used to identify not only a sifter but the braided hairstyle worn by most male possession priests. It is also known as *ṣùkú* (Abraham 1962:391). The priestesses thus detail metaphorically how their actions make Afolabi a mighty king and how his instrumentality makes them mighty as well. This circuit of power, in effect, makes them all possession priests. Afolabi's supporters in the Yemoja priesthood bring *through* him the powers of Yemoja, Afolabi's mothers, and the hill god Abẹnugbọ́rọ́.

According to this "naming," the Onigboho's authority is independent neither in its origin nor in its exercise. It depends on women from every side. His matrilateral pedigree is indicated as far back as his great-great-grandmother—the person who reincarnated as Yede. Among patrilineal forebears, only his father is mentioned explicitly. Among his children, only a daughter is named, and none of his sons.

These women—the priestesses of Yemoja—credit themselves and other women with his election and the security of his rule. He is a vessel and conduit of their goddess. At the same time, he is threatened implicitly with slapping down or outright possession (*gigun*) by Yemoja should he disregard the priestesses' will.

The priestesses' "naming" is effective. Yet, like mothers and wives, the chief stands at the juncture of multiple "naming" practices. Panegyrics express a range of historical, political, and personal assertions, whose meaning and outcome panegyrics alone do not determine. If at some point titleholders in Igboho regarded submission to Sango priests as obligatory or beneficial, they do not practice that submission now. Alepata did not prostrate to any of the dozen or so possessed priests who called on him during the 1988 cycle of Sango festivals. Indeed, one Sango manifest in a junior possession priest squatted, in a gesture of submission to *Alepata*. Those who did show submission to these manifest gods were young and middle-aged women seeking fertility. They sank to their elbows and knees and removed their head ties. *Old* women, by contrast, did not regularly submit in this way. Nor did men.

On the other hand, if the reports of the current Oníkòmọ chief and of members of Onigboho House are true, those chieftaincies associated directly with Yemoja acknowledge—through reciprocal gestures of submission—some dependency on the goddess and the forces represented by the possessed Yemoja priestesses. These dynasties' very distance from the sanction of the New Oyo palace is now the measure of the Yemoja priesthood's authority in Igboho. In Oke-Igboho, the present efforts of Oyeboode sublineage member Adewọle Laṣebikan[23] to combat Alepata and reach the throne have reinforced the strategic place of his matrilateral priestly kinswomen.

These women articulate, at once, the common interests of women against residential exclusion, of matrilines against the new patriliny, of Oyeboode sublineage against marginalization from the chieftaincy, of Onigboho House against Oyo sovereignty, and of the possession religions against a new class of Muslim and Christian chiefs. The power of the Nigerian state will overdetermine the conjoint outcome of a variety of these conflicts. The Chieftaincy Affairs Division of the Oyo State government and the Oyo palace will not recognize anyone as the next

Onigboho chief until the house has officially recognized the supremacy of the Alepata in the town. In the meantime, the elderly female leadership of the Yemoja priesthood will remain the ranking resident leadership of Oke-Igboho quarter.

The Ọmọ Oṣú

The new nerve center of Oke-Igboho quarter is Olówó Bar, which stands at the summit of a hill dominating the rest of the quarter. Most of its business and the activities of its occupants take place on the front veranda, overlooking the unpaved main road and offering a clear view of almost all motor and pedestrian traffic from Ona-Onibode chief's Mọdéké quarter and Alepata's loyalist quarters into Oke-Igboho. Across the road and equally at the summit of the hill is the house of the Mọ́gàjí, or lineage head, of Onigboho House—Charles Akinbami. He holds his office by virtue of seniority rather than election. His direct kinsmen tell me he is the eldest male member of Onigboho House, although literally he is not. He may, until recently, have been the most mentally competent among the eldest males, but now he is as exhausted as his business. The hotel he ran in the house is defunct, and his son supports him through farming.[24]

Titilayo lives in the house of which Olowo Bar takes up the two front rooms. After losing one husband to death and divorcing another, she and her children moved into this house built by her senior brother, M. T. Akintayọ, who has long been living and doing business at the Aflao border crossing in Ghana. Also living behind Olowo Bar is M. T.'s wife, Iya Tunde, whom Titilayo governs, for Titilayo is Iya Tunde's classificatory husband (oko) and Iya Tunde her classificatory wife (iyawo). Titilayo's daughter Joana lives in a room with Akintayo's daughter Comfort, who has not yet married but lives there with her daughter. Joana's full brother Gabriel, Titilayo's son by the same husband, lives in the same nearby apartment building as M. T.'s son Tunde and his wife Carol. Titilayo's son by another husband was crippled in a building accident; he lives in a nearby house built by Titilayo's prosperous second cousin, Adewọle Laṣebikan.

Adewole stays there when he comes home on business. His sister Yetunde also lives there. Between that house and Olowo Bar lives

Lasisi, son of a daughter of Onigboho House. Adewole is usually called "Omooyè," meaning "prince," affirming the expectation that he will be the next Onigboho. However, a wife of the house once said privately of Titilayo, "If she were a man, *she* would be the next Onigboho [chief]." Across the street, but under Titilayo's charge as well, lived the wife of another of Titilayo's sons, along with her own two-year-old son. However, the wife departed, complaining of financial neglect, and left the two-year-old with Titilayo.

The junior *arumi* possession priestess of Yemoja, Orisagbemi, occu-pies a room at the rear of the bar with her son's teenage daughter. After three divorces and a stint of trading in Tamale, northern Ghana, Orisagbemi retired to this (her junior brother's) house. She continues her petty trade in ash-roasted peanuts and Cadbury buttermints from the veranda of the bar but depends financially on the generosity of Titilayo and a son working in Ibadan.

Like many houses built with the trade wealth of expatriates in what was then Gold Coast, this house does not center around a courtyard, nor is its life concealed from the street. Three doors open onto its front veranda, one from a sitting room attached to the master bedroom. The sitting room and master bedroom are together; they are easily closed off and were apparently intended to be reserved for the migrant owner's private belongings. Now they are occupied by Titilayo.

Almost every member of Onigboho House who returns home first calls at Olowo Bar to announce his or her presence and pick up any news. Its proximity to the road leading from Ibadan makes it a natural place to stop. The Onigboho palace is two buildings down the road and far from the street. Like most old compounds, it is structured around an open impluvium.[25] Even when Onigboho Jeremiah was alive, in 1983, visits to Olowo usually preceded visits to the palace. Now that the king is dead, no one calls at the palace except occasionally to visit his widow. She reports, with a laugh, that she is under her husband Titilayo's charge. The other main occasions to visit the palace are the New Yam Festival (*Iṣu Lílà*) and the annual festival (*ọdún*) of Yemoja, whose main shrine remains in the palace (see Appendix III). Although Orisagbemi is the junior of two living *arumi*, it is at her personal Yemoja shrine that elderly women of Onigboho House generally conduct weekly services (*ọsẹ̀*) for the goddess. Orisagbemi's shrine has the virtue of being centrally located: it is in the back of Titilayo's bar. Matters may have been different when the senior *arumi*, Adewoyin, lived nearby. She has moved from her junior brother's house in Oke-Igboho to a bungalow built in a neighboring quarter by her migrant Muslim son.

These women—Titilayo, Orisagbemi, Adewoyin, and the *mógbà Yemoja*, or nonpossession priestesses—are the *omo osú*, women who return to their father's house for ceremonies or after divorce and widowhood. The foremost *mógbà Yemoja* is Oládùnní Àsàbó Awo.[26] She came home years ago when her husband died. She resides in a house diagonally across the street from Titilayo's bar. To support herself, she sells the stacks of firewood that her grandson fetches from the forest. One of her sons died in recent years; his widow and a half dozen of her grandchildren therefore live with her, along with some of her brother's grandchildren.

The gravity of this kingdom of "owners of breasts" is constituted not only verbally, through the eloquence of Yemoja's panegyrics, but through ritual icons and actions, by which Yemoja's authority is extended far beyond Oke-Igboho. Whereas the graves of dead Yemoja priestesses remain in Oke-Igboho, stationary hubs of sacred activity, the Yemoja calabashes move around the village space when women marry or their parents die. These calabashes accumulate the powers and icons of various patrilineages and pass them on through female lines unsanctioned by the new patrilineal order and its publicly monotheistic expositors.

It is not obvious from their biological sex whether the *omo osú* are mothers, daughters, or wives to the agnatic lineage, or whether they are husbands or wives to the Onigboho titleholder, or whether the king is father, wife, or husband to the priestesses. Indeed, all that is obvious is that the *omo osú* are *husbands* to the wives of the house. The gendered order of authority in Onigboho House thoroughly undermines biological sex as the idiom or referent of salient gender categories. The continual "naming" and re-"naming" implicit in the panegyrics of Yemoja define gender according to diverse conduits of power and axes of resistance. These verbal "naming" practices illuminate the technical operations of Yemoja worship. In turn, these technical operations give an alternative, material gloss to the gendered roles continually re-negotiated among the members of Onigboho House.

The Yemoja Altars

Aside from the chief's own wifely head, Yemoja's sacred calabashes are the foremost site of collective, intergenerational subjectivity in Onigboho House. Within these visibly hollow icons of community, however, the priestesses nourish images of *motherhood* in the service of healing and the projection of female priestly lineages across the landscape of the new patriliny. They are switching stations of intergenerational stuff, where old money and barter are used to reclaim the signifiers of maternity from the patrilineage. Except during the festival season, the Yemoja shrine in the Onigboho palace houses the two most important Yemoja calabashes (*igbá*) in the town (figure 8). During rites, the *arumi* Adewoyin addresses them as "the first road [or way]" and "the second road [or way]" (*ònà kinní* and *ònà kéjì*) of Yemoja. They are full of river stones, cowries, and larger *cypraeidae* shells, and they sit atop large, whitened clay pots. One stone in the "first road of Yemoja" is shaped like Sango's "thunder axes" (*edùn àrá*) and was said to have resulted from lightning striking the water, one among many sacred incorporations and transformations of imperial power. The "first road" also contains four and the "second" five small enamel, metal, or calabash containers, each containing numerous cowries and sometimes a stone as well. The entire contents are covered with windings of white cloth (*àlà*) and woven trays under the calabash lid.

"The second road" of Yemoja belongs to "the dead" (*àwon òkú*). On occasions like the fixing of the festival date or major sacrifices, when the other Yemoja calabash is brought out, this one remains in the shrine room. This "second road" of Yemoja contains the shells and stones of three dead people whose children did not want to take care of the calabashes of the deceased. When the children of the deceased become Muslim or Christian and are not willing to care for the dead parent's sacred calabash, they are supposed to bring the calabash and a chicken. The chicken is exsanguinated, as in burials, and the contents of the calabash are poured into this single, now-heavy calabash that sits in the palace shrine room.[27] Next to the calabashes are the pot full of Sango's stones and a set of four long, spiraling antelope (*ìgalà*) horns painted red with the camwood powder (*osùn*) that is used to beautify babies. They are called Oge, which is here considered an *orisa* in its own right

Fig. 8. The shrine of the goddess Yemoja in the Onigboho palace. Photograph by the author (1988). See also figure 6.

but is noted for the same fecundating power as Yemoja (figures 9 [foreground] and 8 [right side]; see also Thompson 1976, chapter 12:5). With the horns, women dance to pray for children. Each of the Yemoja calabashes and the Sango pot has next to it its own pot (*òtun*) of water—decanted for libation and divination or drunk for purposes of healing, particularly when women want to conceive.

Most other Yemoja shrines in Onigboho House contain similar objects. Unlike those in the palace, these others are passed by each *arumi* possession priestess to her successor or to a *mogba* of the next generation. The second-ranking *arumi*, Orisagbemi, inherited her entire Yemoja calabash from its previous caretaker, the *arumi* Oyeyemi. The pan of Sango stones and the Yemoja calabash in the hands of the *mógbà Yemoja* Oladunni, with all their contents, belonged to her "mother's mother(s)," she says. This Yemoja altar belonged at one point to the earliest identifiable *arumi* in Onigboho House, Olómidé Àsàkún Awọ.

These calabashes are indeed monuments to their deceased caretakers and mnemonics for female generations that would otherwise have

Fig. 9. The palace altar of Yemoja spilled out for the setting of the festival date (*idájó*). Note on the left a statue of Yemoja bearing a vessel in her hands. Photograph by the author (1988).

long been forgotten by the patrilineage. They keep alive subaltern claims of belonging and authority in the new patrilineal house. Yemoja festivals invariably progress from the salutation of altars to the salutation of ancestral graves, each performed amid the chanting of Yemoja's and past priestesses' panegyrics. One of those graves belongs to Olomide, whose son Adedigba founded a large sublineage within Oke-Igboho. Adesina, the unsuccessful contestant for the throne in 1952–54, was Adedigba's son and Adewoyin's brother. Olomide's grave sits at the southern edge of Oke-Igboho quarter, closer to Oladunni's house and Titilayo's Olowo Bar than to the compound of matrilateral Adedigba line that Olomide gave birth to three generations ago. Several huge stones and an orange tree serve as distinctive grave markers, among which her granddaughter, the senior *arumi* Adewoyin, paused at length to dance and "press her head to the ground" (*teríbalè*) during the New Yam Festival of 1988.[28] With a sweep of her hand,

Adewoyin declared, for my benefit, "This was the mother of the whole house," a contention that the last Onigboho chief and his supporters resisted violently in the early 1950s.

Not only for contemporary political contenders but for supplicants in need of healing, worship at the calabash is part of an ancestral obligation. Yet the geographical focus of this obligation is as diffuse as the residence of daughters of the house, for women who marry out may also carry their own and their dead mothers' calabashes out. For example, a daughter of Onigboho House named Ọláníiwọ́n Àyìnkẹ́ Awọ took a sacred calabash to her affinal house in Òkè Lóko quarter. It has remained there beyond her death. Even in cases like this—in which the calabash comes to rest in an exclusively Muslim and Christian house—the altars remain pilgrimage sites for the scattered worshipers.

Precisely because they are monuments to the dead, they are instruments of reincarnation and maternity. Indeed, they ignore paternity. Most Yemoja calabashes contain small vessels (*arere* or *ahá róbótó róbótó*), each representing a god to whom some priestesses say Yemoja gave birth—Ọṣun, Èṣù, and Òrìṣà Ńlá (see figure 10). Whereas some Oyo Yoruba identify Orisa Nla as the male lord of the womb, these Yemoja priestesses classify him as a mere "child" of Yemoja. Other priestesses explain that if Yemoja assists a woman in conceiving, that woman must deposit a small vessel in Yemoja's *koto* calabash, itself to be surrounded and filled by the contents of the larger vessel. The child may, in the end, belong to a god other than Yemoja, in which case the objects in the dish must correspond to the child's patron *orisa*. The little headlike vessels of children so born accumulate in the Yemoja calabash. The Yemoja calabash embodies an imagery of Yemoja's responsibility in recycling sacred power, which was once in the hands of female ancestors, into the uterine production of descendants in this subaltern lineage.

Like panegyrics, the contents of sacred calabashes are amended in each generation. For example, the small vessels inside the large calabash are classically small calabashes of the same sort used to give medicine to children (*ahá róbótó róbótó*). Nowadays, they are often made of porcelain, plastic, or metal, depending upon the means of the initial supplicant or the means of the priestess when a preexisting calabash broke in handling. The most numerous objects in the calabash are cowries. They fill and surround the little *ahá* calabashes inside the altar,

Fig. 10. The Yemoja altar of the head possession priestess, Madam Adewoyin, during prefestival offerings. Photograph by the author (1988). See also figure 6.

like a restitution of bridewealth by an ancient and preferred husband. Recall that cowries were money in this region until the beginning of this century, and they retain a name indicative of that fact—*owó ęyo* ("pieces of money"). Shells of the other type used in the calabash shrine are associated with Ajé, goddess of wealth and trade. Yemoja festival songs call on Aje as the principle of their own type of sacred commerce:

> Owner of the *Barter Market*,
> She [Yemoja] comes to the market of Aje,
> She comes to the market for children,
> She comes to the market for immortality,
> Chief of wealth.

> Ọlọ́jà àáro,
> Ó dọ́jà f'Ájé,
> Ó dọ́jà fọ́mọ,
> Ó sì dọ́jà àìkú,
> Bálè ọrọ̀. (emphasis mine)

One daughter of Onigboho House brought a cowry-shell necklace back from the hajj. Given as a gift to the *mogba* Oladunni, that necklace is now inside the *koto* calabash of the earliest-known possession priestess in the house.

The calabashes in the hands of individual priestesses undergo another sort of elaboration that does not affect the palace calabashes. Objects of male worship—inherited from fathers and husbands—often end up inside the Yemoja altars. For example, Oladunni maintains alongside her Yemoja calabash sacred objects in the worship of the hunter god Ọṣọ́ọ̀sì. The calabash of the deceased priestess Olaniiwon Ayinke Awo in Oke Loko quarter now contains not only small dishes for Sango, Osun, Yemoja, and Orisa Nla but a glass bowl of divinatory palm nuts for Ifa and a novel stainless steel emblem of Ogun, added upon her husband's death. He had worshiped Ogun as a member of a hunter's lineage.[29]

The daughter of this Ogun-worshiper's marriage to Olaniwon Ayinke Awo is a Sango possession priest named Móróorẹ́ntí Àjòró Awọ, whose marital residence is at the heart of the quarters loyal to the Onigboho's enemy Alepata. Yet, like the *ọmọ oṣú* of Onigboho House, she traverses the town to wash and sacrifice to a calabash with no remaining worshipers in the hunters' house. Moroorenti says that all the residents of this her natal house are now Christian. This Christian house is one among the many social and religious groups crosscut and perforated by the "roads" of Yemoja.

The intergenerational iconic elaboration of the Yemoja calabashes suggests an intergenerational circulation of important contents of personal identity through female lineages. Male spiritual presences enter but are assimilated to children in Yemoja's body. The worship of Yemoja and the maintenance of her altars in Igboho propagate circuits of female movement that transcend lineages, townwide political factions, religious identities, and, ultimately, age-old politico-religious fissures. The rituals of the festival suggest the calling back of Yemoja herself, the reversal of the goddess's out-marriage and flight. The spilled-out cowries, shells, and stones are washed in herbal infusions prepared amid the singing of sacred songs and fed with hominy (*ègbo*) before being restored to the calabash and to the shrine room at the end of the festival.

In the course of their own out-marriage and flight, women accumulate religious identities, just as Yemoja calabashes accumulate gods. An *arumi* for Onikomo House, for example, said her parents are Christian, and she became Muslim on account of her marriage to a Muslim. Nonetheless, she remains active in the religion of her lineal forefathers. Even when husbands partially succeed at enforcing their religious identities upon their wives, many women remain active in the priesthood of Yemoja, whose nature it is to accumulate and contain ad infinitum in her large collective womb/head. Priestesses then channel the cycle of spirits and identities returning to the world into the reproduction of female-centered groups.

Women's church clubs center on collective financial contributions to the church; participants in *esusu* savings associations likewise base their unity on the circulation of modern cash. The *Oniyemoja*, by contrast, make an advantage of a deficit. Although poor in cash, Yemoja-worshipers create female lineages around alternative heads and through the gathering of alternative money—money removed by time from the authority of the mercantile capitalist state. It is the lucre of past ages: cowries. Rather than from the patrilineage and the kingdom of men, Yemoja-worshipers' corporate identity, power, and wealth derive from the kingdom of motherhood. Yemoja wears the "crown of childbearing women" (verse 52).

Dueling Vessels

Yemoja's iconographic resistance is not arrayed against the new patriliny alone. One of the rams she eats in the river is Sango. Just as an altar of the imperial god Sango sits prominently in the Alepata's reception room, Yemoja rests in the Onigboho's palace. Yet not only the symbolism of "mounting" but the personnel and the icons of Sango are well integrated into the Yemoja cult. Everywhere they are worshiped, myths identify Yemoja as Sango's mother, although Sango and Yemoja priests in Igboho emphasize that claim to different degrees. For at least the three generations I have been able to trace, the Sango and Yemoja priesthoods have overlapped regularly. The Yemoja priesthood of Onigboho House has long had its own Sango possession priests (*elégùn Sàngó*). They are an affine, the sons, and a daughter of female agnates of

Onigboho House who married men of Sango-worshiping lineages (see Appendix II). Whether this pattern of marriage and *orisa* inheritance was planned is not clear. These affinally and matrilaterally related Sango priests may have been invited to stay in the house on the grounds of their religious competence, as a way of appropriating the *ase* (politico-religious power) of the Oyo Empire. Alternatively, or perhaps simultaneously, Onigboho House may have been required by Oyo policy to maintain a Sango possession priest, and preferred its own relatives to any outsiders.

Similarly, the townwide Sango priesthood has an *arumi Yemoja* (possession priestess of Yemoja), and Sango priests usually dance during or soon after each Yemoja festival. They performed in small numbers at the 1988 Yemoja festival in Oke-Igboho—the Onigboho's government-recognized domain—but performed in full force at the subsequent Yemoja festival of the Onigboho's "junior brother," the Onikomo chief, on the other side of town. He is both a Yemoja-worshiper and an Oyo loyalist.

The Yemoja shrines of Onigboho House appear to incorporate her son Sango's power, while apparently stripping it of the imperialist pretenses encoded in the foremost shrines. In leading Sango shrines—like those in Kòso, Ìsàlè Ògèdè, and Àgó Igiṣubú quarters of Igboho and Koso quarter of Oyo town—Sango's stones sit atop an inverted mortar or one that is not even hollowed out, suggesting Sango's own *im*penetrability and the notion that the Sango shrine is self-sufficient in power, requiring input from no higher agent (see figure 11).[30] Sango is, in imperial principle, the paramount divine ruler: he gives power and issues orders rather than receiving them. In less important Sango shrines, like those belonging to individual Sango possession priests, not to mention the Alepata chief, Sango stones are often found in right-side-up mortars, suggesting that their owners receive power from a higher source. This symbolic weakening prefigures Sango's ultimate demotion in Yemoja shrines. There, Sango's rocks and "thunder axes" rest inside simple pots and bowls, inside or, more often, outside and lower in height than Yemoja's calabash. This sequence of iconographic transformations reinforces the image of both increasing distance from the source of Sango's power and diminishing interest in Sango's autocracy.

Fig. 11. The Sango altar in the initiation room of the male initiand (*ìyàwó*). The painted pedestal is the mortar of Sango (*odó Ṣàngó*). Photograph by the author (1988). See also figure 6, site E.

Vessels of Power: Oyo-Yoruba Metaphors of Personhood

Pots, calabashes, mortars, baskets, and sifters are apparently unfamiliar metaphors with a structure quite familiar to Western understandings of agency. The durable Cartesian notion that the body is the detachable and disposable vessel of an invisible mind or soul is what makes possible both our modern notions of the afterlife and the vague credibility of demonic possession. These seemingly innocuous sequelae conceal a political hegemony of great consequence not only in Yoruba villages but in the Nigerian and Western metropolises that ultimately dominate their common postimperial world.

Tropes of containment in the West project the source of historically specific and trained forms of conduct onto an alleged inner essence. The invisibility of the soul removes it from history and places these forms of discipline beyond our capacity to challenge them (see Foucault 1977:29–30). As Butler (1990) suggests, the gendered subject, rather than being an inner essence, is as variable as the disciplinary regimes and signs inscribed *upon* the human body. Indeed, the Oyo-Yoruba village wife is the focus of multiple sartorial iconographies, some of which predicate multiple alien souls into male bodies as well. The ritual iconographies of Yemoja-worship are the material signs of the *hollow self* and the gendered nature of the subjectivity that fills it. What distinguishes these possession religions' metaphors of person-hood from Descartes's is precisely the self-consciously technical quality of the regime creating and installing the Oyo-Yoruba subject. In Yemoja worship, priestly experts replace a received regime of the self with a cooperatively and locally constructed one. Yet these rival regimes maintain certain shared principles: inequality among participants and the privileging of a gendered Other that is *not* defined by sex, as "woman" or "man," "female" or "male."

The Yemoja priestesses "carry water [on their heads]" for the reign-ing Onigboho in his capacity not as a *man* but as a *husband*. As in nuptial ritual, the duty to carry water is coded not simply *feminine* but *bridely*. The king's husbandly role, however, is not fixed; the panegyrics con-struct him too as wifely in relation to Yemoja, "the center of the house." He is a conduit of forces that flow to and through the entire house. Conversely, priestesses who claim ultimate authority in a given context engender themselves husbandly. For example, during prefestival sacrifices in 1988, the head priestess Adewoyin named her relation to the other priestesses present: *Èmi ni jagun; àwọn ni ìyàwó*—"I am the warrior; they are the wives." Significantly, her husbandliness is like that of Yemoja's husbandly persona—the Okere chief of Saki. The sub-ject of action that defines and is defined by the hierarchy of "mounting" is ipso facto husbandly. Priestesses in Oyo therefore address Yemoja herself as their "Husband [and Lord]" (*Oko*), and Igboho priestesses call themselves her "brides" (*iyawo*).

Festival songs further gloss the social hierarchy and symbolic premises implicit in the transformation of priestly consciousness dur-

ing possession. One song gives voice to the perspective of the unpossessed devotee:

> I *use my head* to think of a watery heaven [or other world].
> Instead of water, water covering me over,
> The king's wife [Yemoja] *mounts* my mother [the senior priestess]

> Mo *foríi* mi rò lórun omi.
> Kàkà kómi omi ó *gùn* mí,
> Aya[b]a gun ìyáà mi. (emphasis mine)

Even those who cannot be possessed by the goddess "use their heads"
in connecting themselves to the divine. Yet the very preservation of the
devotee's life depends on her recognition of the senior priestess as the
representative and conduit of a structure of divine and relatively husbandly Others, including Yemoja's husband Okere and Yemoja herself.

Prayers depict the husbandly authority of the goddess in historically
salient terms. In a prayer for an infertile woman, the *mógbà Yemoja* Oladunni addresses

> Yemoja of the sea, *chairman of the Europeans.* . . .
> Help me seek children.

> Yemoja òkun, *alága òyìnbó.* . . .
> Bá mi wómo. (emphasis mine)

In the Age of Abiola, riches are identified primarily with commercial
migrants. Hence, the male Sango possession priest of Onigboho House
prayed to the grave of his father and priestly predecessor:

> Our *travelers in foreign lands* should bring money home and bring their riches
> home.

> Àwọn *èròo wa tí ó wà ní ìdalè* kí wón kó owó wálé, wón kó orò wálé. (em-
> phasis mine)

The desire for children is the most recurrent theme of both song and
prayer. Childbirth is the exclusive means of continuity for the modern
Oyo-North patrilineage, and therefore the focus of its attention to
women. At the same time, childbearing is women's means to ultimate
independence from the patrilineage. As a condition of its lineality, the
Oyo patrilineage conflates female heads and wombs, and, through
bridewealth ("money for the head of the bride"), asserts unique control

over the social identity of a woman's offspring. The Yemoja priesthood reorients this axis of power by highlighting not only the breastlike image of pots (*oru*) but the womblike symbolic potentials of the otherwise skull-like shrine calabashes (*koto*). We saw earlier that the "skull" is called *akotori*—literally, "the *koto* calabash of the head" (see Abraham 1962:383). The polysemy of the calabash altars thus proposes forms of both consent and resistance in Oke-Igboho, through the variable interpretation of the metaphorical vessel in terms of wifeliness or motherhood. However, the constant condition of this polysemy is the hollowness of the self.

Female Centers and the Interregnum

Titilayo's minor but geographically and politically central sublineage is growing. As the de facto leadership of the house grows progressively more female, it seems no accident that the annual Sango festival in Oke-Igboho has only a female *ẹlẹ̀gùn Ṣàngó* and that no effort has been made to replace the male possession priest who long ago converted to Islam and moved away to Ilorin. The ritual act of embodying Yemoja's *ase*, or "power," to the fullest is the carrying of water on their heads by the *arumi* priestesses. During an interregnum, by contrast, the *arumi* do not "carry water." Instead, on the day of the festival, they wear white and receive visitors at home. In one sense the priestesses are immobilized, and they miss the excitement of their earlier power display. They used to carry water and, at the same time, with delicate balance, prostrate before the reigning Onigboho; then the Onigboho would prostrate before them, they recall. They cannot do that during an interregnum, and it may be a while before they can do it again.

In another sense, the *arumi* cease to *bear* loads and become, themselves, sedentary and chieflike foci of other people's movement. Legendarily, Igboho chiefly lines began as itinerant hunters and turned into stationary chiefs. Biographically, contemporary chiefs begin as mobile traders or hunters and turn into sedentary chiefs. Ideally, cycles of exchange revolve around and through such sedentary men. At present, neither chief nor regent (*adelé*) reigns from Onigboho palace. Hence, the cycles of ritual exchange and reincarnation that the priestesses have managed on the chief's behalf now center upon the priestesses themselves. Those cycles center on the priestesses' private residences rather than on the palace.

It is more than the accidental vacancy of the Onigboho throne that has created the new gap between the leadership structures of priesthood and chieftaincy; indeed, that vacancy is itself not accidental at all. It is grounded in resistance to Oyo authority, of which feminine sacred power is a keystone. Thus, this "interregnum" is an element among the progressive changes documented in the leadership of Igboho and Onigboho House over the past sixty years. While the male leadership structure of the house is preoccupied with litigatory battles in Ibadan and Oyo town, a resident female leadership has flourished—nourished by the nostalgia for intact chiefly and husbandly authority but motivated by its own agenda.

The present Oyo king says that Oyo-North possession priests come to the Oyo palace for the final stages of their initiation, but senior Oyo-North priests say that they personally have never gone. This lapse of the Oyo palace as the ritual center of the Sango priesthood and the Onigboho interregnum bear similar structural consequences. They are not simply a falling-apart, for the structure of a past hegemony remains alive in the popular memory. Rather, new unities are modeled on it, as rationales are improvised from the old idiom for the new social circuits that the out-marriage and flight of wives have created. The women and and Sango possession priests of Onigboho House possess a cogent alternative language with its roots in a prestigious history and its proof in impressive material monuments.

These feminine social circuits have become a new local empire, drawing new roads and provinces across a divided town. Its technology of "mounting" and motherhood draws value from the hegemonic Yoruba idiom of authority and social production—lineage reproduction. That technology is equally persuasive to the antisocial agents of private accumulation. Human heads can be bought, emptied, filled, and cut off in efforts to produce, reproduce, or unproduce society. Women are points of enriching contact with the divine in *orisa* ritual. In a more general discourse, because women are the sources of order, they are also potential sources of disorder. It is the disposition of their literal and metaphorical "heads" that makes the difference.

Conclusion

According to Yoruba nuptial rituals and marital norms, motherhood is an inextricable dimension of marriage. Yet the projects of metaphoric "highlighting and hiding" (Lakoff and Johnson 1980:10–13) implicit in priestly assertions use these dimensions to insinuate distinct standards of hierarchy and membership upon the house. Although both the Yemoja and the Sango priesthoods combine the hierarchies of marriage and motherhood, they resolve the dissonance between the two hierarchies in different ways. As we have seen, these resolutions reflect (1) the historical resistance of Onigboho House to the Oyo Empire and (2) the Yemoja priesthood's attachment, albeit now ambiguous, to the patrilineal order. Excluding the Onigboho and Onikomo titleholders, the Yemoja priesthood is exclusively female, suggesting a third motive for the highlighting of "motherhood" as the definitive model of priestly hierarchy. As opposed to the image of feminine subordination in the model of "wifeliness," female dominance is implicit in the hierarchy of "motherhood." The ritual predications of the Yemoja priesthood straddle these three motives, with outcomes contingent upon a changing legal, political, and financial context. As we saw earlier, the authority of "motherhood" is itself subject to diverse normative understandings, with their own ambiguous consequences for women's lives in Igboho.

Like their unity, the differences among Igboho's possession religions are products of history. The Sango and Yemoja priesthoods share various iconographic and mythic images of power, including the imagery of vessels and a complex appropriation of Islam. Although Islam is only one of the politico-religious forces whose opposition has given form to the possession religions, historical conditions have made it emblematic of the tensions that produced royalist Igboho over a long term. The image of gods as foreign and people as vessels is not new; they have required long-term conditions of plausibility. The Oyo Yoruba have witnessed various imperialisms in which those with greater access to imported goods and contacts with racial and ethnic Others came to rule. Oyo North has experienced the codification and depersonalization of the rules governing local social interaction and the increasing autocracy of the Oyo palace. Its people have seen the increasing abstraction of the media of exchange from local products and priorities, as well as their own increasing dependency on remittances from the metropolis.

Objective local conditions of domination and economic marginalization do not alone reveal the symbolic conditions of consent and resistance. However, in the light of those political and economic conditions, local mythology and ritual practice do reveal them. The image of self and community as vessels potentiates particular forms of action, of which women's lives in the patrilineage have become both models and symptoms. Thus, reproducing the terms of their own alienation, certain rural women have become experts in the reification, externalization, and redesign of the subject, as well as its redeposition inside the hollow self.

In its intricate negotiations of power among kingship, priesthood, and empire, the Yemoja priesthood demonstrates the relationality of Oyo-Yoruba gender generally. Neither gender nor sex is the irreducible source of other forms of hierarchy. Indeed, in Oyo-Yoruba society, gender co-varies with the synchronic and diachronic axes of political power. Documented over a much longer term are the conditions and motives of gender transformation among the agents of Oyo imperial sovereignty. Chapters 1, 2, and 3 described a series of long-term political negotiations that have overdetermined the meaning of marriage, birth, and money in the Sango priesthood. In the light of these negotiations, then, we will examine the crowning moment of the Oyo-Yoruba possession religions: the ìdóṣù initiation.

Chapter 6

Re-dressing Gender

No person in Oyo-Yoruba religion is more visually captivating than the senior male *elegun*, or possession priest of Sango. Through him appear the "strongest" manifestations of the fiery god. Thus he is the object of much lore, rumor, and fear. Many believe that his touch to a woman's head imparts uterine fertility. Others accuse him of horrific abuses. One of my informants was a highly educated Christian woman who had grown up in a rural town, to which she returned frequently, not unlike most urban Nigerians. Explaining her lifelong fear of cowry shells, she told me that her family friend was once attending a Sango festival when an *elegun*, wearing his characteristically cowry-studded blouse, approached her and shouted, "You know what you have to do!" The woman stood frozen in apparent puzzlement until the manifest god shouted his cryptic order again and his spell took effect. Wordlessly, the woman sank to the ground, where Sango's mount publicly fucked her. The woman subsequently conceived, but she also became an idiot.

I am disinclined to believe the literal truth of such rumors. More-over, this alleged incident occurred nowhere near Igboho. However, many citizens of Igboho have shared with me less articulate and less specific fears of the Sango priests. What is significant about this rumor is not its truth value but the highly conventional sexual, cephalic, ver-bal, and sartorial signs through which this informant felt the power of the god and his mount. Parallel, and equally striking, is her testimony that she had always avoided palaces because of her understanding that the king (*oba*) could claim as a wife (*gbẹ̀sẹ̀ lé obìnrin*) any girl or woman who caught his eye. These tales derive their own power and efficacy from the same sort of "signifyin' " that Atanda documented and applied in his history of the Oyo Renaissance. My informant proposed no abstract or conceptual explanation for her fear of palaces and cowry-covered gods. Her reflections bore no generalization or theory—only rich visual associations understood implicitly in villages subject to Oyo influence and in their far-flung diasporas. Thus, when they shuttle along the corridor between village and metropolis, when they require healing for medically inexplicable problems, and when they retire to the thrones and family homes of the village, members of the migrant bourgeoisie also face re-"naming" according to ritual and mythic realities that do not always have verbal names.

The rural/urban corridor is but one of the axes along which people negotiate power and identity in the village. People also shuttle between brideliness and motherhood, wifeliness and husbandliness, financial poverty and wealth, nonceremonial and ceremonial seasons, uterine infertility and fertility. The Sango festival displays a unique and synthetic axis of personal and social transformation. Moreover, Sango festivals are the largest ecumenical gatherings in all of Oyo North. They bring together hundreds women of all religions in pursuit of fertility and its many symbolic corollaries. The *hope* and awe of those women are just as powerful and, to them, as inexplicable as are the *fear* and awe of my educated, Christian informant.

Members of the festival audience watch the god's every move, ready to leap out of the way should the god dart unexpectedly in their direction. However, when the god slows down and shows his willingness to bless the hopeful, they quickly kneel and doff their headdresses to await the touch of his hand. Come into this world—modern, rural, and poor—is the apotheosis of an early king of Oyo, the paradigmatic king, authoritarian and virile. Yet he is wearing not only cowry shells but the hairstyle, cosmetics, and jewelry of a woman (see figures 12, 13, and 14). For nearly eighty years, scholarly observers of the *orisa* religions have noted that male possession priests wear "women" 's clothes and braid their hair "like women" (Parrinder 1972 [1953]:20; Drewal 1986:61–62, 67; Lawuyi 1987:253; Babayemi 1979:43; Bascom 1969c:87; Awolalu 1979:37; Peel 1990:344; Gleason 1987:89; Dennett 1910:169). Most recently, M. T. Drewal has written, "Crossing gender boundaries, male priests cross-dress as women" (1992:185). Yet it seems to me that the signs on and around the male Sango priest invite a further decod-

Fig. 12. An ideal image of Sango manifest in his possession priest painted on the wall of the Egungun masquerade headquarters (*ìgbàlè*) in Igboho. Note the priest's
braided hair and the cowry-studded blouse. Photograph
by the author (1989). See also figure 6, site O.

ing, which will, I hope, illuminate the power and depth of the feelings
he inspires in Oyo-Yoruba communities.

Given the length of the precedent for such descriptions of these
priests, it would be tempting to recapitulate what seems to me the foremost axis of debate over the gendered meanings of transvestism. The
preponderance of ethnographic studies elsewhere has suggested that
transvestism and transsexualism reinforce existing binary classificatory
schemes and gender hierarchies (e.g., Berger 1976; Wikan 1977; Peacock

Fig. 13. Male initiand at the coming out of the female
initiand. Photograph by the author (1988).

1978; N. Davis 1978; Mageo 1992). Other studies have suggested, most
convincingly in the field of cultural studies, that, as a form of
classificatory transgression, transvestism *undermines* gendered opposi-
tions and hierarchies by calling to attention their "constructed" nature
(e.g., Garber 1992; Drewal 1992; Whitehead 1981).

The present case differs in a variety of empirical ways from the cases
discussed in these analytic terms and, therefore, does not necessarily
undermine previous interpretations of those cases, though it may provide useful warnings for future studies. Among the empirical differences is the fact that we are not concerned here with theater, the

Fig. 14. Sango manifest in a senior male possession priest (*ẹlẹ́gùn*) on the seventh day of an *ìdósù* initiation. Note the braided hair of the possessed priest on the mortar and of the junior possession priest in daily attire on the left. Computer-digitized image from a video by the author (1988).

purview of most of the existing literature on cross-dressing, and we would be ill advised to subject this case to such an analogy. Oyo-Yoruba cross-dressing generally defines potential or actual spirit possession, which is, to my mind, the very antitype of theater. Most Western actors and audiences understand theater as a form of faking. No matter how profoundly the actor may identify with the dramatic character, she or he always embodies an *as if* clause. It is precisely that clause that Leiris (1989:118) deliberately evokes when he characterizes possession in the Ethiopian *zār* cult as a consensual form of "fakery" (*truguage*) and Drewal (1992: 176–77, 183) assumes in describing the manifest Sango as a woman "portraying" the god or "representing" his actions.

Drewal uses the theatrical metaphor to develop the crucial point that much of Yoruba ritual is ingeniously improvised. In the Oyo-Yoruba case, such an argument has numerous applications but must be adapted to a vocabulary consistent with local ontological categories and the conception of agency implicit in "mounting." Oyo-Yoruba possession is based on the culturally recognized creation and embodiment of a self-aware and distinct subject—a subject ontologically rather than imaginarily distinct from the possessed. Not only do supplicants recognize the presence of a god with every gesture of obeisance, but the possessed declare the absence of their personal subjectivity and agency through reports of amnesia during possession. Rather than inferring that thousands of Oyo Yoruba are engaged in an enduring consensual lie, we might recognize, as I argued in chapter 5, that Oyo-Yoruba conceptions of personhood and agency acknowledge subjects that may occupy a person's body without being that person or a fiction that he or she is conjuring up. Such an ontological reality sets up relational possibilities and formulations of personal gender quite different from those supposed on stage.

This ontological foundation is central to two further differences to be discussed at length in the present chapter. First, the transvestism of Sango priests differs from a number of other cases in the character of the gender categories that it underlines: not "man" and "woman" but "husband" and "wife." Second, beyond affirming or undermining existing gender categories, this sacred cross-dressing finances transformations of gender that make it the densest of all local emblems of power (*ase*) and subjectivity.

The verb *gun* ("to mount") often implies suddenness, violence, and utter loss of self-control—a connotation linking it paradigmatically with *Sango*'s action upon his possession priests and upon the world. Other local priesthoods use a range of terms for their forms of possession, including *gùn*, *wáayé* ("[the god] comes to the world"), and *dé* ("[the god] arrives"). Not only the vocabulary but the iconography and rites of the Sango initiation encode a distinctive political history, in which not only extreme nullifications of personal will but unparalleled invocations of wifely symbolism and, as we shall see, blood sacrifice become explicable. Thus, mounting is an emergent and internally complex type of relationship. It is the focus of a historical project in which gendered categories not only transcend the "man"/"woman" dichotomy posited in previous descriptions of Yoruba priestly dress but acquire their specific shape amid the ritual creation of royal and divine subjectivity. Thus the economic, political, and military conditions that gave rise to the royalist hierarchy of mounting have also overdetermined the meaning of the gender categories that "name" it.

Gender and Metaphor

The initiation ritual creates a new god inside the initiand and designs the reason for supplicants' awe and hope through a complex technical process, which includes exposing the initiand, the priesthood, and, to a degree, the entire community to a highly mixed metaphor; that is, a series of normally incompatible metaphors is combined through their predication upon a single person, who, along with the community surrounding him, senses what each metaphor implies about the initiand as a new social entity and about the kind of social entity that could combine all of those predicated qualities at once (cf. Basso 1976). Properly speaking, the initiand becomes the metonym of a new social *relationship*, which combines all of these qualities but is called by the name of only one of them—being a "bride" and "wife" (*iyawo*), or what I have denominated "brideliness."[1]

If being the bride of human husbands is taken as "literal" brideliness, then an initiand subjected to this metaphor alone has been "named" according to a first-order metaphor.[2] When the common quality among mixed metaphors is attributed to the term "bride," then brideliness has become a metonym and, during possession, a *second-order* metaphor for the new relationship. As we shall see, the postinitiatory development of the priest rehighlights and adds further metaphors to this ironic mix, which comes to be defined metonymically by mounting itself.

If this formulation of the diverse "orders" of metaphor appears obscure at the moment, its concrete significance will become clear through the sequential treatment of the initiation rite. The function of this provisional typology of metaphor is to diagram the dialectical complexity of "gender" in its interaction with other forms of social relationship and, more generally, the transformation of "sources" by their "targets." I am inspired by Strathern's argument (1987:6–7) that in Pacific societies sexual/gender inequality is the irreducible "idiom" in which even inequality between persons of the same sex and gender is understood. Slightly modified, this argument clearly invites application to a range of West African cases as well. The Oyo-Yoruba case suggests, however, that "gender" concepts are reducible: they are subject to prior influences, and they are understood in the idiom of relations between gods and priests, riders and horses, parents and children, seniors and juniors, kings and plebes. Given the centrality of what has been called "gender" in the negotiation of a range of social and political hierarchies, it seems to me that "gender" must be understood as a *product* of such negotiation. "Gender" cannot be understood prior to and apart from the various metaphoric uses that have been made of it.

The initiation and development of these transvestite possession priests specifically resist various common approaches to gender and metaphor. First, the invocation of metaphors is not only a mode of signification appealing to the imagination; their invocation is often a politicized act requiring material conditions of plausibility and enforcement by its expositors against the assertions of other interested parties (see also Robertson 1992). Second, these material predications do not modify only the metaphoric *target* (i.e., the item described), switching it into a new category of which the literal meaning stands unchanged or affirmed. Metaphoric predications also modify the *source* (i.e., the item whose identity is being predicated upon the target). As a *source* of metaphoric predications on political hierarchy, economic privilege, and personal health, "gender" ceases to be gender as we know it. Thrown up into a second order of metaphoric signification, salient gendered signs are transformed by their multiple targets into a new social reality that might invite a description other than "brideliness" if we look systematically at the social, political, and ritual contexts of their invocation. We cannot assume that gender is primarily either the set of symbolic qualities attributed to the two sexes or the irreducible source of other social hierarchies. Gender is historical and is subject to transformation by reigning political and financial interests.

The fundamental question about any given form of transvestism is not "Does cross-dressing affirm or undermine hegemonic *gender roles*?" but "What *boundaries* does the cross-dresser cross?" In this case, it is not in any simple sense the boundary between "man" and "woman." In what follows, we will take a closer look at the categories and boundaries Oyo-Yoruba possession priests *make* through their acts of sartorial crossing. To put it another way, instead of assuming the rules of *classification* expressed or undermined by the transvestite, we will investigate the *process* by which cross-dressing designs new forms of relationship and hierarchy, in the joint service of fecundation and political order.

Sango possession priests must be initiated, and their rank increases according to the length of their subsequent membership in the cult. The highest rank belongs to the god, who manifests himself in priests' bodies. Priests are explicitly possessed only intermittently, but their material link to the god remains *in* their bodies and is indexed by sartorial signs *on* their bodies until old age or death (cf. Butler 1990). Elaborate rituals and verbal utterances cultivate this link, of which the age and quality are formally encoded in long-term stages of priestly dress and grooming. All of these stages are visible during public ceremonies. However, it is private rites that invest meaning and power in the minute signs of dress and grooming. For the multitudes of supplicants, the power (*ase* and *agbára*) of the gods need not be explained. It is seen as if through a prism and, above all, felt through the evocative power of well-financed metaphors. Witnessing the private rites clarifies, in a way indispensable for the outsider, the diverse historical, political, economic, social, and personal tensions that converge upon the transvestite priest.

The Secret in the Making

Two terms are used to describe initiation into the Oyo-Yoruba possession religions: *dósù* and *se òrìṣà*. The first means "to create òsù [a ball of sacred substances] onto the initiand's head." The second means "to do, or make, the god," implying that human ritual effort is required to create a god in the initiand's body.[3] As they "make" the god, they are also engaged in the "making" of a novel and extraordinary category of social relationship, of which the initiand's body is both a metaphor and a metonym.

No full account of the initiation is available in writing, for the Sango priesthood is hedged in by *àṣírí awo* (religious secrets).[4] The secret is not only a limit on outsiders' knowledge but, in itself, a paradigm of personhood and power. As Buckley (1976) points out, even personal health depends on the proper containment of physical and metaphysical substances, including knowledge, will, and "truth." At the same time, the spirit of secrecy competes with the principle of showing others that *there is a secret* and making clear *who is privileged to know it*.[5] For example, on one day of the initiation, the initiand is seated outdoors, where a crowd has gathered. The Sango priests use their bodies and several wrap skirts (*iro*), which the priestesses have doffed to fashion into a curtain, in order to conceal the manipulations inside. Naturally, one wonders why they do not perform the ceremony indoors or in a less populated area, where no crowd would have taken notice. Indeed, the cloth itself becomes a complex public sign of privileged knowledge, bodily containment, social separation, and hierarchy.

To an extent, therefore, curious onlookers like myself are expected and are an institutional feature of the initiation. On the other hand, there are phases of the initiation that the initiate's kin, neighbors, friends, and wives, as well as the investigator, were forbidden to witness in person. Still, many community residents have similar information on what took place beyond their observation. We cannot know if there is an informational secret as such, but whatever detailed information may be missing, the viewer and listener is made plainly aware that an invisible and inchoate divine power (*ase*) is being designed and revealed in a socially legible form (see Fernandez 1986).

I witnessed substantial parts of two Sango initiations in Igboho, one for a man and one for a woman. Between them I observed no procedural differences. Regardless of biological sex, the initiand is called a "bride" (*iyawo*) of the god. I have chosen, advisedly, to use the masculine pronoun in describing the unpossessed novice only because I am specifically discussing male transvestites. Although the male possession priest is not alone in his crossing, it is the ironic image of his *sexual* crossing that alerts us to a semantic order far more complex than sex and sex-based gender. I have inserted an alphabetical *apparatus criticus* of bracketed letters to help the reader correlate portions of the exegesis with events in the narration.

The Initiation

Key Participants

Ṣàngó, the tutelary god of the Oyo kingdom.

Èṣù, the mischievous god of communication, the lord of the crossroads. Christians identify him with the Devil.

Ìyàwó, literally, "bride," or "wife [junior to the speaker]." The male or
female initiand and young possession priest.

Mógbà, the nonpossession priests officially responsible for the initiation of possession priests.

Ẹlẹ́gùn, mature male or female possession priests. A male *elegun* is the
head of the possession priesthood in any given quarter.

Ìyálé, the "senior co-wife," the female *elegun* who takes care of the initiand in the Sango shrine.

Drummers

Audience

Supplicants, those seeking specific assistance from the gods.

The witches, women with the power (*àjẹ́*) to help their allies and, above
all, to kill their enemies.

"Sango does not die; his horse is the one who goes to the other
world" (*Ṣàngó kìí kú; ẹsin rẹ̀ ló ń lọ sọ́run*), said one *elegun* of another possession priest's death. Most Sango priests are recruited from within the
bilateral kindred of a retiring or recently deceased possession priest
(*elegun*). When a "horse" prepares to go to "heaven" or "the other
world" (*orun*), a sacred and immaterial "head load" must be with-
drawn from his head and "tied onto the head" (*di nǹkan rù*) of his nominated successor. Sango's approval of the successor is established
through cowry-shell divination (figure 15).

If the priest's successor has not been prepared before his death, the
egbẹ́ Ṣàngó (the "association of Sango priests") removes the "load" from
the head of the deceased priest but delays the burial of the corpse until
the dead person's family has chosen a suitable successor [A]. Delaying
the burial is a highly feared form of blackmail. The successor is ideally a
young adult. However, much as clitoridectomies are performed earlier
in life than they used to be, so are initiations. The fear that one's children will have adopted other religions before they reach the proper age

Fig. 15. Cowry-shell divination being performed before the objects used in the *di nǹkan rù* ceremony of a prospective possession priest. The sacred head-stuff represented by the bloodied object in the bowl is being fed and transferred from the head of a retiring possession priest and into that of his successor. Photograph by the author (1988).

of initiation has persuaded some priests to initiate prepubescent children.

Priestly recruitment occasionally transcends identifiable heredity, although it did so in none of the cases I witnessed. For example, diviners may interpret a person's illness or misfortune as a calling and prescribe initiation as a cure. Excessive crying or other signs of distress in infants may likewise be diagnosed as a calling. Such children are said to have "brought the *orisa* from the other world" (*wón mú òrìṣà wá láti* ọrun), just as people bring their "heads" from heaven. According to Bascom (1969:43), such cases are usually attributed in principle to inheritance from some forgotten ancestor.

The important phases of the idosu initiation in Igboho can be spread out over a year, but the focus of events is a period of fourteen days, when the initiand sleeps with his female caretaker in the domestic shrine of a *mogba* of Sango. In sum, the initiand begins residence in the shrine room (*gbọngán*) on the eve of what is called the "first day." During this period, the initiand's head is privately shaved, after which sacred substances and large quantities of animal blood are applied to his head and other body parts. His head is repeatedly painted with a series of standardized designs. The initiand participates, alongside senior priests, in a number of public ceremonies as well. Throughout this period, both male and female initiands wear clothing, jewelry, and cosmetics the likes of which only women wear outside the context of the possession priesthoods. The initiand returns home ideally on the "thirteenth day."[6] Various public displays follow intermittently, but years may pass before the initiand becomes a full-fledged *ẹlẹ́gùn Ṣàngó* (i.e., "mount" of the god), responsible for a quarter of his own.

The following extended discussion concerns rites occurring in Igboho in September 1988. It was early in the dry season, about two months after the yam harvest and in the midst of a corn harvest. Food was therefore plentiful and, due to structural adjustments in the import market, the profits from the indigenous cultivation of corn, millet, cassava, and yams had become exceptionally robust.[7] The co-occurrence of two initiations and of preparations for a third in the same three-month period is highly unusual, for the initiations are costly and the residents of the town poor.

The candidate enters the *mogba*'s shrine room (figure 11) on the eve of "the first day," after offerings have been made to the grave of the dead predecessor. Priests circulate money around the initiand's head and deposit it on the grave [B]. Back in the *mogba*'s house, chewed kola nuts (*obì* and *orógbó*) and the blood of a freshly decapitated chicken are applied to various points on the body of the initiand in order to feed the god inside him and to strengthen those body parts [C]. The female ritual attendant (*iyale*) prays as follows upon placing the chewed kola nut:

On the palms of the initiand's hands:
A máa gbowó tó dáa ("We will get a lot of money"),

On the abdomen:
Káa má rí inú rùn ("May we not get a runny stomach"),

On his sides:
Ọlọ́run kò níí jẹ́ káa rí ikú, ẹ jọ̀wọ́ ("God will not let us die, please"),

On his forehead:
Kóoríi rẹ ó má búrú; kóoríi rẹ ó má fọ́ ("Your 'head' should not go bad [i.e., you should not become crazy, stupid, or unfortunate]; you should not get headaches").

The male bride and all the Sango priests stay awake that night. The bride drinks millet beer (*ọtí ọkà*) containing special herbs and bathes in herbal infusions. An age-mate of the deceased priest then shaves the bride's head. In some traditions, a small incision is placed on the scalp, better to allow the penetration of the sacred force that is being inserted there [D]. Some local informants report that the bride swallows certain substances or objects formerly belonging to his dead predecessor.[8] Then the bride sits on an overturned mortar [E] [F], and numerous animals are exsanguinated over his head in a rite called *afẹjẹ̀wẹ̀*—"bathing in blood" [G]. The blood may be painted on with the feather of a vulture (*igún*) [H]. Sango then "mounts" (*gùn*), or possesses, his new bride. From this day until the end of his residence in the shrine room, the initiand is fed, bathed, and led around like a child.

On the next morning (i.e., on the "first day"), a combination of kola nut (*obì*), bitter kola (*orógbó*), and alligator pepper (*atare*)[9] is chewed up by a priestess and applied in a ball called *osu* to the top of the bride's head, just above the suture of the cranium. Again using a vulture feather, that priestess paints lightning- and bloodlike designs on the bride's head with blood-colored camwood (*osùn*) and white chalk (*ẹfun*) [I] (figure 16). The *osu* ball and painted designs will be washed off and replaced on the bride's head at least twice a day for the balance of the first seven days in the shrine room. On this morning of the "first day," the bride carries an offering on his head to the crossroads for the *orisa* Esu—divine messenger and troublemaker—and, according to some local reports, for the "witches" (*aje*) [J]. His female ritual attendant, the *iyale* (literally, "senior co-wife") always leads him to the crossroads.

Fig. 16. Male initiand with his head painted. The henna on his hands is a cosmetic preparation for the public dance of the following day. Photograph by the author (1988).

The bride, his senior co-wife, and the rest of the priests will dance in a circle at the crossroads, which is sometimes the location of the dead possession priest's grave as well. Whether or not the grave is there, the crossroads appears to be a point of contact with the divine.

On the "second day," the priests, who have again spent the night with the bride, awake and chant the panegyrics (*oriki*) of several important *orisa*. On the eve of the "third day," the priests stay awake to divine, with cowry shells, Sango's will in relation to the bride (*wón tẹ òrìṣà fún ìyàwó*) and to determine the bride's taboos (*èèwọ̀*). They also tie the special bead necklaces called *kélé* on the bride [K]. On the morning of the "third day" the bride bears one offering to the crossroads for the witches [between L and M] and another to the river for Sango.[10] At the river, the bride and the priests bathe naked—extremely intimate conduct in this society [L]. Equally shocking to most people, on the afternoon of the "third day" the priests publicly perform ribald songs [M]. They dance to the beat of *bàtá* drums before a serious circle dance takes place, during which both the initiand and his female ritual attendant (*iyale*) are mounted by Sango [N] (figures 17 and 18). Male or female, the bride wears distinctly female clothing (*ìró*, *bùbá*, and *òjá*) [O]—including, in both the initiations I witnessed, textiles covered with images of Nigerian bank notes [P] (figure 13). The predominantly female audience contributes money to the manifest gods' attendants and to the holders of important ritual implements—such as an old razor and the sacred pouch (*làbà*) used to contain Sango's emblematic thunder axes [Q].

Until the eve of the "seventh day," the initiand remains in or near the *mogba*'s room and continues the infantilizing dietary and hygienic routine administered by the female ritual attendant (*iyale*) [R]. On the eve of the "seventh day," more animals are immolated and some of their blood is drunk. The bride's head is reshaved to leave a skullcap-shaped area of stubble, which is then darkened with indigo paint [S].

On the morning of the "seventh day," a ram that has remained captive in the room next to the shrine is brought out and its forehead pressed three times to that of the initiand. The ram is then decapitated [T], as are several chickens. Their blood is collected in a bowl, and several priests use their pinkies to taste a bit of its contents. I am asked to leave for a time that afternoon, during which I believe, based on Verger's (1981) and Salami's (1990) accounts, the blood is applied to the bride's head [U]. More offerings are borne on his head to the crossroads—variously for Esu, the witches, or the dead *elegun*. Then, as we have seen, the bride is seated outside on a mortar [V] and surrounded by the priests and their curtain of wrap skirts (*iro*). After two chickens are killed within the enclosure, the bride comes out staggering [W]. He has apparently bitten off a chicken's head and sucked its blood [X]. The audience sings and signs with its hands that Sango should not kill anyone as he arrives from the other world. In one of the two initiations I witnessed, a second such ceremony was performed later on the same day.

On the afternoon of the "seventh day," a further public performance takes place. It is called *ìkó omo jáde* ("the carrying outdoors of the child") [Y]. Once again, the initiand wears women's clothing [Z]. Before the *iyawo* emerges for his first appearance as an initiated member of the priesthood, the female ritual attendant (*iyale*) washes his feet at the

Fig. 17. Circle dance of possession priests at the coming out of the female initiand. Photograph by the author (1988).

threshold of the *mogba*'s house [AA], where he has resided for the past seven days. The priests collectively dance in a circle, playfully miming public sexual acts and laughing [BB] (figure 17). Then the frivolity ends abruptly, the drums speed up, the dance circle spins like a cyclone, and the god simultaneously mounts bride and senior co-wife [CC]. Before they are sidelined, senior male priests rotate money around the bride's head and place it in front of the drums [DD]. Two senior possession priests are then mounted [EE]—one male and one female—and the manifest gods dance. The Sango manifest in the male priest climbs (*gùn*) onto an overturned mortar to display himself to the crowd (figure 14; see also figure 12). Members of the crowd again give money to the manifest gods' attendants and to the bearers of important ritual implements. Donors then bare their heads to solicit the blessing of the god's touch, from which they expect to obtain uterine fertility, health, and wealth [FF] [GG]. Still later, the taboo of the bride is announced, and people are invited to pay a fee for the privilege of violating it for one last time. In both cases I witnessed, the taboo forbids anyone to strike

Fig. 18. Sango "mounted" on his female possession priest. Photograph by the author (1988).

the priest. Audience members are given pieces of straw with which to hit the initiand as he sits on a mortar. Suddenly, the god mounts the bride and leaps up, enraged. Priests restrain the manifest god and lead him into the *mogba*'s room, where the initiand is called back to consciousness.

In the subsequent days, the special necklaces (*kele*) remain around the bride's neck, and his skullcap of stubble is kept darkened with indigo paint [HH]. On the "twelfth day" of his initiation, the male bride, followed by drummers and priestly attendants, parades around the town wearing feminine clothing and jewelry and bearing in his hands a switch (àtòrì or pàṣọ́n) to fight against the witches. The eve of the "thir-teenth day" will be the last night the initiand spends with the female ritual attendant (iyale) in the mogba's room. On the "twenty-third day" the bride moves about the town bearing a Sango dance wand (oṣé Ṣàngó), representing a human female figure with thunder axes on her head [II], and a crown-shaped and cowry-covered object called Baàyònì, which in some towns used to be conveyed to the site of a house struck by lightning (Abraham 1962:622; Johnson 1880) [JJ]. With it the Sango priests exercised their official right to plunder such a house. Non-religious parties and celebrations may follow the "twenty-third day."[11]

Exegesis

This exegesis is the product of a nonexegetical dialogue. In my experi-ence, officials of the Oyo-Yoruba possession religions are little given to explaining to anyone the rites they conduct and the sartorial conven-tions they follow. Instruction is accomplished by example and correc-tion, and efficacy rather than exposition is the form of Sango's apolo-getics. The ambiguous secrecy surrounding the initiation mitigates further against indigenous exegesis. Although the priests do improvise around the occasional unavailability of certain sacrificial animals, for example, they express a sense that initiations entail a standard se-quence of events, of which elders possess a greater knowledge than their juniors. The convention of secrecy notwithstanding, there is much talk during the Sango initiation. Priests schedule and discuss the events of the initiation in a consistent vocabulary, whose logical relation to rit-ual events and sacred icons is often obvious. At other times, it must be inferred from ideas expressed in the sacred texts recited during the rit-uals and in the well-established mythical, ritual, and social conventions of the surrounding community. Certain indigenous narrative accounts are easily solicited, but the symbolic quality of the initiand's transfor-mation, the sources of its efficacy, and the intensity of audience response await an explanation that conjoins ritual event and iconogra-phy with a wider local ideology. This conjunction is the foremost pur-pose of the following exegesis.

It would be difficult to ignore the implications of this powerful event in relation to issues of central concern to anthropology and Western cultural criticism. Thus I call upon this luminous and semantically centripetal moment in Oyo-Yoruba culture to illustrate three specific implications for the general study of gender and metaphor. First, there are times when "gender" is not gender, when the invocation of gendered terms and, more important, relationships is so overdetermined by relations of class, genealogy, commerce, and empire, for example, that the internal structural "value" of gender in a system of signs (cf. de Saussure 1983) takes precedence over any reference to sex or sex roles.[12] Second, although major works on metaphor have seldom considered the "feedback" effect of metaphoric predications, I would argue that metaphoric predications are never one-way: "targets" (or "defined" concepts) simultaneously predicate meaning and sense upon "sources" (or "defining" concepts). Even as a source, "gender" has been transformed by its metaphoric predicates. Third, the central role of certain gendered signs in these tendentious rearrangements of social meaning called "metaphor" (of which Yoruba possession rituals are but one example) is not primordial or simply semantic. The effective invocation of metaphors depends on a history of material investments.

The Sango initiation retraces a particular, standardized female biography and imposes its constituting ritual signs upon the body of the initiand as a condition of his new relationship to a divine being and his cult. Yet, imposed upon the same person, the biographical metaphors seem to be "mixed," or multiple and incompatible. Although the initiand is addressed simply as "bride," or "wife," of the god, he or she is subject at once to multiple metaphors of captivity, birth, sexual intercourse, consanguineal kinship, and corporal disintegration. The initiand is both the victim and the beneficiary of the most complex form of semantic incest imaginable. Each of these metaphors may be understood in light of an archaeology of seemingly discrete models of relationship, all collapsed within his "brideliness." These metaphors undergo a further collapsing when inscribed on the male body in particular, and still other condensations in the postinitiatory transformations of his attire.

Metaphors of Captivity. The cult seems to understand itself and to be understood by others as the rival of worldly fathers and contemporary families for command over their children, a rivalry that acquires special resonance from the fact that most families prefer for their children to become Christian or Muslim. Sung daily during the initiation, Sango's panegyrics (*Ṣàngó pípè*) thus invoke a past model for this present rivaly:

> When Sango was living at Wanra he was a hunter.
> Tela Afonja[13] used to hunt with a chain.
> He put it in the bathing room *to catch the children of the family head.*

> Nígbàtí Ṣàngó m̀bẹ̀ ni Wánrà, ọdẹ ni ń ṣe.
> Ẹ̀wọ̀n ni Tèlà Àfọ̀njá ń dẹẹ́ ta.
> Báluwè ní í dẹ ẹ̀ sí ọmọ bálé ní í fi mú. (emphasis mine)[14]

Indeed, priests are highly aware that most adults would not voluntarily join the priesthood. Most voluntary recruits are children. Others have been chosen as compulsory replacements for a dead kinsman [A]. Potential priests and viceroys were once recruited, probably amid their own and their families' sense of acquiescence to coercion, from within the populace of chieftaincies and kingdoms under the domination of the Oyo palace. Such a sense of involuntary acquiescence emerges in the image that the initiand has been captured by a royal slave hunter. In sum, the relationship of the god to the initiand is like that of a captor to a captive. This analogy is expressed in the following proportion:

$$\text{god} : \text{initiand} :: \text{captor} : \text{captive}$$

Metaphors of Infancy. During the first seven days of initiation, the novice is configured as a fetus or a newborn. He is rendered bald and nude in semipublic places [L]. He sleeps in the shrine room with a woman who bathes him and attends his excretory functions [R]. The attendant feeds him and ensures that all food has been properly cooled. Hot adult foods like "soup" (*ọbẹ̀*) are forbidden. Whenever the initiand leaves the shrine room, he must wear over his head a white cloth associated with Orisa Nla, the god who forms fetuses in the womb. The interchangeability of wearing the head cloth and being in the shrine room implies that the shrine room is, for the initiand, like a womb. Indeed, the public presentation of the initiand on the "seventh day" is called *iko omo jade*—"the carrying outdoors of the child"—after the name of the first official public appearance of newborns [Y]. Whereas newborn boys undergo this ceremony on the "ninth" day" of life, girls undergo it on the "seventh." Thus, the scheduling of the initiation assimilates the novice specifically to a baby girl. The initiand has been reborn a daughter of the royal house. Hence:

god : initiand ::
royal father : infant daughter

The infantilizing regimen of the first seven days casts the female ritual attendant in the role of the initiand's mother and represents an axis of power rivaling the authority that male priests later assume through another metaphoric assertion. As we shall see, that first axis ultimately gives way to the second.

Blood Metaphors. "Blood" is a prominent trope of vitality, kinship, and reproduction in Yoruba ritual language. "He has blood in his body" (*Ó léjè lára*) means that the referent is healthy and robust. Reified as blood, that vitality can be transferred through sacrifice to the altars of the gods and to the bodies of possession priestesses [X]. As in North American society (see Schneider 1968), "blood" invokes a biological mode of kinship and the code of mutual obligations entailed in it. *Èjè kannââ ni wón*—"they are the same blood"—is a phrase that priests and Oyo Yoruba generally use to describe what we too call consanguineal kin. Conversely, nurses at the Baptist Hospital in nearby Saki say that many of their patients attribute infertility to *èjè burúkú*—"bad blood." Moreover, some men regard sex with their wives as work, believing that it causes them to "lose blood." Sex is a "sacrifice," concluded one English-speaking Yoruba informant.

These verbal usages shed contemporary light on the fact that Sango initiations require the "bathing of [the initiand] in blood"—*afejewe* (see also Verger 1981:39). The bloody deluge in the *mogba's* shrine room [X] appears to be an act of ritual compensation: priests expend vast quantities of animal blood in order to ratify a form of social bond unsubstantiated by the "blood" ties that characterize the canonical site of Oyo-Yoruba social order. Hence, the initiand becomes a mighty kinsman of the royal house, particularly through the "blood" extracted and transferred from Sango's emblematic animal—the ram [T] [U]. Animal blood applied to *heads*—the other canonical Yoruba symbol of kinship—colors a previously nonkin relationship with the kind of realness necessary to justify the highest order of mutual assistance and loyalty—between god and priesthood and among the priests. Indeed, the priesthood adopts for its own purposes a third crucial index of Yoruba consanguineal kinship: exogamy. Thus:

god   :   initiand ::
senior consanguineal kin   :   junior consanguineal kin

According to Buckley's research in Ibadan, Yoruba understand conception as the "coming together of sperm and menstrual blood" (1976:399)—the blood apparently being the mother's contribution to the fetus. I have never heard this belief stated explicitly in Igboho, but its presence in the culturally related city of Ibadan specifies the appropriation to which the relationship of "birth" and "motherhood" itself has been subjected. In the Sango cult, *men* monopolize the redeposition of "blood" and kinship. Only men can sacrifice four-legged animals in Igboho. If a male is present, no matter how junior and inexperienced, he is appointed to sacrifice even the fowls.

Moreover, the logic of "blood" sacrifice and kinship in the Sango cult depends on the hierarchical differentiation between two sorts of blood—the blood of the womb and the blood of the neck. Exposed vaginal blood is explicitly, for the Oyo Yoruba, defiling to all things living and sacred. Blood from the necks of sacrificial victims is, on the other hand, the exemplary source of sacred power. Igboho possession religions thus undo the link between wombs and the blood of kinship and vitality. Indeed, the *orisa* commander of procreation and the womb—Orisa Nla—is male rather than female; he is associated with whiteness rather than with the color of blood. By the same principle, Ajala has taken over a female profession—potting—and taken it up in heaven, where *he* makes heads. Effecting a further abstraction, the blood of the neck is represented on the initiand's head in multiple *vegetable* facsimiles, such as the *osu* ball [I], which reddens as it oxidizes, and painted marks of red camwood pigment (*osun*), which resemble the dripping blood of the "bathing in blood" (*afejewe*) ceremony.

Through imitation, distillation, and displacement, the Sango initiation strips not only motherhood but biological parenthood altogether of its monopoly over the binding symbolism of "blood." Male-controlled sacrifice disrupts that monopoly and shifts blood into a *meta-*reproductive realm that is also concerned with the control and coordination of human "heads." With the capacity to marshal surplus blood and transfer it from one vessel to another, Sango priests empower themselves in multiple ways—not only to "make" gods and priests but to double back and render barren women fertile. In these projects, cerebral "mounting" encompasses and supersedes sexual "mounting." Kinship of the "head" encompasses and outdoes kinship of the womb—but at a great cost in animals, blood, and labor.

Ordinarily, the metaphors of "blood" and marriage are incommensurable in Oyo-Yoruba thinking about social relationships. Known consanguineal kin, no matter how distantly related, are forbidden to marry each other. Yet this clash of metaphors is not randomly ordered. It follows a division of labor and of interests between male and female priests. Over the course of the Sango initiation, metaphors of blood, birth, and infantilization give way sequentially to metaphors of wifeliness. The latter symbolism appears most useful to senior male priests' posture of husbandly authority over the bride, in a logic that carries to its conclusion the female ritual attendant's (that is, the *iyale's*) cession of her authority as the official mother of the infantlike initiand. In Oyo royal history, his mother's death was once the precondition of the prince's accession to the throne. In the initiation, as we shall see, maternal authority is nullified through its transformation of maternal into co-wifely authority, this tranformation being the precondition of the initiand's entry into the priesthood on the "seventh day."

The Oyo Royalist Organic Metaphor. The organic metaphor implicit in Oyo royalism does not assume the integrity of the body. Indeed, both hierarchy and the division of labor and loyalties are rendered in images of butchery (cf. Durkheim 1933:127–31, for example). Through the display of animal dismemberment, priests appear to design and demonstrate the novice's own bodily and social reconstruction. The head is the central vessel of Yoruba personhood. The Sango priesthood's manipulation of its contents and ownership are among a series of such changes in the normal human life, typically mediated by a range of extrabodily social agents. Although they are rivals in the battle for personnel, patriliny and Sango priestly recruitment rest atop the shared premise that the "inner head" (*orí inú*) can be displaced. Spirit possession installs in its place the will and consciousness of a divine Other.

The initiation permanently fixes in the novice's head a new and most powerful being, who, at exemplary moments, takes over from the "inner head," an entity indexing "blood" kinship or individual will. So overwhelming is the invasion of the divine agent that the possessed priest's physical head is said to "swell" (*wú*) (see Drewal 1986:62). This penetration recalls the image on Sango's dance wand (*oṣé*) in which the god's thunder axes, projectiles hurled from the sky, appear poised to enter the possession priest's head [II]. Hence:

god	:	initiand ::
inner head	:	outer head ::
contents	:	vessel ::
heaven (*òrun*)	:	the world (*ayé*) ::
thunder axe	:	Earth

In sacrifice, Sango receives not only blood but heads. The initiatory appropriation of animal heads mimes the appropriation of the initiand's head. Recall that, before the culminating sacrifice, the sacrificers press the ram's forehead against the novice's, apparently establishing an identity between victim and initiand. Then they slip a stone called a "thunder axe" (*ẹdùn àrá*) into the animal's mouth before severing the head [T] [U]. Having been exhumed from the earth after lightning struck, this stone suggests Sango's penetrating power. The severed ram's head, containing the thunder-axe icon of that power, is placed on Sango's altar of head-shaped sacred stones. After being used to mop up stray blood from the floor, the ram's limp body is then thrown out, almost as though the *removal* of the ram's body, rather than the mere death of the animal, has been the objective of the killing. The head is inside the holy of holies; the body is cast outdoors. Hence:

god	:	initiand ::
ram's blood	:	ram's body ::
ram's head	:	ram's body

In a sense, we have witnessed an act of expiation. The late Nancy Jay (1990) argued that much blood sacrifice around the globe is directed toward creating patrilineal groups by expiating matrilateral social identity; that is, it stifles the effect of the mother's identity in order to secure the child's unadulterated identification with and complete membership in the patrilineal house. According to Jay, patrilineal groups affirm their boundaries through the commensality of the sacrificial group. Of course, the Sango priesthood differs from a patrilineage. Indeed, the priesthood is the nemesis of the patrilineal house. Sango ritually *"catches* the children of the family head," as suggested in his panegyrics. What the ram sacrifice expiates must be commensurately different from the contagion of matrilateral identity. The Sango priesthood promulgates rituals of essentialization and directed manifestation, of extraction and subsequent reinvestment. The initiands' bodies and the bodies of a series of sacrificial victims are the instruments of this process of extracting capital, in the sense of essential productive resources, from the patricentric social body, which is drained and thrown out the door like the ram's body. Hence:

$$
\begin{array}{llll}
\text{god} & : & \text{initiand} & :: \\
\text{head} & : & \text{body} & :: \\
\text{patriliny} & : & \text{consanguinity} & :: \\
\text{initiation} & : & \text{patrilineal descent}
\end{array}
$$

Indeed, wearing the *kele* necklaces that visually sever head from body [K], the initiand himself becomes a walking sign of alienation through purchase. Bifurcating the neck, the *kele* necklaces mark transitional sutures between the human head and body in rites elaborately concerned with the transfer of heads from their natal social bodies and into the royal and divine body of the priesthood. In a possession priest's life, wearing them marks those times when his or her head is being transferred out of Sango's service as well. Its meaning enriched by tales probably of recent origin, the central *kele* is identified with Sango's *orisa* wife Oya, who was present when the early king Sango hanged himself, choking off the connection between his own earthly head and body.[15]

These disjunctions and transfers reflect a series of discrete social and somatic relationships, as they are represented in Yoruba history, myth, kinship ideology, and butchering practices. Moreover, in predicating all of these relationships and their metonyms on a single human body, the initiation ritual illustrates the unique and synthetic form of subjectivity by which the initiand will repeatedly be possessed for many years to come. Newly separated are the head from the human body, the inner head from the outer head, the initiand from his natal house, the head and blood from the living animal. Each first term becomes the

metonymic representation of each second term and of its own relationship with the second term. These condensed signs of relationship ultimately converge upon Sango himself. On the altar and inside the head
of the initiand, he is the apical sign of the relationship among relationships. The initiand's body is marked out as a vessel in which the distilled and compounded energy (ase) of all these relationships can
indeed grow before being redistributed.

During the initiation, possession is repeatedly induced, while paintings upon the sometimes surgically opened scalp of the initiand suggest what is being inserted there [D] [E] [H] [I] [N] [W] [CC] [EE]. The
immediate alternation of colors within lines and circles is the visual
leitmotif of these paintings. After the red *osu* ball at the cranial suture
comes a white circle, a red circle, and another white circle (figure 16).
The only explanation I could elicit was that the head painting marks
out which person is the initiand. The name of the vulture-feather paint-
brush (*ìyẹ́ igún*) recalls the verb for "mounting," or spirit possession
(*gùn*)—as do the processes by which birds "sprout" (*gún*) feathers and
by which the flesh of Sango's sacrificial ram is "skewered" (*gún*) before
being cooked and eaten (see Abraham 1962:258). Thus, what is expiated
is ultimately reappropriated, digested, and reformulated in terms of a
new model of social relationship: the nesting relations between container and contained, between mounted and mounter (see Matory 1986:
esp. 53–54; see also Drewal 1986; 1992:75).

Visually, the crisscrossing of the painted designs suggests lightning,
while the combination of red and white recalls fire—both phenomena
ascribed repeatedly to Sango in his panegyrics. The design and its progressive expansion over the course of the initiation suggest the downward radiation of fire- and lightninglike force, as well as their total
appropriation of the bride's head. The initiand undergoes a redesign
not only of his "head" (*ori*) but of his "eyes/face" (*ojú*)—his consciousness, public identity, and chief portals of perception—amid the guided
invasion of Sango's power. Their new design is mimed several times
daily during the first six days of the initiation. The ordered power (*ase*)
of the designs—like that of the other substances applied—is supposed
to seep into the head. Metaphorically, Sango's thunder axe has entered
the *initiand*'s head through the ram proxy; his head has been severed
from its physical and social bodies and reinvested with their power.

The painting on the eve of the "seventh day" appears to seal in what has been deposited. That night the priests shave and dye the initiand's head with indigo, leaving a blue cap much like what appears on the image of Sango's possession priests carved on the sacred mortar (*odo*) in Igboho shrines [S] [HH] (figure 11).

As we shall see, the darkening of the head suggests a feminine containment and sealing in of what has, for several days, been inscribed on the initiand's head in red and white [H] [I]. These manipulations invoke the structural contrast between, on the one hand, the *orisa* (including Sango) and other powerful foreigners—widely conceived of as light-skinned (*pupa*) or white (*funfun*)—and, on the other, the dark vessels of the gods. Blackness is an ancient, if lapsed, ideal of feminine appearance (see Baudin 1885:66–67). Moreover, not only are the shrine pots used to contain most gods' power (*ase*) generally glazed dark brown (*dúdú*), but in many regions they are dyed with indigo to accentuate their dark hue. By contrast, the stones and shells *inside* the gods' pots are light. The consistency of the ritual metaphor becomes obvious when we recall that heads are likened to pots. The ultimate darkening of the head emblematizes the containment and fixing of a dyadic relationship between the vessel-like possession priest and the new divine contents of his or her head. Hair is allowed to grow again in the indigo-painted area, recalling the verses of Sango's panegyrics sung during public and private ceremonies:

> In a place that sprouts hair,
> And also encloses like a tiny farm hut,
> Fire . . . is there with my husband and lord [Sango].

> Níbi tó hun-run,
> Asìfamónra bíi ahéré,
> Iná . . . iná mbè lódò okòò mi.

The ritual ploys of the Oyo imperial palace are the most obvious precedent for the social organization of the modern Sango priesthood. The cognatic workings of priestly succession were institutionalized in the precolonial and early colonial patrilineage, but late-colonial judicial reforms rendered them anachronistic. Such sacred anachronism is, for the Sango priesthood, not a deficit but a source of symbolic power. It embraces the anachronistic quality of the royal village itself.

In the initiand's newly hairy head, Sango's fire is contained as if in a tiny farm hut, as if in the rural outpost of the Yoruba's historically urban civilization. In a parallel manner, the image recalls the possession priest's politico-religious functions in the relations between the imperial capital and its provinces. Often natives of the provinces, possession priests became the king's delegates through the investment of the imperial god in their heads. Thus:

$$
\begin{array}{rcl}
\text{god} & : & \text{initiand} \;\; :: \\
\text{fire} & : & \text{farm hut} \;\; :: \\
\text{light contents} & : & \text{dark vessel} \;\; :: \\
\text{city} & : & \text{farm settlement} \;\; :: \\
\text{capital} & : & \text{province} \;\; :: \\
\text{Nigerian state} & : & \text{royalist village}
\end{array}
$$

Both the priests and the audience of modern spirit possession may construe their marginality in the Nigerian state with reference to an empowering mythohistorical vision. Sango's heavenly and historical empire makes the priesthood an indispensable arbiter of fertility and, metaphorically, of social anatomy and political order.

Metaphors of Sex and Marriage. The terms "husband" and "wife," or "bride," appear to rival many of the metaphoric predications discussed hitherto. Indeed, they are plainly incompatible with the initiand's status as infant daughter and "blood" kin of the husband's house. Yet the initiation and the nomenclature of Sango-worship are suffused with images of both marriage and elaborations on its expected sexual component. During public presentations, the male or female initiand will wear women's earrings and clothes—not only a blouse (*buba*) and wrapskirt (*iro*) but a baby sling (*oja*), used by mothers to bind infants on the back [O] [Z] (figure 13). The *oja* sling suggests the nature of the productivity and power for which the initiand is being prepared—that is, more precisely, the nature of the divine subjectivity being created inside him, to which this productivity and power will be credited. Sango will "mount" the initiand bride, an act whose sexual implications are clear [E] [N] [W] [CC] [EE]. Not only do gods "mount" priests, but male animals "mount" females in the sex act.[16] Sango's fiery penetration of his political domain and of his priest's head invites automatic comparison to the penetration of another "place that sprouts hair"—the vulva. At times when possession is sought, the initiand is seated on a mortar (*odo*) [F] [V]. When spoken, its name can also mean "You fuck" (*o dó*). The visual/verbal pun affirms the brashness, sexuality, and force implicit in his relations to the world. His "brides" are also the objects of that force. The normal action of the pestle (*ọmọ odó*) suggests the phallic character of Sango's penetration of the "bride." Reinforcing the parallel, an apparent pun likens the action of the pestle to that of the god: just as the god "mounts" (*gùn*), the pestle "pounds" (*gún*); although the two Yoruba words differ tonally, they are identical phonetically.[17] According to this circuit of metaphors,

$$
\begin{array}{rcll}
\text{god} & : & \text{initiand} & :: \\
\text{husband} & : & \text{wife} & :: \\
\text{penetrator} & : & \text{penetrated} &
\end{array}
$$

In a sense, the initiand bride will outgrow the status of infant and daughter of the house before truly entering the priesthood. The radical transformation of the infantile initiand into a bride occurs expressly on the "seventh day." As on the night of a worldly bride's initial entry into her new husband's house, the initiand bride will have his feet washed by a "senior co-wife" (*iyale*) in the house of his divine "husband [and lord]" (*oko*) [AA].[18] Like a new bride, the priestly initiand will be exempt from labor for a time. For the initiand, that time is marked by the wearing of three necklaces (*kele*), which are identified with Sango's three mythical wives—Oya, Osun, and Oba [K].

Undoubtedly owing much to its past material enforcement and association with the sovereign, royal state, Sango-worship develops to an extreme the hierarchical quality of the husband-wife relationship in the patrilineal house. Sango's "bride" embodies the complex logic and techniques of Oyo imperial government, of which various forms of "literal" wives (*ayaba*) and wifelike personnel (*ayaba, ilari, elegun*) were the main functionaries, well into the 1960s. The "bride" illustrates the penetrating and fertilizing power of the god. Moreover, he displays the structure of human heredity, group membership, agency, and their capacity for redesign from without—particularly by those who can finance such redesign in the currency of today and, most important of all, the equity of yesterday.

The symbolism of sexual penetration and reproduction is—in rites of both worldly marriage and spirit possession—displaced upward to the head. The groom and his family pay "money for the *bride's head*" (*owó orí ìyàwó*) for title to her uterine production. Possession priests literally rotate bank notes around the bride's head and place them on the grave of the dead predecessor [B] (who possesses an ancestral claim on the initiand's bridewealth) and in front of the drums [DD] (which call the god to mount the bride's head).

The prominent display of bank notes in modern Sango initiations, themselves modeled visibly upon weddings, acquires special meaning in the light of the colonial monetization of bridewealth [B] [P] [Q] [DD]. Coins and paper money became a historically redolent sign of both women's social connectedness and their liberation from the patricentric compound, or "house" (*ile*). The bride's subjection to the god, as well as the bride's consequent prosperity and freedom from the affinal house, are configured conspicuously in monetary signs, helping us to understand why the bride's brocade blouse is covered with images of bank notes (figure 13; see also chapter 2).

Bank notes do not simply draw the ritual or worldly bride *away* from the patrilineage; they also draw him *into* the symbolically structured power of the Nigerian state. Whereas Belasco (1980) and others have underlined the power of money to leach cultural meaning from material exchange and liberate people from existing or "traditional" social relationships, it is equally evident that money can refinance, revivify, reorient, and compound existing sacred and social relationships (see, e.g., Berry 1985). First, the specific bank notes that appear on initiands are themselves icons of an independent Nigerian state that finances and defends the interests of Igboho's trade diaspora abroad and facilitates the repatriation of its itinerant citizens' earnings back to the village.

Second, the bank note represented in brocade depicts General Murtala Mohammed. From 1975 to 1976, he spent less than a year in office, but, under the usual (and often popular) claim of the Nigerian military to rescue the country from corruption, he purged thousands from the civil service without due process. He promised to make Nigeria upright and efficient. His assassination in a failed military coup has long been lamented in Nigeria. As a hero and as the savior that Nigeria lost prematurely, he appears not only on bank notes and cloth but trays, key chains, and glassware. His dictatorship in the service of justice recalls rural peasants' image of Sango, who strikes down thieves and liars with lightning force and restores the property of the deprived. Like Sango, he was a Muslim from the north.

Our final analysis reflects the priests' public "naming" of their product. All the richly biographical and political predications the initiand has undergone are distilled down to one term: he is a "bride" of the god. It is in this final "naming" that a second-order metaphor arises. On the eve of the initiation, a simple, first-order metaphor had identified the initiand. As a metaphorical bride of the first order, he was but an outsider and subordinate newcomer to the groom's house. Then a series of additional metaphoric predications were imposed alongside that first-order metaphor: captivity, infancy, "blood" kinship, corporal containment, economic peripherality, and imperial subjection. The common denominator among all these relationships is, at the end of the initiation, defined sartorially and verbally as brideliness. However, such a complex common denominator clearly differs from the initial, first-order referent of the term. As the lone verbal title and description of the initiand, "bride" not only represents the initiand's likeness to literal brides but becomes a second-order metaphor (see the accompanying chart). The person so named emblematizes a kind of social relationship and reciprocity that logically and materially encompasses but supersedes those enacted in worldly marriage, even though they bear the same name. Moreover, the initiand advertises this second-order brideliness as a paradigm and as a reified instrument of society's relationship to the god, by means of which supplicants who kneel to him can guarantee their own personal and collective health.

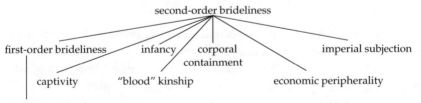

The second-order metaphor inscribed on the Sango priest qualifies him as a technician and an instrument in the cure of literal wives. At the same time, he evokes a model for the curative redesign of the literal wife's own *conduct and subjectivity*. Thus, the gendered contentions of the Sango cult double back on their literal sources.

The Internal Logic of Brideliness

Most ethnographic works on gender still fix their sights on the roles, qualities, and phenomena associated in any given culture with the biological categories "man" and "woman," as though our own binary biological categories were the natural starting point of other people's cultural elaborations. We would do well to recall Ortner and Whitehead's admonition that *both* sex and gender are symbolic constructs. To describe the gender concepts associated with each sex is not to reveal how local people interpret nature; it is to reveal how they relate one symbolic construct to another (Ortner and Whitehead 1981:1–2). Thus, to describe the male possession priest as a "man" dressing or braiding his hair "like a woman" is not erroneous. Indeed, it speaks an unmistakable empirical truth. However, it stops short of identifying local conceptual categories and the symbolic process by which this crossing "names" Sango's power into existence. Precisely what boundary does the Yoruba cross-dresser cross? Need we assume that it is the line between "man" and "woman," or any line most clearly described as "gender"? Might not the line itself shift at different stages of the ritual cycle and of the priestly biography?

There are fundamental differences between the following two metaphoric "sources":

> (1) man   :   woman
> (2) husband :   wife[19]

The first difference is that the second source is invoked far more often than the first in Yoruba ritual evocations of the sacred. The second difference rests on logic. Whereas the category "man" might logically imply the category "woman," one can imagine any particular woman and describe her without reference to any particular man, or even to men altogether. By contrast, one cannot imagine, logically or empirically, any "wife" without a "husband" or vice versa. Third, source 1 calls to mind *contrast*, whereas source 2 calls to mind *relationship*. In literal marriage, a husband and a wife constitute each other as such. This quality of relationship and mutual constitution is, I think, what makes the "husband"/"wife" pair such a central and generative metaphoric source in so many Yoruba ritual and mythic operations. "Rider"/ "horse" is an interstitial case. So is "mother"/"child." As in English, a young orphan is a "child" (*omo*) without any mother in the world, and a "mother" in Yoruba (*iya*) does not necessarily have children. For example, *Ìyá Alákàrà* (a female seller of bean fritters) could very well be childless. In short, not every child is constituted as such by a mother or every mother by a child. Nonetheless, goddesses are called *Iya*, or "Mother," with significant affective and logical implications. The distinctive feature of the title *Oko*, or "Husband," is that it can be used to address both gods and goddesses. It names a universal quality of the possessing *orisa*'s relations to human beings.

In this case, the rich scholarship distinguishing the social construct of "gender" from the biological construct of "sex" seems somewhat irrelevant. Westerners often justify particular actions or rationalize particular social arrangements by claiming that they are "natural," while they condemn other actions and arrangements as "unnatural." Talk of the "natural" is Americans' favorite "officializing" discourse (Bourdieu 1977). Hence, for Western feminists and other social critics, it has been important to demonstrate to the public that objectionable aspects of the status quo are not "natural," but rather are "constructed." Our officializing discourse, however, might do little to illuminate the dynamics of ideological hegemony and resistance in a West African society.

It is not particularly revealing to observe that the Yoruba recognize that the "man"/"woman" dichotomy is "constructed" and is therefore not made compulsory by a sense of its "naturalness." "Naturalness" is not, in Oyo-Yoruba society, the attribute that makes any given behavior compulsory or preferred for a normal person. Yoruba people are little given to justifying their social conduct on the grounds of its biological or natural foundations. Therefore, Western feminist critiques of biological determinism are ill suited to revealing the concealed axes of power in Oyo-Yoruba society. The persuasive force behind the "husband"/ "wife" metaphoric source is not that it "naturalizes" social hierarchies but that it socializes and civilizes nature in a paradigmatic way. It predicates cultural order upon natural disorder, a duty far more central to the Yoruba religious project than is, say, behaving "naturally." Nature, or that category of things sharing the qualities of the "bush" (igbó), is not for the Oyo Yoruba the paradigm of social order; it is the origin sof the inchoate forces (see Fernandez 1986) that must be contained, dressed up, and reconstituted in the Oyo-Yoruba politico-religious project. The sexually integrated nude bathing [L], the sexual joking at private cult parties, and the ribaldry at the beginning of public performances [M] [BB] are followed by a dressing-up that makes inchoate power socially usable. The containment, regulation, and social transformation of Sango's stormy, extrasocial force is predicated in the idiom of marriage. It is his wives who must contain and transform the wild.

Other Femininities

Amid its prescriptions of "brideliness" as the ultimate metonym of personal health and sociopolitical order, the initiation addresses another female relational posture: witchcraft (aje). The "witches" are fearsomely independent women empowered, like "brides," by their capacity to contain, but they use it mainly to *devour* others (see Matory 1986). According to some, they receive the offerings of food and money carried to the crossroads during the Sango initiation [J]. Their independence from the patricentric arrangements of empire and rural house calls to mind wealthy market women. Indeed, the witches hold their nocturnal meetings at the market, which in Yorubaland is a predominantly female space even during the day.

Like the king (oba), the Sango priesthood must respect and negotiate with the witches, for the witches are experts at creating chaos through killing and reproductive sabotage. Their power of containment is denominated in terms not of "brideliness" but of a nefarious "motherhood." The initiand himself is vulnerable to their power. To put it another way, they rival the order of power with which the initiand is being invested. Therefore, he makes a public show of driving them away on the "twelfth day" of the initiation, a ritual statement upon which the priesthood publicly bases its claim to authority and efficacy. Yet the "motherly" authority of the witches is not as easily superseded as is that of the iyale (female ritual attendant) on the "seventh day" [AA] [DD]. The priesthood's nonpublic offerings to Esu and the "witches" underline a major threat to the priests' public efforts at control and healing. Only when paid or fed does Esu allow clear communication between gods and people. His connection with the witches suggests a further form of social linkage as an objective of these offerings. The market and the crossroads are the paradigmatic sites of anonymous and ill-defined interaction *among people*. The repast at the crossroads appears to bridge the radical social disjunctures and failures of patri-centric and kin-based authority of which witchcraft is still richly emblematic in capitalist Nigeria.

Although many of those disjunctures are market-inspired, the mar-ket has also provided indispensable resources toward the realization of sacred linkages. Therefore, the witches turn out to be not so much the priesthood's enemies as its alter egos in the pursuit and management of market-borne riches. Some say it is the witches who receive the offer-ings at the crossroads; others say it is Esu. Thus a pact is made with the lord of communication, enabling the priests and their god, this world (*aye*) and the other (*orun*), to commune. He too is said to preside over the crossroads, and some call him the very "father of witchcraft (*aje*)" (Abraham 1962:167). He and the witches also share the marketplace, of which some say that Esu is the lord. Oyo royal officials used to propiti-ate his effigy in the marketplace, that he might not provoke disorder there (Morton-Williams 1964a:258–59). He also presides over the cowry-shell oracle that enables Sango and Yemoja priests to divine the will of the gods. Likewise, he receives a piece of every divinatory bitter kola, kola nut, and yam. The reader will recall that cowry shells are lit-erally called "pieces of money" (*owó ẹyọ*), which Esu himself is said to have brought to the Yoruba (Belasco 1980:122). The money of the mar-ket potentiates both disorder and order. However, as the foremost instruments of divination in the possession cults, cowry shells recom-mend communication as a form of commerce, and money as the very essence of communication.

The initiand's sartorial brideliness emblemizes a complex social and sacred relationship that imitates, distills, and supersedes a series of its worldly metaphoric "sources," investing their compound power metonymically in the initiand's head. Brideliness graphically encom-passes and resocializes, or remythologizes, the transformative potential of money. We have seen so far that paper money and its representa-tions signal the nature of the new priest's participation in a sacred, royal lineage and its hierarchy. As we shall see, the difference between cowries and the specie of the Nigerian state also indexes a major transition within the hierarchy of initiated priests. Sartorial images of paper money not only index low rank in the priesthood but emblemize the antistructure in which priests will participate fully during the nonceremonial season—Nigerian market exchange. Yet, like the bush itself, the market fuels the ritual pursuit of desirable ends. The bank notes that Sango's blessings enable them to earn in the market transform women in particular from the nonsubjects (or antisubjects) of patrilineal reproduction into the subjects of ownership and active motherhood.

The bank note is already an abstraction of labor-power, of which its representation on cloth is even more abstract. Invisibly contained within this representation is a further abstraction—the ultimate subject of exchange. That subject may look like Murtala, whose reduced and stereotyped face appears at the center of the bank note. Only through his wifely vessel do we darkly spy Sango. The possessed priest is the hub of much the same circulation of spirits and communal resources that kings represent. Unpossessed, he is blessed with the mastery of market circulation. Not only does his dress entitle him to others' surplus cash and to a temporary exemption from labor, but as long as he serves Sango he is marked out as a professional manager of others' social production and reproduction, a trader of futures in "blood" and money. As the healing powers of the initiate come to fruition through the years, the sartorial tokens of that commerce will illustrate a further order of condensation, abstraction, and empowerment, which we will examine in the next section.

Other Transvestisms

The initiation is really the first in a series of personal and social transformations registered in priestly dress and grooming. Not one but three styles of cross-dressing therefore outline the stages of the "made" god's manifestation: the attire of the "bride," of the unpossessed senior "mount," and of the possessed senior "mount." Simultaneously visible in the priesthood's public presentations, they illustrate the character of Sango's relation to the "present" world and the arrangement of priestly hierarchy. The dress of the ranking possession priest, that is, of the male *elegun*, defines the ultimate nature of Sango's healing power in the world and participates in a newly mixed metaphor that sets second-order brideliness alongside horsemanship, the relation between divinized ancestors and their descendants, and the relation between ancient and modern commerce.

We have seen that, in the worldly house, recently married wives are the foremost referents of the title and description "bride" (*iyawo*). Unlike the comparable English term, it may remain in use for years after the wedding, especially by a woman's male reproductive partner and by affines much older than she. Once the bride bears a child, she will receive a fitting teknonym. As she gains a professional competency, she will be called "Mother of [that profession]." For the same reason, senior *orisa* priests may be called *Bàbá Oníṣàngó* ("Father-Owner of Sango") or *Ìyá Oníṣàngó* ("Mother-Owner of Sango").

The analogy of kin status titles to priestly titles lapses in the middle. There are no counterparts in the priesthood to teknonyms related to childbearing. The dominant metonym of priestly accomplishment comes from a different semantic domain, created through a new synthesis of signs, which "hides" the extant qualities of second-order brideliness while "highlighting" new qualities and a new order of relationship between god and priest, priest and supplicant (Lakoff and Johnson 1980). We might denominate this newly mixed metaphor "mountedness," from one point of view, or, more generally, "mounting."

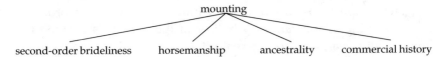

The initiand wears wrap skirt (*iro*), blouse (*buba*), and baby sling (*oja*) throughout the month of the initiation, whether possessed or conscious. Older possession priests and priestesses are called not "brides" but "mounts" (*elegun*) and "horses" (*esin*) of the god, recalling the equestrian means by which Oyo, in the eighteenth century, became the largest royal empire in Yoruba history. The verb for possession (*gùn*— "to mount") may refer to horseback riding, as well. Thus:

$$\begin{array}{ccc} \text{god} & : & \text{initiated priest} \quad :: \\ \text{rider} & : & \text{horse} \end{array}$$

Postinitiatory changes of title, clothing, and coiffure specify not only changing "highlights" in the invocation of the relationship between god and priest but a wholly new constituent of the mixed metaphor. Some years after initiation, priests begin to don not only a different and especially historically redolent title, but a different form of money, and the god comes to speak through them in archaic Oyo language.

Moreover, from the time of initiation until the priest renounces his sacred "head load" upon retirement or death, his hair must never be cut. Possession priests are the only Oyo-Yoruba men I know who braid their hair, often modeling it on an archaic bridal coiffure (àgògo; see Abraham 1962:30; Thompson 1969:166–67). Sometimes they follow more recent fashions, creating elaborate coiffures by winding black thread around carefully parted bunches of hair. Male *elegun* are also among the very few Yoruba men who wear earrings or adorn their hair with trinkets, such as safety pins. Since at least the 1950s, the weaving of narrow-loom cloth, or strip weaving, has been a female profession in Igboho and neighboring towns. The only man who remains engaged in strip weaving is, almost predictably, a Sango priest. In few other respects is the daily postinitiatory dress or conduct of male priests feminine or bridelike. They regularly have multiple wives and children, and no one even seems to wonder if they engage in sex with other men.

Yet during festival seasons, the signs of their femininity multiply in selective ways. They tend to wear antimony eyeliner (tìróò) and dye their palms and soles with henna (làálì), which no other men do, as far as I know. Spirit possession alone requires a change from ordinary men's clothing. If the gendered indices of the "bride" 's clothing are immediately clear, those of the senior "mount" require a more careful reading. Once manifest in the priest, the god is taken indoors to be dressed in a cowry-studded shirt and wàbì—appliquéd panels that resemble the full-body outfits of fine ancestral masquerades, or Egúngún. Just as the god manifests himself contained in the body of his possession priest, so the ancestral spirit manifests itself inside such *wabi* cloth outfits, its own physical form invisible through the cloth. Sango not only partakes of the ancestral nature of *Egungun* masquerades, but, as we have seen, his cult projects the model of "mounting" upon the structure of agency in Yoruba masking, which was also integrated into the Oyo imperialist order (Johnson 1921, 29–30). Surrounded by old money and clothed in ancestral cloth, the perfect priestly sign of Sango's imperial power culminates on the *elegun*'s head. Unlike that of the initiand bride, the senior priest's gendered cross-dressing is concentrated above all on his head, through hairstyles, earrings, and eyeliner. This cephalic transvestite is the ultimate proof of the reification, extraction, appropriation, and condensation of wifely fertility. Thus:

$$
\begin{array}{rcl}
\text{god} & : & \text{initiated priest ::} \\
\text{ancestral spirit} & : & \text{cloth mask} \\
& \text{and} & \\
\text{initiated priest} & : & \text{initiand ::} \\
\text{head} & : & \text{lower body ::} \\
\text{old money} & : & \text{new money}
\end{array}
$$

The Economics of Sacred Power

I would like to consider the further hypothesis that the density, frequency, and contemporaneity of *material investments* in a given form of social relationship profoundly affect its gravity as a metaphoric source. Suggested and affirmed graphically in this modern Yoruba case, the hypothesis invites critical testing in other contexts as well. Money is both economically and iconographically central in the initiation and ritual dress of Sango possession priests. Postcolonial naira have succeeded colonial pounds sterling and precolonial cowries as the currency of literal bridewealth and commercial exchange. Priestly marriage to the god, the feeding of the god, and the festival cycle in which the god is made real and effective for the public all depend on the availability and affordability of numerous animals, most of which must be bought at market. The new *iyawo*, possessed or conscious, wears industrially manufactured brocade emblazoned with images of new Nigerian money. On the other hand, the senior "mounts" (*elegun*) of the gods dance in cowry-studded blouses. The prominence of cowry shells suggests that money has long been an important attribute of Sango's earthly manifestation. Shells have acquired distinctive value, however, now that they are out of circulation. Perhaps *because* they are out of circulation they have become something like an essence of money, a metacurrency in the same sense that the "blood" produced through sacrifice is metablood.[20] They are the "money of the gods" (*owó òrìṣà*), as a Sango priest in Kétu put it in 1988—the apotheosis of money.

At the heart of Sango ritual is a consciously economic understanding of the sign and its social efficacy. Indeed, Yoruba ideally mark *every* rite of passage and important social accomplishment—births, funerals, weddings, the completion of a house, and so on—with "the spending of money" (*ináwó*), the defining feature of hospitality. It takes money and labor to settle the meaning of the polysemic sign, to define the inchoate identity of the subject, and to compel the human conduct so prescribed. It must be remembered that literal marriage in Igboho also costs a lot of money, in bridewealth, gifts, and entertainment. What it produces in the absence of monetary exchange—the bastard (*ọmọ àlè*)—is forever incomplete in his or her social being. Moreover, the production of animal blood, the other major signifier in the priestly marriage, is a capital-intensive commercial project, just as its transformation into "blood"— the reified form of kinship and vitality—is a labor-intensive project.

"Blood" and money are not simply illusory representations of human productive activity, in the sense that Marx described as "fetishization." They do not naturalize the social sources of inequality. Indeed, as we have seen, much in Oyo-Yoruba discourse credits human beings explicitly with the "making" of gods. Rather, as human-manufactured signs of relationship, "blood" and money create productive order out of socially unproductive relationships. They integrate under a single author contrary norms of hierarchy and responsibility, which otherwise would, and do, divide the village-centered community. Those newly integrated norms include seniority, sex, *relational* gender, heredity, wealth-in-people, and cash wealth.

In the Age of Abiola, money is the paradigmatic capital in metaphor creation. It is presently the most "generalized medium of symbolic communication" (Munn 1973) and almost a sine qua non of effective "naming" strategies. With the assent of the most diverse set of actors and believers, it can be used with compelling force in the creation of wealth-in-people and the restoration of social and personal health (*àláfíà*), not to mention the acquisition of horses and guns, wives and taxis. "Blood" has a long history of *generalization* in Yoruba religion, medicine, kinship and politics. Yet no matter how *generalized* either becomes, the performative meanings of both blood and money remain bound to their histories and to the social institutions that guarantee their value as metaphors. The Oyo-Yoruba economy has a rich and specific cultural history.

Sango initiations carefully display a principle of restricted access and use, a hierarchization of collective subjectivity. The senior male possession priests monopolize the labor of blood sacrifice. Moreover, during public ceremonies, they alone circulate bank notes over the head of the possessed initiand and deposit them in front of the drummers, who are also uniformly male. No one would explain the practice, aside from saying òrìṣà ni—"it is [because of] the orisa." It seems that senior male possession priests hereby interpose themselves, as seconds of the divine groom, into the marriage between god and initiand, by pantomiming the payment of this "money for the bride's head" (owó orí ìyàwó).

The postinitiatory status terminology enables this interposition: the possession priests of sufficient seniority to circulate money around the initiand's head are themselves no longer classified as "brides." They are "mounts" and "horses," highlighting the equestrian dimension of the "mounting" metaphor. In tandem, their difference from the "bride" is given precedence over their subordination to the god. Yet, just as the money of the state symbolizes the senior male priests' role as husbands to the new bride, the "money of the gods" festooning the senior priests' clothes and their archaic bridal hairstyles represent them as the most perfect order of the god's wives.

Re-dressing "Gender"

Cross-dressing in the Sango cult differs from a range of cross-dressing phenomena seen elsewhere. It is not a carnivalesque mockery of women. Nor does it appear to be a ritual inversion intent on manifesting the power of disorder. Nor does it seem to be an antitype or transgression of proper manhood and womanhood that ultimately affirms "normal" gender categories. Nor does it appear to undermine gendered power inequalities (by contrast, see esp. Whitehead 1981; Drewal 1992). If the present case bears a general warning, it is that "gender," as we see it, emerges from a historical and social process rather than from the necessity of "male"/"female" difference as such. Much of the gender-studies literature on transvestism is intent on the detection or deconstruction of "gender categories" construed as the proper behaviors of "men" and "women." To paraphrase Garber (1992), that literature often looks *through* rather than at the transvestite. Even those who study transvestism as the transcendence of categories must be alert to the possibility that biological sex and the gender categories "man" and "woman" are not what is being transcended through acts of transvestism. Yet I remain convinced that the *relational* gender categories "husband" and "wife" illuminate the forms of crossing ritually and sartorially engineered by the Sango priesthood.

I do not conclude along with Garber that the transvestite necessarily motivates social change by undermining all categories, nor with Drewal that he illustrates the freedom of the Yoruba to ignore gender stereotypes. Sango initiations and possession rites are not acts of "self-fashioning" (Greenblatt 1980) but of collective healing and reproduction, processes no more essentially progressive or conservative than any act justified by "tradition" (in this case, *àṣà* and *nñkan bàbá wa*). As Natalie Davis (1978) has shown, transvestism can even structure cultural logics and occasions of rebellion while *affirming* existing gender stereotypes.

These ritual operations do not guarantee social change insofar as they cross relational gender lines but insofar as their predications about social health and personal integrity are better financed than rival predications. The transvestism of Sango priests does materially build up the authorizing and healing power of second-order brideliness and "mounting" in the cult's sphere of influence, while revising rather than undermining local women's enactment of literal wifeliness. Women who submit to healing by the Sango priesthood also finance the ritual and logical connection between their own successful wifeliness and the captivity, the riddenness, the hollowness, the penetrability, and, in a word, the mountedness of the self of Oyo-Yoruba subordinates generally. At the same time, the afflicted supplicant finances the link between husbandliness and divinity. Male and female priests and supplicants, as well as their families, invest their limited money and resources in the efficacy of "mounting," but in capitalist Nigeria the Sango cult competes against spheres of social action where paper money itself is the *central* trope of relationship. Moreover, the possession religions' growing nemesis—reformist Islam—is well equipped to finance a vision of authority that excludes both women and transvestite priests as a matter of principle (see also Peacock 1978).

Conclusion

The Sango initiation highlights a series of social relationships, extracts from each a material essence, and lays them one by one upon the body of the initiand. The public representation of the priest, the manifest god, and their efficacy take form through the mixing of metaphors. Yet the process of initiation and priestly maturation illustrates the orderly layering and "feedback" by means of which new powers and relationships are created. Metaphoric "targets" transform their "sources" into second-order metaphors, which synthesize the qualities of Oyo-Yoruba marriage, "blood" kinship, commercial exchange, horsemanship, bodily existence, sexual intercourse, containment, clothedness, consciousness, political delegation, and the striking of lightning. Like single metaphors, mixed metaphors generate "novel semantic categories" through "the interplay between discordant meanings" (Pesman 1991: 237; Basso 1976:111, 116–17). Indeed, they may create or reproduce novel forms of social relationship as well, which do not then necessarily invent new names for themselves.

Therefore, we cannot assume a priori that we know which categorical boundaries the cross-dresser is crossing. Even in cases when the stated motive of cross-dressing is the concealment of the dresser's biological sex, there is no simple sense in which a man's donning women's clothes and hairstyle makes him culturally convincing as a woman. He has not crossed the line between "man" and "woman." Nor is he "representing," "acting like," or "dressing as" a woman, except, I might imagine, in the context of some particular forms or readings of the theater. Rather, the *conjunction* of particular classes of male body with particular classes of female dress and hairstyle, where they are classified as female, is itself a sign that demands reading. For example, in the West we allow ourselves to distinguish between sartorial "transvestites," on the one hand, and hormonally, surgically, and sartorially prepared "transsexuals," on the other. I suppose "she-males" fall somewhere in between. In no simple sense is any of the three a "woman," since the *irony* of their having *changed* or of having *deceived* some otherwise intelligent social interlocutors remains key to their social role, their classification by others, and their personal identity. The semantic category the male cross-dresser has entered is conditioned from the start by irony, an irony that becomes *part of the sartorial sign itself.*

All the cases that we call "transvestism" embody such irony, but not every cultural system of transvestism defines the categorical boundaries thus crossed in the same way. In some such systems, the transvestite's occupation, role during intercourse, or state of consciousness may be defining indices of the categories between which s/he switches. The Oyo-Yoruba Sango initiation provides an extraordinarily rich hermeneutic for a local reading of transvestism, as well as its ritual and, in Latin-influenced languages, its etymological cognate—the trance. I would argue that the transvestite male Sango priest has crossed the line not between "man" and "woman" but between consanguinity and "mounting" as the primary structure of his social self. He also advertises and affirms the premise of the Oyo royalist order: that the person, like the god and society itself, exists in the quality of nesting *relationships* between "mounter" and "mounted," and that every being involves a conjunction—though not a mixture—of the two. Ritual enactments of mounting even feed back and highlight those dimensions of Oyo-Yoruba kinship ideology most consonant with spirit possession and the alienation of personal will—that is, the notion of the physical head's occupation by the ancestral or heavenly "inner head." The lapse of mounting relationships, and especially of the state-sponsored ones, is associated with personal barrenness, social decay, and politico-religious disorder. Persons long invested in the Oyo royalist order will not find this association or the forms of mounting intended to cure it ironic, but their poetic and mythological claims to power exploit the knowledge that their contemporaries of other religious and political convictions do. Not only do they turn others' shock and fear into their own power, but they define a seductive order of resistance to the power of the metropolitan state.

I do not imagine that such involved readings are possible in cases where cross-dressing is a form of personal rebellion or carnivalesque mockery or, as in the case of the Native American "berdache," the evidence has already been crushed under the weight of a Western category-mistake (Ryle 1949; see Whitehead 1981). This story of the ritual making of a transvestite differs from the many autobiographical narrations available in the West, in that Oyo-Yoruba transvestism is not a marginal phenomenon. It is a central one, once codified and disseminated by an imperial state and now answering to the deepest aspirations of hundreds of thousands of Nigerians, Béninois, and, as we shall see, Brazilians. Hence, the warning it bears is more difficult for students of collective social action to overlook.

Instructed by the semiotics of dress itself, we must assume that not all crossings dressed up in "gender" are essentially about men and women. Indeed, the overwhelming authority of men in a cult that valorizes "brideliness" in its priests seems to lie in the fact that transvestites are the most permanent emblems of the god's own dressing across boundaries—in the bodies of human beings.

Chapter 7

Conclusion: Dialogue, Debate, and the *Chose du Texte*

The politico-religious order of Oyo North is under debate, and debate is the very structure of that order. It is a debate over the proper historical model for contemporary society and the proper relations of production and reproduction. The possession religions have developed amid the transformative antagonism of various nonpossession religions. I follow Henry Louis Gates, Jr. (1988), in positing that traditions of creative expression, and therefore the object of the foregoing description, are constituted less by consensus than by fields of intertextual contradiction, which Gates calls "signifyin'." The "texts" I am discussing are configurations of ritual and narrative tropes that generate advantage by differentially highlighting, hiding, and mixing the sources of their meaning. In every local context, the interlocutors command different means of enforcing such configurations, the outcome of which affects the balance of power in daily life.

I have been concerned specifically with tropes of gender in the historically changing production of Oyo-Yoruba political order and personal action. A hegemonic project in the Age of Sango, spirit possession and its gender-bending axioms anchor an important set of moral communities within a bourgeois-dominated nation-state. The social-status transformations of wives define, in the kingdoms and the possession religions, the structures of both male and female agency. Hence, these religions allow some women highly public and influential roles in negotiating the sociopolitical order of the village.

We are not led obligatorily from here to the conclusion that the possession religions are a feminist discourse. Indeed, their symbolism is structured by the assumption of husbandly dominance. Moreover, male Sango-worshipers draw strength from the male absolutism and

216

sexual literalism of Islam and missionary Christianity. However, *orisa* ritual metaphors authorize some women to lead not only as mothers but as husbands and the agents of ranking husbandly authorities, thereby often reversing metropolitan sexual hierarchies.

Although kings and chiefs are husbands and fathers writ large to their subjects, they are as wives and children to the *orisa*. Their heads are subject to takeover by gods through the proxy of the priestesses. A priestess places upon the new Oyo king's head his first ritually charged crown, which contains powers beyond his control and supervision. Chanting priestesses announce their metaphorical "braiding" of the Onigboho chief's head, and they intone a threat to have Yemoja completely take over his head if he fails to cooperate. To priestesses who initiate a male into the Sango priesthood, the latter is still a "wife." Whether through metaphors of shaving or braiding, painting or *osu* application, mothers and female husbands use their *hands* to exercise divine will over the *heads* of biologically male and female subordinates.

The urban vocabulary of "mounting" at once embraces and signifies on these rural symbolic endeavors. Whereas "mounting" defines productive networks of authority in the rural outposts of Sango's spiritual empire, it is reclassified as a mechanism of derangement in the individualist language of Ogun's urban regime. A variety of contemporary bourgeois expressions suggest the arbitrariness of royal authority and the emergence of homologous new forces and means of self-aggrandizement:

Ṣó tún gùn ẹ́?—"Have you gone crazy again?" (literally, "Is it mounting you again?")

Kí ló ń gùn ẹ́?—"What's gotten into you?" or "What has made you angry?" (literally, "What is mounting you?")

Ṣé owó ń gùn ẹ́?—"Does your money make you feel that you can behave in this inappropriate way?" (literally, "Is money mounting you?")

Ṣé ẹwà ń gùn ẹ́?—"Do you think just because you are pretty you can act that way?" (literally, "Is beauty mounting you?")

The detachment of "mounting" from the order of royal and lineal social ties seems implicit in recent commentary detaching the metaphysical "head" from any implication of familial inheritance. Whereas some tales report that heads are inherited from one's dead forebears, others discard the idiom of inheritance and suppose that individuals simply *choose* their heads in heaven (*orun*). In the latter tales, one's success or failure in life is no longer bound to the network of support, responsibility, and rights of which lineal ancestry is a metonym. Some tales even specify the need to bribe Ajala, the heavenly maker of heads, to get a good one (Eades 1980:121; see also Abimbola 1976:118). One suspects the recent origin or elaboration of tales that ignore inheritance and acknowledge graft, which is the definitive means of access to today's most powerful institutions—the federal and state governments.

What English-speaking Nigerians call "corruption" acts toward collective institutions as if they are arenas for zero-sum competition among individuals—whether these be individual persons or individual towns, which benefit from having sons or daughters well placed in the government. *Lukudi* and *eda* moneymaking magic are the ultimate development of selfish acquisition. The heroes of the Age of Abiola attracted almost celebratory headlines in the 1980s concerning their theft of ever-larger sums of money from government coffers. In Oyo North, these "*Alhajis, Alhajiyas,* and ministers" are mythologized as mass murderers. The rich perpetrators of such larger-than-life crimes might have seemed exceptional had the narrator of the tale recorded in chapter 3 not prefaced his remarks with the claim that "almost everyone uses rituals to get money. It usually involves killing a small child." Hyperbole reflects the speaker's impression of the homogeneously cannibalistic character of modern wealth. I have argued that religious cycles, biographical cycles, mythic processes, historical cycles, and residential cycles regularly parallel each other and draw on each other's symbolic terms. In Yoruba history, hunters and wanderers become sedentary chiefs and kings. In contemporary royal and chiefly biographies, hunters and itinerant businessmen—some of Ogun's worldly personae—return home to assume the throne. The kingship remains, though tattered, a central and redolent piece amid the various cultural and historical crosscurrents making up modern Nigeria. If any site in Yorubaland is credited with moral and social orderliness, the kingship is understood to be its hub. The king personifies the "unity" of the people, the denial of moral and sociopolitical chaos. Therefore, by the end of their bodily lives, even the most corrupt urban businessmen seek the legitimizing imprimatur of hereditary office.

Like urban businessmen, the *orisa* too are often credited with audacious and destructive behavior. However, the worshipers of any given god simply endeavor to socialize that behavior for their benefit, to insure that it will be directed against the outward and in the defense of the cult. Worshiping an *orisa* restores her or him to a sedentary place— reversing her or his mythic flight into the nonsocial and immoral wilderness. Inviting the return and regulating the power of a further ambiguous and itinerant character—the emigrant businessman—has meant just as much to the creation and enforcement of political order in modern Oyo-Yoruba society. In the Oyo Renaissance, the British be- came the apical source of royal power. Kings had to manage that power ritually in order to make it efficacious in governing the peasantry and subordinate chieftaincies. These powers are part of a precedented func- tional category in Yoruba ritual discourse, whose membership derives less from any conception of European *racial* superiority than from Yoruba perceptions of foreigners' role in the transport of resources into local hierarchical systems. From a modern perspective, *oyinbo* (whites, Europeans, Westerners) are salient in their unsocialized quality—man- ifest in the violence and disorder that bourgeois Nigerians detect in their image of North American society, now the prevailing exemplar of the West. The very word *oyinbo* means to some Yoruba etymologists "peeled people," that is, people without integument, lacking the con- tainers that transform gods from wild forces into socially useful pow- ers. It is the function of Yoruba royals and entrepreneurs to introduce these powers and the goods associated with them into social usage, to tame them for local benefit. Only insofar as these Yoruba actors can perform or mobilize the symbolic functions of wives—productive con- tainers and transformers of the wild—are these actors successful in the modern royalist sphere.

A New Politics of Ethnography

The context of this investigation is the religious history of the Oyo Yoruba. What distinguishes it from a more conventional history *of* reli- gion is that it posits the worth of Yoruba verbal and ritual tropes as organizing features of the historical narrative itself, for local concep- tions of action, responsibility, and personhood regularly differ from those that organize indigenously Western constructions of global politics and change, such as "class," "women," "patriarchy," "homosexual-ity," "dependency," and "oppression." This effort follows the lead of Sahlins (1985:53) in specifying local "historicities" and of the Comaroffs in locating the terms of local historical consciousness "not in explicit statements . . . on the part of a social group, but in the implicit language of symbolic activity" (Comaroff and Comaroff 1987:192–93). What Sahlins has described in terms of myth and called "mytho-praxis" I have sought to describe in terms of rituals and icons, in what one might denominate "*icono*-praxis." It is not, however, the scarcity of explicit historical narratives in Yorubaland that motivates this approach. Rather, what motivates it is the superabundance and controversy-rid-den diversity of Yoruba historical discourse.

Like the longtime rival factions in the struggle for sovereignty among the Oyo Yoruba, I have structured my argument loosely around the mythic tension between the *orisa* Sango and Ogun. They differ with respect to their sacred emblems, their behavior in relation to mythic women, and the roles women play in their priesthoods, as well as the geopolitical regions and historical periods in which they have reigned. I have argued that Sango and Ogun personify developments in the changing creation and management of power among the Oyo Yoruba. In their contrast, they illuminate the historical role of spirit possession in the imperial Age of Sango and the political conditions of its develop-ment; the unmarking of gender differentiation and complementarity in the politics of the nineteenth-century Age of Ogun; the use of transves-tite political agents and the ambiguous consequences of codifying indi-vidual women's rights during the colonial Oyo Renaissance; and the murderous and misogynistic acts of ritual entrepreneurs and the gen-dered foci of royalist communities in the contemporary Age of Abiola. In writing an *icono-practical* description of religion and politics in Oyo North, I implicitly propose a new politics of ethnography, which is ulti-mately transatlantic in scope.

Two of the best recent ethnographies on Yoruba religion raise a question of conscience that weighs heavily on the anthropological en-terprise, and they flag it with their common citation of V. Y. Mudimbe's widely praised *Invention of Africa* (1988). M. T. Drewal's *Yoruba Ritual* (1992) begins with an epigraph:

Until now, Western interpreters as well as African analysts have been using categories and conceptual systems which depend on a Western epistemological order. [. . .] Does this mean that African *Weltanschauungen* and African traditional systems of thought are unthinkable and cannot be made explicit within the framework of their own rationality?

V. Y. Mudimbe (1988:x)

Drewal (1992:xiv) defines "the central problem of ethnography" as "translation"—a problem she treats with great sensitivity. Should we translate Yoruba terms dense with local implications into English terms with another set of implications? Drewal says she does so on the grounds of "readability" and, more importantly, because English-speaking Yoruba themselves translate into English terms laden with Christian and European connotations. It is difficult to tell whether Drewal thinks that fact misleads the scholarly translator or, indeed, reflects the historically changing realities of what we call "Yoruba religion."

There is considerable evidence for the latter posture, which undermines the study of "Yoruba religion" in isolation from wider ideological currents in Nigeria's cosmopolitan society. Its implications deserve further attention. English is a local language among Nigerian Yoruba, and local "translations" have not only acquired meaning from but have *transformed the meaning* of Yoruba terms. For example, bilinguals translated the Bible into Yoruba, hammering, as best they could, the meanings derived from their British educations into preexisting Yoruba religious and proverbial language (see Ajayi 1965:128). The Yoruba Bible is one of the oldest and certainly the most pervasively influential written text in the language. Moreover, its having been written essentially in Oyo dialect has added new contrast values to religious and nonreligious verbal communication throughout Yorubaland.

"Translations" and glosses are faits accomplis in Yoruba religion and its "dialogic" realization (Bakhtin 1981) in contemporary Nigeria. Therefore, the terms we use to draw other contemporary Westerners into this dialogue bridge a *cline* rather than a *chasm*. But certain techniques of writing ethnography create the impression of a chasm and verticalize it, not after the manner of missionaries preaching to "pagans" but worse, like conquistadores hoisting the flag over a "New Spain," wholly renaming the realities of a local dialogue. This time the flag usually says "Marx," "Weber," or "Durkheim," but there are other Western standards of salience as well, such as "art," "theater," "under-development," and "women's position." Such rubrics often have great utility for laudable didactic and political projects. Yet unless we are conscious of the awesome power of such "naming," we drown out the local dialogue, and the priorities that emerge from it, instead of involving our readership in the dialogue.

Apter (1992) also introduces his concern in this regard by quoting Mudimbe:

> Is not this reality distorted in the expression of African modalities in non-African languages? Is it not inverted, modified by anthropological and philosophical categories used by specialists in dominant discourses? (Mudimbe 1988:186)

Yes, answers Apter, but, given the political benefits of communication between Africa and the West, the scholar must not give up. She or he must instead strive for "more culturally accurate, less ideologically loaded" translations (Apter 1992:226).

There remains the more minute question of how to represent the constituent voices in this dialogue, especially when such voices appear to speak through allegory, metaphor, self-contradiction, or irony. Suppose such "voices" are silent and gestural rather than verbal? And what about the silent premises taken for granted in local verbal discourse? Drewal simply observes that to represent local voices in writing is an awesome act of authority, which, Apter would agree in principle, must be scrutinized continuously to ensure against the dictatorship of our own Western conceptual priorities. In order to do so, I would add, we must carefully consider not only our means of checking such dictatorship but the institutional incentives not to do so at all.

Mudimbe's sense of anthropology's interpretive failings is premised on a radical division between literate analysts and their texts, on the one hand, and, on the other, the *chose du texte*—that is, the "primordial African discourse" and "African indigenous systems of thought" (see Mudimbe 1988:186, 200). Indeed, the politics of publication and tenure require ethnographic arguments to subsume African ritual, political, and cognitive projects under models familiar and fashionable in the academy. However, the best of anthropology practices the reverse order of integration as well, allowing *emic* constructs to overdetermine the choice and ultimate form of analytic models. To do so is both a virtue and a necessity, for to my mind "the primordial African discourse" is both illegitimate and impossible as the object of ethnography. Moreover, to reconstruct some pre-"translated" contemporary Yoruba episteme (which it is then our lonely task to translate) is an exercise in imagination, which seems to invite our own idealist projections about an Africa that is not and, most likely, never was.

No dialogue simply reveals the predialogic understandings of its interlocutors—whether we are considering Africa and the West or the anthropologist and her informants as the interlocutors. The ethnographic record can reveal only transformed and postdialogic understandings (or simply "dialogic" ones, in Bakhtin's sense). I wish to call attention to the peculiarly macroscopic character of the dialogue on Yoruba religion, which has been particularly productive of mutual understandings and is unanticipated in Mudimbe's chasmic and vertical dichotomy. In both Drewal's and Apter's introductions, it is treated as background, when in fact it deserves recognition as a central empirical dimension of the very phenomenon we document.

The worship of the *orisa* is now a world religion, with tens of millions of practitioners on three continents who recognize their kinship to one another. Since 1981, it has been the focus of at least four world conferences of worshipers and scholars in dialogue.[1] Some of the most influential scholarship on any one of these continental traditions has been informed by field research on two or three of thóse continents. Consider the work of Herskovits, Bascom, Verger, Abimbola, Thompson, Drewal, Juana and Deoscóredes dos Santos, Omari, Barber, and myself, not to mention Gates. For example, Robert Farris Thompson's analytic concepts of "hot" and "cool," which have now become shibboleths in studies of the West African Yoruba, are clearly and profitably inspired by a mid-twentieth-century Afro-North American aesthetic idiom (see Thompson 1973).

My own recognition of the significance of pot and calabash symbolism in Nigerian *orisa* religion came not directly from my first Nigerian field research in 1982–83 but from an encounter in Lawrence, Massachusetts, in 1984. There, Puerto Rican, Cuban, Lebanese, Italian, and African-American *santeros* led me to bow down before *orichas* in porcelain *soup tureens!*—the likes of which any prolonged visit to the Candomblé will also reveal. Pots and calabashes visually melt into the background of most Nigerian rites and shrines—only one of the many differences among these divergent continental traditions. It was the shock of this *intermediate difference*—between pots and calabashes on the one hand, and soup tureens on the other—that led me to what these traditions had in common, and therefore to a hypothesis about what really mattered in the symbolic expressions of Nigerian *orisa* religion. In the china cabinets of North American *santeros*, the familiar glimmer of porcelain illuminated an unfamiliar metaphoric iconography of selfhood. The most widely cited among previous studies on the *orisa* (e.g., Ellis 1964 [1894]; Morton-Williams 1964a; Idowu 1963) have diagrammed not shared iconographies but hierarchical "pantheons" and chains of being, consciously highlighting the likeness of Yoruba theology to Christian and Greco-Roman formulations. In an earlier work, I proposed that models systematized in this way represent not what is universal in Yoruba religion but the particular syntheses of Yoruba Christian apologists and interested assertions of the sort that particular kings and priesthoods make in order to enhance their own esteem in a competitive local context (Matory 1986:18–21; see also Apter 1992:237).[2] Although Apter, Drewal, and I have found the iconographic hypothesis useful (see Matory 1986; Apter 1992:98–114; Drewal 1992:73–75, 180–86), my intention here is not to insist upon its correctness or constant heuristic relevance. I simply wish to point out the complex and intermediate epistemological quality of this and other interpretive models of Yoruba religion.

Despite anthropological claims of documenting the voice of the Other, all that we can do is summarize a particular intercultural dialogue. Instead of concentrating on the chasm our translations must cross, we should recognize the intermediate models Yorubanists have regularly traversed. We recognize them at a cost to our highly prized "experiential authority" (see Mudimbe 1988:199) but with even greater benefits to the accuracy of our account of "Yoruba religion" as we know it today. The models that guide the interpretive study of *orisa* worship are both local and international. They are forged where scholars and worshipers of diverse origins meet, debate, and read each other's work. Such intermediate models acknowledge the reality of a sizable international community of *orisa*-worshipers and their pursuit of mutual understanding, rather than the Western academy's institutional aspirations to universalize its "truths" in the name of Marx, Weber, and Durkheim.

Diaspora: Exploring the Breadth of the Model

There is no denying that this account is deeply engaged in the dialogue among university scholars. It also attempts to expand upon Yorubanists' exemplary involvement in a grass-roots dialogue. I hope that it will join the company of scholarly works read and employed critically by believers. One of the most involved interlocutors in this exchange has been Thompson, who has coined the rubric "Afro-Atlantic" for those religious and aesthetic traditions around the Atlantic perimeter that have, for centuries, imitated and transformed West African prototypes. Within the blended and creolized civilizations of the Americas, he argues, certain ancient features of Yoruba civilization have served as a "canon" and formal vocabulary of creative endeavor (Thompson 1983).

As in aesthetic endeavors, so in religious ones modern worshipers of the *orisa* have consciously manipulated Yoruba prototypes amid cataclysmic social change and the vast international exchange of cultural influences. Modern West African Yoruba religion has been no less subject than its American counterparts to such change and exchange. What we know of New World transformations illuminates the processes of change in an Old World civilization, and vice versa (see also Herskovits 1966 [1948]). We might, then, gloss the hermeneutical context of this study as the *Yoruba-Atlantic* complex. The identification of enduring, common symbolic elements among these traditions clarifies worshipers' means of handling, and prompting, social change.

A high proportion of slaves alternately called "Yoruba," "Nagô," and "Lucumí" in the New World originated from the Oyo Empire's southwestern domains, bordering on the kingdom of Dahomey (see figure 1); many more came from the heartland of the empire, whose collapse created military turmoil after 1830. Moreover, Oyo colonists and administrative delegations carried Oyo *orisa* into the empire's domains, especially in the southwest (Morton-Williams 1964b:40–41), and various groups voluntarily adopted those *orisa* that they might share in the Oyo prestige (Apter 1992:36, 51). Hence, the *orisa* of Oyo-Yoruba origin are more widely worshiped than those of any other single group in present-day Yorubaland. Likewise, a disproportionate number of *orisa* that reached Brazil and Cuba (and Cuba's United States diaspora) originated among the Oyo Yoruba.

According to Curtin, about 3.5 million Africans were taken by force to Brazil during the entire Atlantic slave trade; 1.2 million of them, or one-third, landed in Bahia. Although the vast majority of captives sold on the Brazilian market originated from central Africa, captives from the Bight of Benin formed the plurality among those entering Bahia during the nineteenth century, coincident with the fall of Oyo. Bahian shippers enjoyed a great advantage in the Bight of Benin because consumers there preferred Bahian tobacco. The number of Oyo Yoruba intercepted by British antislavers and resettled in Sierra Leone in that century vastly exceeded the number of any other Yoruba or non-Yoruba groups, strongly suggesting that Oyo Yoruba predominated as well among the West African captives who reached both Brazil and Cuba during the nineteenth century. Nina Rodrigues's late nineteenth-century interviews in Bahia confirm this inference (Nina Rodrigues 1945:52–53; Curtin 1969:239–42, 260, 264, 291–98, esp. 292; see also Braz do Amaral [1915], cited in Cunha 1985:103). The recentness and concentration of forced immigration by Oyo-Yoruba captives are two factors accounting for the disproportionate influence of their culture on such Afro-Latin religions as Cuban Santería and Brazilian Candomblé. Despite the numerical prominence of central African captives during the slave trade and the strength of their cultural influence throughout the diaspora, Oyo-Yoruba gods are the core of a "metalanguage" (Risério 1988), or lingua franca, according to which even religious groups consciously opposed to the Yoruba—such as Bahian Candomblé Angola, Umbanda in Rio de Janeiro and São Paulo, and Cuban Palo Mayombe—feel obliged to identify the beings they worship.

Prominent in that "metalanguage" is the hunting god Ọ̀ṣọ́ọ̀sì (Portuguese Oxossi), the tutelary god of the Béninois Yoruba kingdom of Kétu. Indeed, from 1789 onward, Ketu was subject to repeated attacks by Dahomey, which delivered much of Osoosi's priesthood into slavery in Brazil and Cuba (Smith 1988:58; Verger 1981:113). Moreover,

Brazilian observers have taken the prominence of the term "Quêto" (Portuguese for Ketu) in the historical and musical references of the Bahian Candomblé as an indication of the *preeminence* of the Ketu influence on the Afro-Bahian religion (see, e.g., dos Santos 1976:28), an inference no more justified than the one that posits the predominance of Dahomean influence from the use of corruptions of the Fon and Ewe term *vodun* in Haiti (see Mintz and Price 1976:8–9). In Bahia, as in Cuba, it seems more evident that the Ketu Yoruba were a minority within an array of peoples subject to Oyo influence and, often, imperialism. Indeed, Ketu had come under Oyo imperial control by the seventeenth century (Smith 1988:35). Costa Lima, one of the premier researchers on the Candomblé, produces evidence that Bahia's oldest temple and the root of the Candomblé Quêto had been the Oyo palace official in charge of Sango worship (Costa Lima 1977:24–25; Abraham 1962:20). As a result of this West African imperialism and its towering importance until about 1830, the Oyo influence is so strong in many Brazilian states that the entire array of local practices—from those allegedly most "purely African" to those alleged to be most innovative—bears the name of Oyo's tutelary divinity. *Xangô* (Yoruba, Sango) is the name for Afro-Brazilian religion in the northeastern states of Sergipe, Pernambuco, and Alagoas (Dantas 1988:26 n, 39). Indeed, throughout Brazil and Cuba, Sango is the most widely worshiped of all African divinities. In contemporary Nigeria, his following is second in size only to that of Ogun.

The foundation of my own transatlantic fieldwork, in Nigeria, the People's Republic of Benin, Brazil, and the eastern United States, has been the identification of those symbolic elements whose coherency might be overlooked—and generally had been—in any single context. I do not automatically regard the common elements among these cognate traditions as central elements in any one tradition. For example, the presence of Kardecist spiritism in both modern France and Latin America does not in itself prove the centrality of Kardecism in French culture. However, the ideological and socioeconomic conditions of its popularity in nineteenth-century France do illuminate the conditions of its arrival, expansion, and interpretation in Latin America—and vice versa (cf. Comaroff 1985:177ff.). Indeed, the *intermediate difference* among Yoruba-Atlantic practices can underline widespread implicit axioms.

We have seen as much in the symbolism of vessels, a case I have discussed at great length elsewhere (Matory 1986). Similarly, the contrast between Sango and Ogun first became apparent to me in the New World context. Like Candomblé Quêto, Cuban Santería explicitly emulates Yoruba models, and the worship of non-Oyo gods has undergone the strong influence of Oyo religious practice. In Santería, many initiations (*asientos* or *kariochas*) require the initiand (also *iyawo*, or *yaguó*) to sit on Sango's sacred mortar (*odó* or *pilón*) (see Brown 1989:387ff.; Cabrera 1974:162–63). Virtually all require the shaving of his or her head and its feeding with animal blood. This initiatic tradition also underlines the tension between Ṣàngó (Spanish, Changó) and Ògún (Spanish, Ogún). For example, Ogún's initiands are forbidden to sit on the mortar (Cabrera:162). If the two gods "mount" their "horses" simultaneously at a sacred festival, they are bound to fight. *Santeros* cite as proof of their antagonism the fact that thunderbolts, which are sent by Changó, regularly strike iron, which is Ogún's main symbol. Even in the present Oyo capital, the head of the Ògún-worshipers, the *Aṣípa* Ọlọrunọṣebi, is the avowed enemy of the royal dynasty. He played a role in the dethronement of the present Alaafin's father.

Also mutually illuminating are the gender correlates of possession in diverse Yoruba-Atlantic locales. Indigenous and foreign commentators have noted the prominence of homosexual men in the Brazilian Candomblé, relating it variously to the mental illness, deviancy, and liminality of Candomblé practitioners generally (e.g., Landes 1947 and 1940; Ribeiro 1969; Fry 1982). I have argued that their prominence emerges from the conjunction of peculiarly Brazilian gender categories with Oyo-Yoruba metaphors of "mounting" (*gigun*) in politico-religious delegation (Matory 1988). Since before the nineteenth-century European categories of "homosexual" and "heterosexual" reached the bourgeoisie of southern Brazil, northeastern Brazilian folk have recognized two male gender categories: (1) *homens* or *machos*, who penetrate others during intercourse, and (2) *bichas* or *adés*, who are penetrated.[3] Not only are *bichas* understood to be like women in affect and dress, but they are physically and, by extension, spiritually "mountable." Indeed, the verb "to mount" (*montar*) is used for possession in various Afro-

Brazilian religions, as it is in Cuban Santería, Brazilian Umbanda, and Brazilian Candomblé de Caboclo.

An anatomical conception that recognizes anal penetration as a form of sexual conduct and as an index of gender identity also posits for the system a new category of priests. The vocabulary of sexual relations among these Brazilian gender categories illuminates social and spiritual relations in the Candomblé as well. Key to these relations is a sharp power differential, whereby the *homem* "dominates" (*domina*) the *bicha* just as he "dominates" women. As the *homem* "dominates" his *mulher* and *bicha* partners, so the *orixá*, or god, is said to "dominate" his possession priest (Matory 1988; Fry 1986). Alternate, Kardecist-influenced vocabularies of relations to the *orixás*, such as *influência* ("influence") and *irradiação* ("irradiation"), posit similar conceptions of the body as receptacle in the context of bourgeois worshipers' visions of an egalitarian spirituality, even in the midst of military dictatorship and U.S. imperialism.

The contextual political entailments of other widespread and durable metaphoric sources in the Yoruba-Atlantic complex invite investigation as well. Some of them I have touched upon in the West African context. One is the widespread equestrian vocabulary of possession. Although present in Brazil, Cuba, the United States, Benin, and Nigeria, the metaphoric references to "horses" and "mounts" are surely subject to varied styles of "highlighting and hiding," conditioned by the equally varied ideological and political conditions of their predication. The variable attribution of uterine, cephalic, and breast-related meanings to ritual vessels would seem to allow for similar explanations, as would the foreignness of the gods. For example, the contrast between the "Africanness" of the gods and the "Brazilianness" of the lesser *caboclo* spirits has structured a range of white-financed hierarchical privileges for certain "purely African" religious houses, in which both university scholars and the Brazilian state have been complicit (see Matory 1993; Dantas 1988, 1982; Fry 1982:49–50; Henfrey 1981).

Exploring the Limits of the Model

Although the Yoruba-Atlantic complex is its hermeneutical context, this book is about the Oyo Yoruba as they have negotiated their place in a cosmopolitan society. It bears direct implications for Oyo's former subjects in Egba and Egbado communities, but should not be used to generalize prematurely about the subjectivity of women, men, husbands, and wives in, say, Ekiti or Ijebu. Nor does it address the highly visible commercial accomplishments of Ijebu women in Lagos or Ibadan, which still require analysis in gender-sensitive terms. A vastly wealthy Lagosian woman once told me, Èmi ọkùnrin!—"I am a man!" The priests and priestesses who have taught me in Oyo North are physical emblems of morally central but economically marginal communities with their own distinctive logic of gender and politics.

It is natural now that I should turn in conclusion toward Ile-Ife, lest I be accused of endorsing, rather than reporting, the Oyo Yoruba's conviction that theirs is *the real* Yoruba monarchy. Of course, I will stop short of bourgeois Yoruba's sense that Ife is. Despite the international breadth of Oyo's influence, the case of Ife demonstrates the temporal and regional limits of this gender-based model of authority and tropic signification. The bronze and terra-cotta artifacts of ancient Ife (eleventh to fifteenth centuries) reveal nothing of the more recent obsession of Yoruba and particularly Oyo-influenced artists with kneeling, vessel-bearing, and fecund women.[4] Horsemen too are absent among the more ancient Ife artifacts. This observation cautions us against the imposition of "mounting" symbolism upon ancient Ife government—whose reputation for authoritarian and expansionist politics is dwarfed by that of Oyo. At the same time, it strengthens our sense of the very *suitedness* of that symbolism to Oyo-Yoruba royalists and to those who still implicitly regard Oyo as a divine prototype of world order.

Appendix I

Oriki Yemoja (Yemoja Panegyrics)

1   Drenching water under the leaves,
   Eats in the house, eats in the river, wife of the king
      Òkèrè.
   One who listens to our complaints,
   My mother kills, [but] we call her a woman.
5   Mighty water of endless expanse is the home of Yemoja,
      who eats two rams in the river.
   I [eagerly] watched for the arrival of Water; I
      prepared yam paste, and Yemoja spoiled it.
   I added a calabash [of pounded yam]; our mother has
      made pounded yam turn into water [i.e., she
      accepted it as an offering].[1]
   Opeepee Yemoja who has the back to carry Sango.
   The baby sling of that youngster is like a shining baby
      sling, Owner of breasts of honey, there
      is no hill as nice as Ìgbàdì Hill.
10 The center of the house is the river.[2]
   There is just no road that is as good as the road to
      [the town of] Sà*à*rè.
   The center of the house is the river.
   My mother kills people, [but] we call her a woman.
   The center of the house is the river.
15 Mighty water of endless expanse is the home of Yemoja,
      who eats two rams in the river.
   The center of the house is the river.
   The great collector, our mother with breasts that go
      all over her chest.
   The center of the house is the river.

My spectacularly fierce mother, who eats people in the
    manner of the stinging caterpillar.

20   The center of the house is the river.

When mother is eating [them], they will think it is a
    stinging caterpillar that is eating [them].

The center of the house is the river.

They will take up the sleeping mat, and shake their
    clothes.

Water-Stops-My-Weeping [Yemoja], they will think the
    stinging caterpillar is eating them.

25   The center of the house is the river.

They will take up the sleeping mat and shake their
    clothes.

The center of the house is the river.

Yemoja Opeepee who has the back to carry Sango.

The center of the house is the river.

30   No breast is as sweet, Ojerinade [someone in the
    audience whose family worships the Egungun masquerade],
    as my mother's breast.

The center of the house is the river.

When it is deep red, the red will be really deep.

The center of the house is the river.

I met Yemoja enthroned, child of "Puny Fruit Bats" [a
    praise name of Onigboho House].

35   Owner of white teeth, who is a trader,

The center of the house is the river.

No baby sling is as good as [Yemoja's] shining baby
    sling.

The center of the house is the river.

My Mother, no hill is better or more beautiful than
    Igbadi Hill.

40   The center of the house is the river.

There is not a single road as good as the road to Saare
    [town].

The center of the house is the river.

The one with white teeth, who is a trader in laughter,

The center of the house is the river.

45   My mother, do you hear my complaints?

The center of the house is the river.

Sea-dye water,[3]

Ọlabenwa is the king Okere.

The center of the house is the river.

50   Ọjẹniran [someone in the audience who worships
          Egungun], like Water-Is-Prestige [praise
          name for Yemoja or her worshiper], Àwùyó Ọgẹ
          [praise name for Yemoja],

The center of the house is the river.

The receiver of the crown of childbearing women, who
          has breasts of honey,

The center of the house is the river.

The great collector Yemoja, owner of extensively
          collecting breasts [i.e., they can feed
          multitudes],

55   The center of the house is the river.

It is only a small river that we can dam up with a fish
          trap.

The center of the house is the river.

Water-Is-Prestige, Okere-of-the-Sea [Yemoja], who [has
          the power] to dam up the mighty, rolling
          water for them?

The center of the house is the river.

60   I will never [dare to try] to dam the mighty water,
          which carries away fish traps.

The center of the house is the river.

The owner of the Kalanchoe plant, owner of the land in
          Irá [Yemoja's hometown and the place of
          Sango's birth], Water-Is-Prestige, Awuyo
          Oge,

The center of the house is the river.

Olubọ became the owner of the land at Érìn.

65   Greetings! [archaically]

Bááyárìn-Èjìdé became the owner of the land at Sèlé-
          Ilé.

The center of the house is the river.

The Arsonist-Who-Won't-Deny-It became the landowner in
          Kòso.

The center of the house is the river.

70   The son of the houseowner would not like his house to
          burn.
        The center of the house is the river.
        My mother became the landowner in Oke-Igboho.
        The center of the house is the river.
        My mother Bean-Curds-in-the-Water.
75   The center of the house is the river.
        The sea that avenges like a medicine man,
        The center of the house is the river.
        If you send evil medicine against Bóoyíkáà [Yemoja's
          praise name], Yemoja will spoil it.
        The center of the house is the river.
80   The one whom water gives prestige is my mother.
        The center of the house is the river.
        When you take liquor [to her], it will change into water.
        The center of the house is the river.
        Opeepee Yemoja who has the back to carry Sango.
85   The center of the house is the river.
        The child that has a house at the place where it is
          impossible to have a house,
        The center of the house is the river.
        My mother kills people, [but] we still call her a woman.
        The center of the house is the river.
90   Greetings! [archaically]
        If you have (a) head(s), hold it/them in your hands
          [i.e., be careful].
        [You] Sea, who hear our pleas,
        The head that I entrusted you to plait, don't unravel
          it on me.
        Magical finger ring that can kill twenty [people], that
          can kill thirty,
95   Eats in the house, eats in the river.
        The voice I hear right now is that of a loud bell.
        Afolabi [the Onigboho present at this recitation],
          thank you, son of Alaatipo [his father and
          eponym of Afolabi's royal line].
        Greetings to you who wake to honor your father [i.e.,
          he honors his father's religion].

Your forefathers are the ones who strengthen your hand
[i.e., assist you].

100   Afolabi, child of Fǫlasinyẹn [his mother],

Jeremiah [Afolabi's first name], child of Ǫtẹ [the
father of this mother],

They held a conference and fixed it, child of Yede [the
name of Afolabi's mother's mother].

Àdìgún Èrán [Alaatipo's praise name and, by extension,
Jeremiah's], they agreed that Jeremiah would be
the king.

Each and every elder,

105   They said that Jeremiah would have this honor [that is,
had won the chieftaincy title].

Jeremiah, who is never crooked [that is, has never
wavered from the elders' expectations],

Afolabi, child of Alaatipo, Adigun Eran became the person who bathed
among the royal wives.

Sifter, father [or male user] of the sifter, Jeremiah,
father of Sẹgi [his daughter],

Sifter, father of the sifter.

110   You sifter, Adigun, as we have been doing to you, so
the sifter does to yam flour in Igboho.

Onigboho, you are greater than all the [other] kings
who have ever reigned.

Afolabi, child of Abẹnugbǫ́rǫ́ [a hill worshiped by
Onigboho House], Jeremiah, son of Ote.

From Wale-Wale [a town where Afolabi lived in Gold Coast (now
Ghana)]
you brought the title home, child of Yede.

Éébùkí [a poetic distortion of Afolabi's personal
praise name—Áíbùkí], God has approved of our
plans.

115   Afolabi, child of Alaatipo,

The head load of the elder[s] who has [have] no head
cushion [i.e., a serious burden for which
there is no easy solution], Adigun, your
father's "head" will help you to lift it.

Adigun, your job will not become another man's job
[i.e., no one will take your job].

In the presence of the Owner-of-the-Baby-Sling-Full-of-
    Kindness [Yemoja],

A stroke resulting in paralysis will not take away your
    luck.

120   Whoever wishes troubles upon you will himself have troubles.

A dog does not have the option to put its child in its
    armpit [i.e., a dog cannot carry its child,
       because a dog is not built that way. Thus, your enemies cannot escape
    their troubles].

1   Omi rẹrẹ lábẹ́ ewé,

Jẹ nílé, jẹ lódò, ayaba Ọ̀kẹ̀rẹ̀.

Elétí ìgbáàròyé,

Ìyáà mi ń pa, a lóbìnrin ni.

5   Omi alagbalúbú omi òréré yèlú Yemoja tí í gbódò jẹ̀jì
    àgbò.

Mo ṣọ́mi lọ́nà dé; mo yíkà, Yemoja bà á jẹ́.

Mo rígbá sí; Ìyéè wa tí sọyán domi.

Ọ̀pẹ́ẹ̀pẹ̀ẹ́ Yemoja tí réḥìn pọn Ṣàngó sí.

Ọ̀já ọ̀dọ́ bíi ọ̀já ororo, ọlọ́mú oyin, òkè kan kò sunwọn bíi
    Òkè Ìgbàdì.[4]

10   Ààrin ilé lódò.

Ọ̀nà kan kò sáà dára bíi ọ̀nà Sàà rẹ,

Àà rin ilé lódò.

Ìyáà mi ń pani, a l'óbìnrin ni.

Àà rin ilé lódò.

15   Omi alagbalúbú omi òréré yèlú Yemoja tí í gbódò jẹ̀jì
    àgbò.

Àà rin ilé lódò.

Ikókó ìkó, ìyéè wa ọlọ́mú akún-gbáàyà.

Àà rin ilé lódò.

Ìyáà mi òrorò ajẹni-bíi-ìtalẹ̀.

20   Àà rin ilé lódò.

Bí Ìyá bá ń jẹ wọn, wọn ó ṣebí ìtalẹ̀ ló ń jẹ.

Àà rin ilé lódò.

Wọ́n á máa ká ẹní, wọ́n á máa gbọn aṣọ.

Omìírànlẹ́kún, wọ́n ṣebí ìtalẹ̀ ló ń jẹ wọ́n.

25   Àà rin ilé lódò.

Wọ́n á máa ká ẹní, wọ́n á máa gbọn aṣọ.
Ààrin ilé lódò.
Yemọja Ọ̀pẹ́ẹ̀pẹ̀ẹ́ arẹ́hìn pọn Ṣàngó sí.
Ààrin ilé lódò.
30 Omú kan kò dùn, Ọ̀jẹ́rìnádé, bíi ọmú Ìyáà mi
Ààrin ilé lódò.
Bó pọ́n roro, á kàn roro.
Ààrin ilé lódò.
Mo bá Yemọja lórí ìtẹ́, Ọmọ Àdán Gèrèjìn.
35 Eléhín funfun tí í ṣòwò,
Ààrin ilé lódò.
Ọ̀já kan kò dára bíi ọ̀já oróro.
Ààrin ilé lódò.
Ìyéè mi, òkè kan kò sunwọ̀n bíi Òkè Ìgbàdì.
40 Ààrin ilé lódò.
Kò sọ́nà kan tó dára bíi Ọ̀nà Sààrẹ.
Ààrin ilé lódò.
Eléhín funfun tí í ṣòwò èrín,
Ààrin ilé lódò.
45 Ìyáà mi, ṣé o gbọ́ àròyéè mi?
Ààrin ilé lódò.
Omi aró ibú,
Olábéñwá l'ọba Ọ̀kẹ̀rẹ̀.
Ààrin ilé lódò.
50 Ọ̀jéníran bíi Omiléyẹ Àwùyó Ọgẹ,
Ààrin ilé lódò.
Olówó gbadé abiamọ, ọlọ́mú oyin,
Ààrin ilé lódò.
Okókó ńkó Yemọja ọlọ́mú akógbádọ̀,
55 Ààrin ilé lódò.
Odò kékèké ni sédò-sédò ń sé.
Ààrin ilé lódò.
L'Omiléyẹ, Ọ̀kẹ̀rẹ̀ òkun, tání bá wọn sé alagbalúbú omi?
Ààrin ilé lódò.
60 Èmi ò jẹ́ sé alagbalúbú odò tí ń gbé ìgèrè lọ.
Ààrin ilé lódò.
Ọlọ́ọ́dán onílẹ̀ n'Írá, Omiléyẹ, Àwùyó Ọgẹ,[5]

Àárin ilé lódò.

Olùbó di onílè l'Érìn.

65   O kúúúúúú!

Bááyárìn-èjìdé di onílè ni Sèlé-Ilé.

Àárin ilé lódò.

Akunlé-má-sèrùú di onílè ni Kòso.

Àárin ilé lódò.

70   Omo onílé tó nílé kò níí fé kí ilée rè ó jó.

Àárin ilé lódò.

Ìyáà mi di onílè l'Okè-Ìgbòho.

Àárin ilé lódò.

Ìyáà mi, Òlèlè lómi.

75   Àárin ilé lódò.

Òkun asànyà bíi olóògùn,

Àárin ilé lódò.

Bó bá se oògun àìsàn fún Bóoyíkáà, Yemoja bà á jé.

Àárin ilé lódò.

80   Omo l'Ómiléye ni ìyáà mi

Àárin ilé lódò.

Bóo gbé otí á domi.

Àárin ilé lódò.

Òpéépèé Yemoja tí réhìn pon Sàngó sí.

85   Àárin ilé lódò.

Omo tó nílé síbi tí a kò [l]è ní iléè sí,

Àárin ilé lódò.

Ìyáà mi ni ń pani, a sì lóbìnrin ni.

Àárin ilé lódò.

[New solo enters]

90   O kú o!

Elérí kó fowó mú erí.

Òkun elétí ìgbáàròyé,

Orí ti mo fún o dì, má bá mi tú[u].

Aluwó tó ń pogún, tó ń pogbòn,

95   Je nílé, je lódò, ayaba Òkèrè.

Ohùn wàsìkò tí mo gbó ohùn aláro.

Afolábí, osé, omo Aláàtípó.

O kú o, ajísáajo bàbáà re.

Àwọn bàbáà rẹ náà ni oníràn lọ́wọ́ọ̀ rẹ.

100   Afọlábí, ọmọ Fọlásinyẹn,

Jeremiah, ọmọ Òtẹ̀,

Wọ́n pé súúrú, wọ́n dì í, ọmọ Yédé.

Àdìgún Èrán, wọ́n ní Jeremiah ní ó jọba.

Àwọn àgbà kan àgbà kan,

105   Àwọn ní Jeremiah lọ́wọ̀ yìí.

Jeremiah tí kò wọ́ rárá,

Afọlábí, ọmọ Aláàtípó, Àdìgún Èrán di ẹnití ń wẹ̀ láàrin
    ayaba.

Kònkòsò, bàbá kònkòsò, Jeremiah, bàbá Sègi,

Kònkòsò, bàbá kònkòsò.

110   Kònkòsò Àdìgún, bíi a ń tí ń ṣe ọ́ ló ń ṣe èlùbọ́ ni Ìgbòho.

Onígbòho, o pọ̀ ju gbogbo ọba tí ń tí ń jẹ lọ.

Afọlábí, ọmọ Abẹnugbọ́rọ́, Jeremiah, ọmọ Òtẹ̀.

Wàlà-wálá ló ti mú oyè wálé, ọmọ Yédé.

Éébùkí, Ọlọ́run rí sọ́rọ̀ wa.

115   Afọlábí, ọmọ Aláàtípó,

Ẹrù àgbà tí kò lóṣùká Àdìgún oríí bàbáà rẹ yóò bá ọ
    gbée.

Àdìgún, iṣẹ́ẹ̀ rẹ kò níí jẹ́ iṣẹ́ oníṣẹ́.

Lójú ọlọ́jàá aájò,

Ègbà kò níi gba ire ọwọ́ọ̀ rẹ dànù.

120   Ẹni tó wí pé kóo máà rójú eléyìí ni ò níí rójú.

Ajá ò rójú gbé ọmọ́ọ̀ rẹ̀ sí abíyá.[6]

Appendix II

A Partial Genealogy of the Oyebọọde Priests[1]

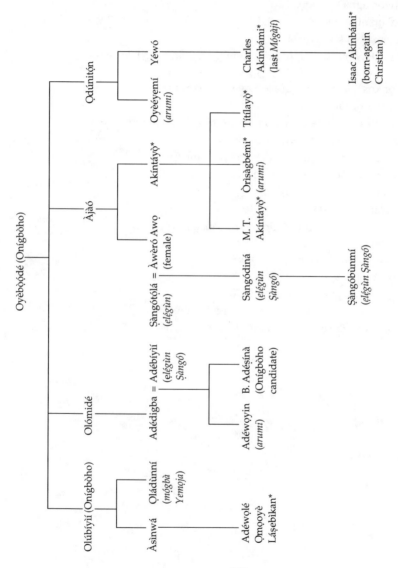

*pseudonym

Appendix III

Yemọja in the Kingdom of Ṣango:
The Ritual Calendar

Sociologically, the collective rites of Yemoja-worship in Oke-Igboho are as notable for their inclusions as for their exclusions. They follow the generations-old ritual map of priestly graves and the more recent migration of the sacred calabashes; they also follow the will of certain classes of contemporary women to be together and "support" one another's projects. The ritual calendar of the Yemoja priesthood predicates a religious community but not a community that is religious alone. Many Muslim and Christian women participate, although it invites the antagonism of Muslim men. Cutting across the apparent unity of Yemoja-worshipers, the priesthood of Onigboho House maintains a rigid separation from the priestesses of its dynastic "junior brother," Onikomo House in Ọba Ago quarter. All of the priesthoods receive the "support" of the town's Sango priests.

Each god with a priesthood is the object of a weekly service, that is, once in the four-day Yoruba week (ọṣẹ̀). The weekly service for Yemoja is called the "week of Yemoja" (ọṣẹ̀ Yemọja), just as the annual service is called the "year of Yemoja" (ọdún Yemọja). Adewoyin's and Orisagbemi's Yemoja altars receive kola nut (obì) for Yemoja and bitter kola (orógbó) for the associated Sango on Ọjọ́ Jàkúta, the day of the week consecrated to Sango. These condiments are split and used to divine whether the two gods are satisfied with affairs in the house. Sometimes hominy (ẹ̀gbo) is offered as well. Adewoyin often neglects her weekly duties, whereas Orisagbemi conducts hers without fail at around 9 A.M. Various mọ́gbà Yemọja (nonpossession priestesses of Yemoja) regularly accompany her in the rite in the rear bedroom of Olowo Bar.

Titilayo tells me that when there was more money, presumably during the oil boom of the late 1970s and early 1980s, the priestesses celebrated *Jímọ̀ Olóyin* ("Sweet Friday") services for Yemoja in the palace. King Jeremiah was still alive then. "Sweet Friday" is the day when the major Muslim prayer day coincides with *Ojọ́ Jàkúta*. These services invariably included offerings of hominy, and sometimes fowls.

Igboho's major *orisa* festivals (*odun*) of 1988 began in May, with the Egungun festival and a minor Ogun festival conducted simultaneously. The Sango festival season followed, from 14 June to 29 July. It began with sacrificial rites and a small festival (*odun*) for the *orisa* Àyàn, the god of the *bàtá* drums, which must be played at Sango festivals. This year, Sango festivals occurred in nine quarters: Àgọ́ Igiṣubú, Ọba Ago, Ìsàlẹ̀ Bọ́nní, Òkè-Ìgbòho, Ẹ̀bẹ̀di, Igbópẹ̀, and Mọdéké. The male *ẹlẹ́gùn Ṣàngó* (Sango possession priest) of Onigboho House washed his Yemoja and Sango stones on 15 June in preparation for Sango's dance in Oke-Igboho on 18 June. It was not he but a young female *elegun* of the quarter who was mounted by Sango on that date. She is unrelated to Onigboho House. The Ṣàngó Kòso festival in Kòso quarter occurred on 10 August, distinct from the series of town Sango festivals. Ṣàngó Kòso is said to belong to Alaafin rather than to Igboho and its authorities.[1] Yemoja festivals occurred on 7 September in Oke-Igboho and on 11 September in Ọba Ago quarter. From 7 July to mid-September, a series of festivals honored Òrìṣà Oko, and the year ended with a lengthy Ifá festival. The townwide Sango priesthood attends virtually all major *orisa* rites in the town, whereas the Yemoja priesthood is absent from most. An Òrìṣà Oko priestess, and mother of Oke-Igboho's active female *ẹlẹ́gùn Ṣàngó*, feted the Òrìṣà Oko altar left in the quarter by her dead mother on the same day as the Yemoja Onígbòho festival, implying that she acknowledged no social relationship at all to the Onigboho priesthood.

The New Yam Festival

The Yemoja priestesses and the female *elegun* of the house consecrated the harvest of the new yam (*iṣu lílà*) on 9 July, in a rite of concern only to Oke-Igboho quarter. *Ọmọ oṣú* (daughters of the house) came to the palace shrine room from all quarters, bringing hominy and new yams for Yemoja. At least one contributor of new yams was an *Alhajiya*, a female pilgrim to Mecca. During the rite, Adewoyin cut off the end of each yam, split the end in half, pinched off a morsel for the god Esu, and used the two large pieces like the lobes, or cotelydons, of a kola nut to divine whether the goddess was satisfied with or had advice for the contributor of that yam. She would present the two yam pieces to the Yemoja calabashes, place them on the ground before the raised altar, sprinkle water on them, and cast them. As long as at least one convex peel side landed downward, the cast was considered propitious. She then chewed alligator pepper (*atare*) and presented kola nut (*obi*) to the Yemoja calabashes, saluting Yemoja as "the Mother of Children" (*Ìyá Ọmọ*). Amid the loud chanting and affirmations of Orisagbemi and the half dozen *mogba* crowded inside the shrine room, Adewoyin exhorted the goddess not to let any of her wards die arbitrarily and, yes, to protect her emigrant children, including the collective *Alhaji* and *Alhajiya*, the Muslims in general, and the Christians. Adewoyin shouted that "the Mother" (Yemoja) is *also* holy (*mímọ*), ending an ecumenical litany always heard in her prayers, and told the goddess to bring them money, to keep evil people from "getting" (*gbà*) the supplicants' children, and not to "fight" (*jà*) against her worshipers. One *mogba* shouted *Ẹ kí Ìyá!* ("Salute the Mother!"), which brought the reply *Ikúúúú!* ("Death!"). The talking drums outside reproduced the *oriki* chanted by the chorus.

Adewoyin deposited half kola nuts in the small dishes within each calabash and distributed the other halves among the *mogba* and the *elegun* for them to eat. She mixed the melted shea butter (*òrí*) into each bowl of hominy with the handle of Yemoja's sacred bell (*ìrònẹ̀n*). From each bowl she scooped out a handful, tasted a bit, and deposited the lump on the raised altar in front of one of the two Yemoja calabashes (the "first road"). These were offerings on behalf of each woman who had brought a bowl of hominy. The priestesses themselves had eaten much of the remaining hominy before Adewoyin exited the shrine room to salute the tomb of King Jeremiah through the door of the neighboring room.

Together, the priestesses left the palace, danced behind Adewoyin to the accompaniment of talking drums (*dùndún*), and proceeded to visit and "press their heads to the ground" (*teribale*) over the family graves around the quarter. Descendants of the dead would emerge from their houses upon hearing the drummed praise poetry of their ancestors and give money to the priestesses and drummers. The senior *arumi*,

Adewoyin, insisted on collecting and distributing all money according to her own judgment. After saluting Olomide's grave, the priestesses left the drummers and went to present the new yam to the Yemoja calabashes of the *mogba* Ọladunni, of the *arumi* Orisagbemi, and of Adewoyin herself.[2] Later in the day, these priestesses gathered again in the palace, joined by the male *elegun* of Onigboho House and Moroorẹnti, the female *ẹlẹ́gùn Ṣàngó* who takes care of the Yemoja calabash in Òkè Lọ́kọ quarter. They ate boiled and salted yam with a stew of *elégédé* (the inner flesh of a type of calabash) and ground *ẹ̀gúsí* melon seeds.

Setting the Festival Date and Washing Yemoja

Not until 22 August did they set the date (*dájọ́*) of the main festival. They invited the town's senior-most *elegun*—a male bearing the title *Jagun*, or "Warrior"—to divine the proper day by means of the sixteen-cowry oracle.[3] The *elegun* of Onigboho House participated only marginally in this procedure. Not only blood sacrifice but the bathing of sacred objects in herbal infusions is indispensable in annually renewing the power of an *orisa* in its shrine. The selection of herbs used in those infusions is a matter of ancient tradition and is secret in most parts of the Yoruba-Atlantic complex. The washing and feeding of the Yemoja stones of Onigboho House's *ọmọ oṣú* spanned from 30 August to 6 September. The *mogba* Oladunni trekked about, despite her twisted leg, hunting down the various leaves that would have to be strained to make the solution to wash the stones. What she forgot, she sent her grandchildren back out to find. One of these girls will probably inherit responsibility for these altars. Preparations for the festival combine elements of fun, instruction, public display, and the *semantic replenishment* of the sacred collective self.[4] The last of these is structured by a ritual logic of punning and a worldly logic of competitive acquisition. Both the *koto* calabash and the human head, which mimic each other, are bathed in fluids semantically full of the power and qualities of the *orisa*.

In preparing the solution for the main set of stones, shells, and beads in her calabashes (which once belonged to Olomide), Oladunni simply crushed and twisted the following leaves in a solution of black lye soap (*ọṣẹ dúdú*) and water: *ọdándán* (elsewhere called *ọdúndún*—*Kalanchoe crenata*), *ewé àgbàdo* (corn leaves), *tẹ̀tẹ̀ pọnlá* (elsewhere called *ètì pọ́n ọlá—Boerhavia diffusa*), *léélé*, *yérí*, *ewé igbá* (calabash vine leaf), and *ewé ìrókò* (iroko tree leaf), *àjàdẹ*, *ewé Ògún*, *eèsún* (*Pennisetum purpureum*, used in making mats; Abraham 1962:165–66), *òrúwa* (or *òrúwọ*—the brimstone tree), *ewé pákí* (cassava leaf), *ewé ọkà bàbà* (guinea corn leaf), *níní*, *pèrègún*, *kẹ̀kẹ́*, *ọ̀pọ̀tọ́* (female fig tree), and *akòko*. The resultant solution is called *àgbo* (herbal medicine). With it, she and her granddaughter washed the shells, stones, bead chains, and the cowry chain from Mecca and then dried them in the sun. Then they washed the metal enamel pans and the *koto* calabash itself, rewhitening the latter with chalk (*efun*). With the remaining solution, Oladunni wet her own, my own, and her grandchildren's heads.

Not until a day later would Adewoyin and Orisagbemi come and help her prepare a new solution to wash the contents of the small dishes (*ahá róbótó róbótó, arere*, or *àwo kékeré*) that rest inside Oladunni's calabash. The three women sat around a metal bucket of soapy water. Adewoyin would hold a leaf or several leaves in her right hand and, speaking each leaf's name aloud, beat them gently against the rim of the bucket. Once Adewoyin began her song, the other two women would sing—sometimes simultaneously, sometimes in chorus—and grip the leaves. Together they twisted and tore apart (*já*) each leaf and dropped the shreds in. Some songs simply invoked an *orisa* without reference to the leaf, but many a song was identifiably specific to the leaf whose tearing it accompanied.

Medicinal value is attributed to many of these leaves. For example, *odundun* is credited with curing smallpox, headache, earache, and ophthalmia, while *ètì pọ́n ọlá* is believed to reduce fever and convulsions in children (Abraham 1962:168, 505).[5] There is an element of preventative health care in the washing of these divine and human heads, but the logic of its efficacy is not simply pharmaceutical.

Another logical element of this rite is that obtaining valued states and objects is like plucking leaves or fruits from a tree. The verb used for that "plucking" is *já*, which describes the "plucking" of valued things in the following song:

Whatever you can pluck
Go ahead and pluck (chorus)

With the kind of plucking that brings money
Go ahead and pluck (chorus)
With the kind of plucking that brings children
Go ahead and pluck (chorus)

Ijákújàá
Ẹ máa já ǹsó (chorus)
Ajálówó
E máa já ǹsó (chorus)
Ajálómọ
E máa já ǹsó (chorus)

Trees, like people, have heads (orí); orí igi is the leafy top of a tree. This parallel provides one hint as to why the "power" (ase) in trees should be transferable to the headlike calabashes that house the goddess's power. While applying these herbal infusions to their own and their children's heads, the priestesses pray for others not to harm them. The plucking and steeping of leaves instantiates a zero-sum game, in which some "heads" gain from others' loss. Hence, a song for the corn leaf asks the goddess not to "wrench off" (ṣe àyàmu) the sacrifiers' affairs as they have "wrenched off" the corn leaves:

Mother, don't wrench off our concerns,
[Like leaves] wrenched from a cornstalk.[6]

Ìyá, má fòrò wa ṣàyàmu,
Àyàmu igi àgbàdo.

Inversely, but by a similar logic, corn leaves (ewé àgbàdo) are sometimes used to attract good luck, since their name contains the verb "to grab" (gbà) and a near homonym of "two hundred" (igba) (see Verger 1967: 14–15).

The priestesses themselves offer no explicit rationale for the selection of leaves. But the efficacy of the leaves is clearly connected to their semantic qualities. Punning, metonymy, and metaphor are major vehicles of performative force in Yoruba ritual utterances generally. The texts of sacred songs indicate that leaves are vehicles of many tropes, adding concrete imagery to the thematic repetitions central to most Yoruba ritual (see Buckley 1982).

For example, like the inner flesh of the calabash, eaten on the day of the Yemoja festival, the leaves of the calabash vine recall the sacred con-

taining qualities of calabashes themselves. Like the calabash itself in *èdà* (moneymaking) magic, the leaves are used in connection with incantations to draw wealth (Verger 1967:50–51).[7] *Kẹ̀kẹ́*, one of the leaves used, is also the word for "bicycle," which a rider "mounts." A peculiarity of the local dialect is that the edible leaf elsewhere called *ètì pọ́n ọlá* is here called *tẹ̀tẹ̀ pọnlá*, potentiating another pun. One song for the tearing of *tẹ̀tẹ̀ pọnlá* plays on the tonal and phonetic similarity of *tẹ̀tẹ̀* to *tètè*, "to hurry":

> We never hear of the death of a hoe
> We never hear of the death of a grinding stone
> We never hear of the death of a cloth
> We never hear of the death of earth
> Just that they grow old [i.e., last a long time]
> They did not *suddenly* arrive such that they will go away *suddenly*
> Only lately did I just arrive.

> A ìí gbọ́ 'kú ọkọ́
> A ìí gbọ́ 'kú ọlọ
> A ìí gbọ́ 'kú aṣọ
> A ìí gbọ́ 'kú ilẹ̀
> Àfi kó gbó
> Wọ́n ò *tètè* dé tí wọ́n *tètè* lọ ni
> Kẹ̀hìn-kẹ̀hìn ni mo tó dé.

Hence, goes the incanted argument, the speaker should remain alive much longer.

Another song for the steeping of *tẹ̀tẹ̀ pọnlá* leaf appears to play on the word *pọnlá*:

> *Tẹ̀tẹ̀ pọnlá* leaf is good, good for food,
> It's good, good for children.

> Tẹ̀tẹ̀ pọnlá ó dáa, dáa fún ọ́njẹ,
> Ó dáa, dáa fún ọmọ.

As a verb, the syllable *pọn-* can mean "to carry [a baby] on one's back." The leaf's name might be transliterated as "vegetable that carries 'honor' on its back"—a child on the back being a woman's foremost honor. Ifá oracular verses specify the value of this leaf in attracting money, apparently because its name contains a near-homonym of both "tomorrow" (*ọ̀la*) and "wealth" (*ọlà*) (see Verger 1967:34–35).

Through "washing," Yemoja absorbs anew the qualities of various gods associated with these leaves; mythically, Yemoja is the mother of all *orisa*. For example, *ewé Ògún* clearly belongs to Ogun, as does *peregun*, according to some priests. Some say *akoko* belongs to Sango. It is placed on heads of recipients of chieftaincy titles. The tones and phonemes of the word *akòko* resemble those in a common Yoruba expression: *Ojú ẹ̀ le kókòkó bíi ẹlẹ́gùn Ṣàngó*—"His face *is hard and cruel* like a Sango possession priest's" (Adedoyin Ṣoyibọ, personal communication, November 1988).[8] The botanical name *yẹrí* is virtually identical with the word for the women's undergarments worn by possessed *ẹlẹ́gùn Ṣàngó*. The priestesses believe that they themselves absorb the power and semantic qualities of Yemoja as they "tear the leaves" (*já ewé*).

In the following days, Adewoyin and Orisagbemi would prepare similar solutions to feed and wash all Yemoja calabashes, along with their contents, in Oke Loko and Isale Bonni quarters, often with the joyous assistance of the children of each house. After the washing, the calabashes are set up for display in public reception rooms until fifteen days after the Yemoja festival day.

A Dual-Purpose Sacrifice

Blood sacrifices preparatory to the 1988 Yemọja Onígbòho festival occurred not in the palace but in Adewoyin's new residence, the recently completed house of her son, *Alhaji* Sule Ajibade. Although absent from Igboho, he is very much present in Adewoyin's public prayers among the *orisa*-worshipers. She seems proud to refer to him as *"Alhaji"*—a title associated, in a hybrid Yoruba discourse, not only with Islam but with extravagant wealth. Orisagbemi, the *mógbà Yemọja* Asumawu, the Jagun, and a contingent of other *elegun* gathered in the room of *Alhaji's* house reserved for Yemoja. This day's ceremony not only prepared for the festival but celebrated (*wẹ̀*—literally, "washed") Adewoyin's new home. The "washing" of new acquisitions in Yorubaland is celebratory, but the great generosity entailed also seems to be intended to diffuse the potentially dangerous envy of others.

The Oya priestess of the town's Sango priesthood intoned the praise poetry of deceased *arumi Yemọja* as Orisagbemi beat the sacred bell (*iro-*

nen). The *arumi* Adewoyin, *mogba* Asumawu, and *arumi* Orisagbemi all doffed their head ties, and Adewoyin touched her forehead to the front of Yemoja's unlidded calabash before praying aloud briefly. Then she took Orisagbemi out of the room with her to fetch the chickens. Adewoyin kneeled and presented one chicken to the calabash full of stones, shells, and small dishes, saying she hoped the chicken would please the goddess and make her want to be present. She uncovered a basketfull of wrapped yam paste (*ọkà*) and offered this further incentive, asking Yemoja not to fight (*jà*) them. In the meantime, the Ṣàngó and Ọya priestesses added volume to their chanting, and the Yemoja priestesses repeatedly answered *àmín* ("amen") to Adewoyin's prayers.

Orisagbemi passed the second chicken to the *mọ́gbà Yemọja* Asumawu to free her hands for divination. The kola-nut (*obi*) oracle answered propitiously, and the priestesses prostrated themselves in the feminine manner (*yíkàá*). According to the bitter-kola oracle, Sango too accepted the chicken brought for him. The young male *ẹlẹ́gùn Ṣàngó* 'Dare was then called upon to kill the chicken for Yemoja first. He passed its head three times under his left foot, stepping on the neck on the third pass. Thus pinning the neck to the floor, he pulled the chicken's body free from its head. From the headless stump he wiped a bit of blood on the front edge of the Yemoja calabash and on the front edge of the sculpted clay pot underneath. Orisagbemi and Adewoyin touched the neck stump and sucked a bit of blood from their fingers. 'Dare mistakenly repeated his entire first procedure with the next chicken, but the women directed him to go back and spill the second chicken's blood over the bowl of Sango stones. Adewoyin meticulously scrubbed the blood off the floor. As she then swept out the house, the Sango and Oya priestesses intoned the family and personal *oriki* (panegyrics) of each person in the shrine room, causing them to beam with gratitude and pride. Wearing her black head scarf, Orisagbemi divined again with kola nut to assure that Yemoja was satisfied. The initial throw was negative. "What's wrong?" she asked before tossing again. The second toss was propitious, so she prostrated herself (*yikaa*). The group danced and sang entertaining songs while Adewoyin cooked the chickens. An hour later, she presented the stew and yam paste to the gods and to the guests (figure 10).

The Annual Yemoja Festival (*Odun*) in Oke-Igboho

The Yemoja Onígbòho festival took place on 7 September. The *mogba* Oladunni conducted a ceremony in the palace shrine room mostly for nonpriestly daughters of Onigboho House who sought good fortune by bringing gifts of hominy and kola nuts. Early in the ceremony, a woman dramatically narrated a dream (*àlá*), in which the ancestors of Onigboho House rose up and counseled all the Muslims and Christians of the house to resume their devotion to Yemoja, so that the house might become great again. The *mogba* Oladunni affirmed the message and prayed for its realization "by the power of our father Tondi [the first Onigboho]" (*lágbára bàbá wa Tóńdì*) and of a series of female ancestors, beginning with Olomide Asakun Awọ, the earliest *arumi Yemoja* I have been able to identify. Using kola nut, Oladunni divined various women's fortunes. Whenever she received a negative combination, she cast again until a positive one appeared, for which the gathering thanked Yemoja. At the conclusion of each consultation, half of the kola nut was deposited in the "first road" of Yemoja.

Adewoyin and Orisagbemi remained in their homes waiting for visitors, while the various *mogba* and a retinue of women, children, and drummers called at the riverine shrine (*ojúbọ*) at Omi Tàtàlà, the local tributary of the River Ògùn. Most of the priestesses wore white that day. Oladunni's youngest granddaughter—who, I was told, is a virgin—bore the effigy of Yemoja on her head to the river. Except for the drummers, we all waded across toward a stone ledge on a rock face dripping with water. This was the sacred place, where the *mogba* Oladunni set down the statue, prayed, offered hominy, and divined with kola nut. She determined that the goddess was satisfied. In the midst of the rite, half a dozen female *ẹlẹ́gùn Ṣàngó* arrived. As a group, we paraded to the Òkè Lókọ shrine of the dead woman's Yemoja. There the *ẹlẹ́gùn Ṣàngó* Moroorenti "sprayed" the praise singers and drummers with money for so honoring her dead mother. We danced to rhythms for Ògún in honor of her father and his line. The priestesses "pressed their heads to the ground" over the grave of the dead *arumi* and paraded back to Oke-Igboho quarter, singing and greeting bystanders on our circuitous route.

Several Muslim men emerged from a mosque and told the drummers to stop drumming as they passed, out of respect for the mosque. What pause there was in the drumming was perfunctory. One Muslim woman, on the other hand, came out of her house and poured water on the feet of a dancing celebrant to "cool" her path and honor Yemoja. "She was really dancing!" the Muslim woman observed. In Oyo town, this gesture is meant to bring fertility to the childless festival participant whose feet are wet. It recalls the wetting of a bride's feet as she enters her groom's house on the wedding night, as well as the wetting of a king's feet as he first enters the palace. The Muslim woman, who is somehow related to Onigboho House, presented money to the *mogba* and then danced herself. All the other money donors as well were women.

Once the parade reached Oke-Igboho, the priestesses saluted various graves and disbanded until the afternoon, when businessman Adewole *Omooye* Lasebikan, Titilayo, and Orisagbemi hosted a feast for the *orisa*-worshipers in Adewole's new house. The cooked food was delivered from Olowo Bar next door. Most of the guests were Sango priests. Two were Yemoja priestesses from other quarters, and one was the late Onigboho Jeremiah Afolabi's *elegun* daughter, on a visit from her affinal home in Modeke quarter. The Yemoja priesthood of Onikomo House, which has taken Alepata's side in the ongoing chieftaincy conflict, was wholly absent.

The two *ẹlẹ́gùn Ṣàngó* of Onigboho House rendered sacrifice to their altars that evening and on the subsequent day, recognizing calendrically their institutional connectedness to Onigboho House and their subordination to the Yemoja priesthood proper. However, the Yemoja *arumi* and *mogba* failed to attend either of these Sango rites. Only the townwide Sango priesthood "supported" these Onigboho House *elegun* by attending their sacrifices and subsequent feasts. The Sango-worshipers as a corporation are omnipresent in the celebration of the town's *orisa*. They are the largest corporation of priests. The reason for the Yemoja priestesses' nonsupport of their kinsmen and members of the same family priesthood this year was not explained, but their rank, particularly in the midst of the interregnum, appears to require *their fixity* and the mobility of their subordinates around *them*. What is clear is that Yemoja's local priesthood is highly sectional and hierarchical, whereas Sango's habitually transcends quarters and kin groups.

Five days after the Yemọja Onígbòho festival came the Yemọja Oníkòmọ festival of Onigboho's "junior brother," on 11 September. This scheduling respects the Onigboho title's seniority. Not until 22 September did the priestesses come around to wash the Yemọja and Sango stones in the Onigboho palace. The "seventeenth-day" feast concluding the Yemọja Onígbòho festival occurred on 23 September. On the "seventeenth day," Orisagbemi and various *mogba* also sacrificed a baby he-goat to Òsányìntà, the sacred hill behind Olowo Bar. Women are forbidden to sacrifice with the knife. Since no *orisa*-worshiping men were available, the priestesses recruited a Christian kinsman to perform the killing. Once the live kid was hauled up the hill, Orisagbemi used kola nut to divine the goodwill of the hill god. She wiped shea butter (òrí) on a stone face and ledge some fifty feet up the hill and said the shea butter was really camwood (osùn). I received no explanation for this traditional ritual misnomer. Amid cries of Ẹ kókè! ("You all, greet the hill!") and replies of Ikúúúú! ("Death!"), the Christian cut the kid's throat and spilled its blood on the rocks. Orisagbemi cast a split kola nut on the rock ledge, and the hill, she discovered, had approved.

Appendix IV

Ṣango Pipe (Ṣango Panegyrics)

Recorded on 13 September 1988, on the "third day" of the initiation of a male *iyawo*, in Isale Bonni, Igboho.

Every day is like a festival for Ọba Kòso [Ṣàngó], King of Koso,
Praised throughout the world, like Almighty God.
Husband of the mother on the hill. The ball is now in your court [I have
    handed the problem over to you], Needle-sharp Sango inevitably
    amazes.
You have mercy for everyone, my husband, please have mercy on me,
One who fights with fire, One who shows off with fire.
He carries the important fire all over the world like God himself.
In the present world, it is only the warmth of the smoke that we feel [i.e.,
    Sango's worldly manifestation pales before his heavenly one].
In a place that sprouts hair,
And also encloses like a tiny farm hut [i.e., the vagina or the head],
Fire, my mothers, fire is with my husband and lord.
Many different types of fire are with Sango. . . .
He shares money so the thief needs not steal. . . .
When Sango was living at Wánrà he was a hunter.
Tẹ̀là Àfọ̀njá[1] used to hunt with a chain.
He put it in the bathing room to catch the children of the family head.
When Sango was living in Sálúù he was a Muslim,
Who ate dog's head with pounded yam,
And pig's head for breakfast during Ramadan to break his fast. . . .
One who fasts during Ramadan. . . .
The husband of Ọyadolu,[2] who carries balls of pounded yam to eat under
    his clothes [during the Ramadan fast]. . . .
I do your bidding today, *orisa* from the beginning of the world;
Do my own bidding for me. . . .

253

Ọjọ́ gbogbo bíi ọdún Ọba Kòso,

A níyì káyé bíi Olódùmarè.

Ọkọ ìyá orí òkè, ó dọwọ́ọ̀ rẹ Ṣàngó abẹ́rẹ́mú tojú timọ́.

Ènìọ̀n gbogbo lo ń ṣàánúu ọkùnrin-ìn mi, ṣàánúù mi,

A-gbéná-jà, a-gbéná-yan.

Ò gbé iná àtàtà káyé bíi Olódùmarè.

Èéfín iná la ń yá láyé.

Níbi tó hun-run,

Asìfamọ́nra bíi ahéré,

Iná, ìyá, iná ḿbẹ̀ lọ́dọ̀ ọkọ̀ mi.

Iná iná ḿbẹ̀ lọ́dọ̀ Ṣàngó. . . .

A bá wọn pínwó olè má jà. . . .

Nígbàtí Ṣàngó ḿbẹ̀ ní Wánrà, ọdẹ ni ń ṣe.

Ẹ̀wọ̀n ni Tẹ̀là Afọ̀njá ń dẹ́ẹ ta.

Báluwẹ̀ ní í dẹ ẹ́ sí ọmọ bálé ní í fi mú.

Nígbàtí Ṣàngó ḿbẹ̀ ní Sálúù tí ń fi ń ṣe Ìmàle,

Tó bá forí ajá jẹ iyọ́n,

Àti orí ẹlẹ́dẹ̀ jẹ sààrì. . . .

Àgbà àwẹ̀. . . .

Ọkọ Ọyádolú, akó iyọ́n rúgúdú bọ abẹ́ aṣọ. . . .

Tìyẹ lèmi ṣe lónìí, òrìṣà ìsàndàáyé;

Bá èmi náà ṣe tèmi. . . .

Appendix V

The Naming Ceremony

The "naming ceremony" (ìsomo lórúko) and "the carrying outdoors of the child" (ìkó omo jade) are alternate terms for the first official public presentation of the child to the community; it includes far more than announcing the name of the child. Classically, a boy's naming ceremony takes place eight days after his birth (called the "ninth day"), and a girl's takes place six days after her birth (called the "seventh day"). Naming ceremonies generally begin early in the morning, before people have gone to work. The wives of the father's house have woken up before dawn in order to prepare the meal for the guests, who will eat rice, àmàlà (yam paste), or èbà (cassava paste) along with vegetables and a stew of ègúsí (melon seed) or pepper, onion, and tomato sauce.

All the family members, friends, and neighbors of the new mother and father gather, usually outside the front door of the father's natal house. If they live in Lagos, the gathering is more likely to take place inside the private home of the couple. A religious leader of the father's faith or an elder of his family will preside over the ceremony. Family members may wear a common uniform (aso ebí) if one has been prepared for a previous occasion. The father and the mother wear their own distinctive matching outfits and sit before the crowd with the baby. The officiant begins the ceremony by taking the baby and leading everyone in prayers and sometimes songs about the god they worship and the benefits he or she bestows.

A variety of items have been assembled on a table. These are touched one by one to the child's lips in order to illustrate and give specific force to the prayers uttered at that moment. They center on certain common metaphoric themes and illustrative proverbs but may vary:

Water (*omi*). The officiant says something like "Water has no enemies. Everyone needs and loves water. So everyone will like you. Like water, your life will be cool."

Salt (*iyọ̀*). "You will live long. As salt is a preservative, so your life will be preserved. As salt makes food 'sweet' [i.e., good-tasting], your life will be sweet."

Kola nut (*obì*). "Kola nut is a sign of hospitality, offered to guests. So you will always be welcomed. If anyone feels anger toward you, he or she will get rid of it as if vomiting." (Uttered slowly, the word may also mean "You vomit.")[1]

Bitter kola (*orógbó*). "As the bitter-kola tree is long-lived and hardy, so you will live long." (The last syllable of this word, *gbó*, means "to grow old.")

Sugar (*adùn*). "As sugar is sweet, so your life will be sweet," or

Sugarcane (*ìrèké*). "As sugarcane is sweet, so your life will also be sweet."

Honey (*oyin*). It is used alongside sugar or sugarcane, with the prayer "As honey is sweet, so your life will also be sweet."

Seeds of the alligator pepper (*atare*). "As the alligator pepper contains many, many seeds [*ọmọ*; literally, "children"], so you will be fecund and bear many children when you grow up."

Schnapps (*ọtí òyìnbó*; literally "white people's liquor"), preferably Dutch. "As the elders drank Schnapps in the days of yore, you will acquire the wisdom of the elders."

Portions of each item are distributed for everyone to taste.

The officiant then asks the father to bring a sum of money, according to his means, in exchange for the privilege of naming the child. After placing coins into a bowl of water or a twenty-naira bank note into a dry bowl, the father announces the name the parents have chosen. This name will be registered with the state and will appear on all documents. It may indicate the circumstances of the birth (twin birth, cord around the neck, caul over the head, foot first, etc.), the day of birth (Sunday, Monday, etc.), the parents' financial status at the time (e.g., "Ajeiigbe" for recent financial recovery), the recent death of a grandparent (i.e., "Father-Returned" or "Mother-Returned"), the religion of the parents (Sikiratu [Islam], Ezekiel [Christianity], etc.), the *orisa* responsible for healing the mother's difficulties with conception (e.g., Ṣangobunmi, "Sango-Gave-Me"), and so on. Other persons in attendance are then invited to donate money in exchange for the privilege of giving the child a pet name. Children thereby end up with a score of names, reflecting the memories and preferences of those who love them. People give the names of deceased relatives, the names of the mother's imaginary childhood playmates, endearments, and so on.

Then, as the wives of the house distribute meals and drinks, various guests come forth to greet the parents. Elder guests pray further over the child. Wives and daughters of the house may chant the *oriki* (panegyrics) of the child, which will include the *oriki* of the father, the mother, their families, and, in some cases, their *orisa* or their professions. Children may acquire a one- or two-word *oriki* of their own as well, which indicates nothing about their personalities and accomplishments but simply expresses the parents' love and the child's paternal ancestry.

The wives of the father's house demand gifts of money from members of the father's house, usually while chanting the *oriki* of the paternal house. Prosperous families and their close friends have commissioned commemorative gifts. At the end of the ceremony, they distribute buckets, cups, matchbooks, address books, enamel pans, and so on, imprinted with words and photographs recognizing the date and nature of the ceremony. The female guests regularly take home parcels of the food served.

Notes

Chapter 1. A Ritual History

1. See especially Wafer's 1986 review of this literature.

2. "Tapa" is the Yoruba word for Nupe, a major ethnic group to the north.

3. Isola blames this distortion on the Church Mission Society School headmaster who published the *Iwe Kika Ẹkẹrin Li Ede Yoruba* in the 1940s, and Abimbola cites the drummed renditions of the two phrases in Yoruba to prove that *Ọbaa Kòso* ("The King of Koso") does not refer to suicide by hanging. Although perhaps products of a nineteenth-century missionary revision, Sango's alternate tragic flaws of tyranny and inadequate control over his own power live on in modern, particularly bourgeois, discourse, popularized by Duro Ladipo's play *Oba Koso* (1964). These forms of disorder lie just beyond the stability and prosperity that his uncontested authority can bring.

Unlike Abimbola and Isola, I decline to take sides in the debate over which myths are true and false, biased and unbiased. I simply take this conflict as evidence of a widespread and enduring tension among visions of supreme authority in Nigeria. Chaotic tyranny and authoritarian order are alternate visions of both Oyo imperialism and modern dictators' attempts to rescue the Nigerian state from civil disorder and politicians' corruption.

4. Priests of Ogun and other divinities in the Oyo-ethnic towns of Ọ̀yọ́, Òkèihò, Kísí, Ìbàdàn, and Ìgbòho have also told me repeatedly and insistently that Ogun does not "mount" (*gùn*).

5. M. T. Drewal reports instances of Ogun possession in the unusual Egbado town of Igbogila, and Verger in an Ọ̀họrí-Yorùbá town, both among the southwestern Yoruba of the People's Republic of Benin and distant from the Oyo heartland (M. T. Drewal 1989; Verger 1981:86–94, 103 [Illustrations 55 and 56]; Verger 1970:150ff.). I was told in Kétu that the Ogun who possesses people is distinct from the far more common Ogun of the hunters and blacksmiths.

One lay informant in Igboho informed me that the only occasion of Ogun possession is the *ìgbẹ́ ìwọ̀* ceremony, in which an Ogun-worshiping hunter or blacksmith is buried. I have not yet been able to confirm this report with the priests. Ajuwon reports that the head of the hunters in Oyo town, the Aṣípadẹ, "is thought to become Ogun himself and, therefore, he is offered respect and deference which exceed the normal amount given him at other times" (1989:178). Ajuwon's description does not, however, suggest that the Asipade is possessed on such occasions. The son of the last Asipade, Wande Abimbọla, denies that Ogun possesses people at all (personal communication, 12 October 1990).

6. Occasional male cross-dressing does occur during the Ogun festivals in the non-Oyo-Yoruba towns of Ire-Ekiti and Ondo; and trance, if not possession, occurs in Ondo (Ibigbami 1978:53; Akinrinsola 1965:87, 94). However, I have no general data specifying the gender indices of *possession* or the significance of transvestism in these towns.

7. Female and male husbands are equally likely to say such things about wives as a lot. See chapter 4.

8. As we shall see in chapter 6, the application of blood to the heads of certain palace "wives" appears to have turned them into "blood" kin of the royal line as well, recommending dramatically a novel standard of identity and personal agency for palace wives. Johnson's description of their initiation does not reveal the detailed attention to blood evident in twentieth-century Sango initiations (1921:34–35). It is difficult to say whether the initiation has changed or Johnson was kept partly in the dark about nineteenth-century initiation procedures. Yet the prominence of animal blood in all the modern *orisa* initiations all around the modern Atlantic perimeter—in Cuba, Brazil, the People's Republic of Benin—suggests that the practice is at least as old as the large-scale transatlantic dispersion of the *orisa* and their Yoruba-speaking worshipers in the eighteenth and early nineteenth centuries.

9. Johnson says that the term *ilari* refers to the treatment of the messenger's own physical head. However, he also says the male *ilari* were called the "keepers of [the king's] head," suggesting that they bear some special metaphysical relation to the king's own "inner head"—the invisible substance of his consciousness, competency, and luck (see chapter 4 of this volume). It seems possible that the *ilari* were regarded as, in effect, possession priests of the king's "head."

10. Belasco (1980:160) also posits the salience of a historical period of which Ogun is emblematic, describing the eighteenth and nineteenth centuries as "Ogun's era," in contrast to the sixteenth- and seventeenth-century "age of Obatala." Not only the timing but also the principle distinguishing Belasco's ages differ from the ones I am proposing. Whereas trade prevailed over war during Belasco's "age of Obatala," war prevailed over trade during "Ogun's era." Moreover, whereas Belasco intends for his historical model to cover the entirety of Yorubaland, I posit the relevance of my own for the Oyo-Yoruba alone.

11. In the mid-nineteenth century, Abeokuta and Dahomey overran Oyo's corridor to the Atlantic ports (Morton-Williams 1964b:42).

12. That is not to say that Ibadan's economy was based exclusively on warfare. Like Oyo, it possessed important agricultural and manufacturing sectors (see Falola 1984).

13. Although this description concerns the camp of Ibadan's major enemy, Akintoye argues at great length that its politico-religious conduct closely assimilated that of Ibadan. Like those in Ibadan, the generals of the rival Ekitiparapo Alliance effectively displaced the leadership of royals in the region they defended. The measure of their debt to Ibadan's "revolution" is the fact that their leading general, Ogedemgbe, like many of his allied contemporaries, was trained at Ibadan (Akintoye 1971:59). In Ibadan, one famous general actually had ritually treated iron objects inserted in his body to increase his military power (Awe 1975:278; Barnes and Ben-Amos 1989:55).

14. Both menstruation and recent sexual contact with human husbands are defiling to women immediately engaged in *orisa* rites. The chief priestess of Yemoja in Abeokuta, Madame Omileye, told me that only a postmenopausal woman can occupy her office.

15. The National Archives, housed at the University of Ibadan, contain a large number of colonial government documents. Although such documents usually escape the atten-

tion of anthropologists, they contain invaluable information on the social changes witnessed and wrought by the British colonizers. At the risk of putting off the general reader, I will record in these notes the exact location of my archival sources, in the hope that other researchers will be able to explore them further. In this case, for example, see Oyo Prof. 1, file no. 1048/13, p. 93—discussed in detail in Matory 1991:254.

Chapter 2. The Ọyọ Renaissance

1. Long before Lord Lugard articulated and popularized the theory of "Indirect Rule"—found in *Political Memoranda* (1906 and 1919), *The Dual Mandate* (1922), and news articles of the period—British African colonial administrators had accepted the premise of ruling through "native agencies." Indirect Rule saved money and averted the need to deploy numbers of European officials unavailable for service in Africa. Moreover, Lugard had written of East Africa, "An arbitrary and despotic rule, which takes no account of native customs, traditions and prejudices, is not suited to the successful development of an infant civilisation, nor, in my view, is it in accordance with the spirit of British colonial rule" (from *The Rise of Our East African Empire* [1893], quoted in Atanda 1979:87).

2. In the colonial context, all Yoruba hereditary authorities and ranking Ibadan officials were classified as "chiefs" of one grade or another. Among these, however, Yoruba distinguishes between, on the one hand, *oba* (crowned and sometimes uncrowned town sovereigns) and, on the other, *ijoye* (subordinate chiefs) and *bálẹ̀* (town sovereigns recognized as subordinate to some specific *oba*). Few Yoruba hereditary officeholders are not subject to some higher officeholder, but communities with a strong sense of local identity or a strong desire to claim independence tend to call their rulers *oba*, or "kings" when speaking English. Throughout this book, I will reproduce the usage I ordinarily heard, and will explain only those controversies relevant to the immediate argument.

3. As the source of this quote, Atanda cites Oyo Prof. 4/7, file no. 275/1918, National Archives, Ibadan (hereafter N.A.I.). Extract from Enclosure in Parliamentary Paper no. 434.

4. "Awa ki jagun l'Ọyọ o / Aiye at'ọba la a jẹ" (quoted in Atanda 1979:74).

5. Particularly irksome to Ibadan was the British reform that established a hierarchy of "Paramount," "District," and "Village" chiefs, each presumed to stand in a hierarchical relation to all others. All orders were assumed to pass down and all responses to pass up through this chain of command (Atanda 1979:133–34). In this way, Alaafin came to rule over the "inferior" chiefs of its former subjects in Ibadan.

6. Public Health Ordinance of 20 July 1917, in *Nigeria Ordinances* 1917, N.A.I.

7. Oyo Prof. 1/840, file no. 1207, p. 10, N.A.I. In 1906, Alaafin Lawani had issued a similar order, in Ross's words, "to prove his authority," and met Pinnock's vocal opposition.

8. Letter from Johnson to Wright in *Annual Report*, January 1880, Church Missionary Society (London) Archives CA2/056 Nigerian Mission. The Sango priests evidently firebombed the house of a converted Ifa divination priest.

9. Memo no. 51/981924 from District Officer, Ife Division to Resident, Oyo Province, Oyo, dated 16 June 1927, in Oyo Prof. 1/833, file no. 1205/1, N.A.I.

10. See, for example, letter no. 740/17/26 from the Oyo District Officer to the Senior Resident of Oyo Province, in Matrimonial Rules, Oyo Division, Oyo Prof. 1/834, file no. 1205/1, N.A.I. Men seldom divorced their wives because, except in the odd statutory

marriage, they had no legal obligation to remain faithful to a single wife. They could divorce wives who kept them constantly in debt, who were regularly unfaithful, or who "made medicine" against their co-wives. Nonetheless, divorce proceedings were almost always initiated by women because they could marry only one man at a time. Several Oyo provincial officials, probably following hegemonic Yoruba assumptions, nonetheless conceptualized women's chief motive for divorce as "adultery" and "seduction" by another man (see letter no. 1352/69/1926 from Assistant District Officer Osogbo to Senior Resident, Oyo Province, dated 28 July 1931, and letter no. 337/0056 from the King of Ifẹ, Ọ̀ọ̀ni Aderẹmi, to District Officer, Ife Division, reported in District Officer's letter to Resident, Oyo Province, dated 21 March 1932—both in file no. 1205/I, Oyo Prof. 1/833. See also letter no. 3828/123/1 from Senior Resident, Oyo Province, to Secretary of the Southern Provinces, Enugu, dated 25 November 1930, and letter no. 51/98/1924 from District Officer, Ife Division, to Resident, Oyo Province, dated 16 June, 1927—in Oyo Prof. 1/833, file no. 1205/1, N.A.I.

11. Memo no. 705/17/26 from District Officer, Oyo, to President and Judges, Native Court, Oyo, dated 6 June 1927, N.A.I.

12. "On Divorce in Oyo Province," Oyo Prof. 1/833, file no. 1205/1, N.A.I.

13. See memo no. 256/123/21 from Senior Resident, Oyo Province, to Assistant District Officer, Osogbo, dated 22 May 1929—in Matrimonial Rules, Oyo Division, Oyo Prof. 1/834, file no. 1205, N.A.I.

14. Young and middle-aged women from one non-Oyo community told me in 1992 that they still fear to pass palaces, because they have heard that a king can *gbẹ́sẹ̀ lé obìnrin*—literally, "place their feet on top of a woman"—and thereby force her to marry him.

15. Women who escaped to these chiefs' houses and successfully "held the post" (*dipomu*) could not legally be removed again to the husband's house. The inauguration of this system by the British seems partly accountable for the Iseyin-Okeiho uprising of 1916 (see Atanda 1969:503).

16. Memo no. 1064/15/27 from Assistant District Officer, Osogbo to Senior Resident, Oyo Province—in Oyo Prof. 1/833, file no. 1205/1, dated 10 May 1929, N.A.I.

17. Letter no. 97/126/32 from Resident, Oyo Province, to Resident, Oyo Division, dated 19 January 1933—in Matrimonial Rules, Oyo Division, Oyo Prof. 1/834, file no. 1205/1, N.A.I.

18. See letter no. s.p. 7197/16 from Secretary, Southern Provinces, Enugu, to Resident, Oyo Province, dated 31 July 1930—in Oyo Prof. 1/840, file no. 1207, N.A.I.

19. Document 1A by W. A. Ross, Resident, Oyo Province, dated 7 September 1920—in Oyo Prof. 1/840, file no. 1207, N.A.I.

20. For example, the Attorney General proposed that a mother "might keep custody of her children, provided that, in the case of female children, dowry on marriage was paid to the family of the deceased father and not to the mother and, in the case of boys, compensation is paid by the mother to the deceased father's family for loss of services." He believed that widow inheritance by the husband's "pagan" relative should not be a problem if the widow refunds to her in-laws the bridewealth paid on her by the deceased husband's family. These are the broad outlines on which District Officers were instructed to resolve matters. (See letter no. L. 271/47 from Attorney General Donald Kingdon to Bishop of Lagos, dated 25 May 1926—in Oyo Prof. 1/840, file no. 1207/1, N.A.I.)

21. Letter no. L. 271/27 from Attorney General Donald Kingdon (Lagos) to chief secretary (Lagos), dated 25 February 1925—in Oyo Prof. 1/840, file no. 1207, N.A.I.

22. Memo from W. A. Ross, Senior Resident, Oyo Province, to Secretary, Southern Provinces, Lagos—p. 6 in Oyo Prof. 1/840, file no. 1207, N.A.I.

23. Colonial officers had set out systematically to replace one with the other in commercial transactions (Hogendorn and Johnson 1986:148ff.). Yoruba, as well as Ashanti, Hausa, and numerous other languages in the region, identify cowries and state-issued specie by the same term: *owó* in Yoruba, *cedi* in Ashanti, and *kud'i* in Hausa, for example.

24. Although I am aware of debates over whether the cowry is "money," as opposed to a more "symbolic" or "special" medium of exchange, my own argument implicitly undermines any such dichotomy. I believe the changing religious and commercial meanings of the cowry are so mutually influential that they are not distinct. Moreover, as we shall see, the Oyo Yoruba invest state-issued specie with a variety of sacred meanings intimately wrapped up with its commercial value. See contributions to this debate by Belasco (1980) and Falola (1984:123 n).

25. The Ọ̀ọ̀ni (King) of Ife fixed the sums in the mid- to late 1920s as follows:

a) Girl up to one year of married life—£15.0.0
b) Woman from 1 to 5 years of married life—£10.0.0
c) Woman 5 years and over—£7.10.0. . . .

Either party may take action . . . to collect any substantial debt from each other [*sic*]. . . . A woman against whom any order is made for debt shall be allowed £ 2.10.0 for each child she has living for the divorced man ("Divorce Rules," 98a in Oyo Prof. 1/833, file no. 1205/1, N.A.I.).

26. Letter no. 2114/123/21 from Senior Resident, Oyo Province, to District Officers, Ibadan and Ife Divisions, and Assistant District Officers of Osogbo and Ilesa Districts — in Oyo Prof. 1/833, file no. 1205I, N.A.I.

27. For example, the opening of the railway line from Lagos to Northern Nigeria before World War I enabled young men to travel and earn in one year of wage labor what a rural father earned in three years of farm work. In no position to migrate themselves, rural men sought to extract their share of the new cash wealth through bride money. Young men complained. Even the Depression of the 1930s did not reduce fathers' extortionate demands (Fadipe 1970:92–93).

28. "Bride price for a virgin girl shall not exceed £12.10.0. . . . The bride price recoverable on divorce if divorce takes place within 3 years of marriage shall not exceed £12.10.0 or the actual amount paid as bride price whichever is less. . . . The bride price recoverable on divorce after 3 years of marriage shall not exceed £6.5.0 and or the actual amount paid, whichever is less" (file no. 1205/1, Oyo Prof., N.A.I.).

29. In the 1920s and 1930s, it was common for people to provide labor in lieu of the payment of debts incurred by themselves or their senior relatives. Often held in the custody of the creditor, these laborers were known as *ìwọ̀fà*, or "pawns." In the twenties, Ross justified the persistence of the system on the grounds that the state guaranteed the *iwofa*'s right to terminate his service whenever he chose. Eventually, Ross would prohibit the use of minors as *iwofa* and fix the rates of compensation for *iwofa* farm labor. Ross fixed the value of *iwofa* farm labor as follows: "In Oyo Div. 2d per 100 heaps [of earth for planting yams] / In Ibadan Div. 3d per 100 heaps / In Ife Div. 3d per 100 heaps" (Oyo Prof. I, vol. 1, file no. 1028, N.A.I.). Individuals characterized as "domestic slaves" were directed to the native court when they wished to free themselves by paying the long-rec-

ognized fee of £3.15.0. Although the fee was not legally required, the "domestic slaves" understood themselves to have incurred a debt for the food and clothing they had received during their service and preferred to pay the money (see also "On Iwofa" in Oyo Prof. I, vol. 1, file no. 1028, N.A.I.).

30. File no. 1205/1, Oyo Prof., N.A.I.

31. Letter no. 97/126/32 from Resident, Oyo Province, to Resident, Oyo Division, dated 19 January 1933—in Matrimonial Rules, Oyo Division, Oyo Prof. 1/834, file no. 1205/1, N.A.I.

32. See Fadipe 1970:67ff. See also Letter no. 10/52/1927 from District Officer, Oyo, to Senior Resident, Oyo Province, dated 25 July 1931—in Oyo Prof. 1/833, file no. 1205I), N.A.I.

33. From the 1920s to the 1950s, codified lists of women's legal grounds for divorce remained almost unchanged. See, for example, *On Divorce in Oyo Province*, p. 98a—in Oyo Prof. 1/83, file no. 1205/1.

34. Memo no. 51/98/1924 from District Officer, Ife Division, to Resident, Oyo Province, dated 16 June 1927—in Oyo Prof. 1/833, file no. 1205/1, N.A.I.

35. Ibid.

36. In the present understanding of *magun*, the danger is not only to those who sleep with married women but to innocent women too. If someone applies *magun* to a woman and she commits no act of adultery, she is thought to die from it.

Chapter 3. Igboho in the Age of Abiọla

1. The Federal Land Use Decree of 1978 threatens to transfer the ultimate authority of chiefs and kings to local government bureaucrats. However, "traditional authorities" in Oyo North have retained their jurisdiction over land use due to the extralegal assumptions of their subjects and uncertainties about the permanence of federal law (see Francis 1984).

2. However, the last Onigboho had stopped attending its sessions before his death.

3. I owe this insight to Dr. Jacob Kehinde Olupona (1983:491), who applied Bellah's concept to the *orisa* rites of the Ondo Yoruba. See also Olupona 1991.

4. *Lukudi* comes from the Hausa word for "cowry" and "money" (*kud'i*), and *eda* means "[money-]doubling."

5. Yoruba men are loath to carry loads on their heads. Among adults, only women carry water from the river or the well. The role of this act in wedding ceremonials recommends it as a defining responsibility in a wife's relation to her husband's house. In wedding rites described by Fadipe in the late 1930s, a new bride was required to fetch water for a wide circle of the husband's kin soon after her entry into his compound (1970 [1939]:85).

6. Recall that the application of the term "Yoruba" collectively to the Ọ̀yọ́, Èkìtì, Àwórì, Òǹdó, Ìjẹ̀sà, Ẹ̀gbá, Ẹ̀gbádò, and so on, is of nineteenth-century origin.

7. See Apter (1992:13–34) for a brilliant discussion of the precolonial precedents for the use of Ife-centric mythology in resistance to Oyo imperialism. See also Peel (1990:342).

8. In 1972, the Nigerian Enterprises Promotion Decree required the management and capital of a range of existing foreign-owned enterprises to pass into Nigerian hands.

9. Oyo Prof. 1, file no. 1048/13, p. 12, National Archives, Ibadan (hereafter, N.A.I.).

10. Ibid., p. 43.

11. See also *Igboho Chiefs and District* and "On Igboho Chiefs and Government"—in

Oyo Prof. 1, file no. 1048/13; Oyo Prof. 1, file no. 1048/12; Oyo Prof. 1, file no. 4162/2, N.A.I.

12. Peter Clarke (1982:193ff.) has discussed other West African instances in which Islam constituted forms of opposition to European colonial authority.

13. Letter from Waibi Akanbi, Laisi Akande, and the young men of Iseyin town, on behalf of the Ilutoro Society. Oyo Prof. 2/3, file C226, entitled "Witchcraft in Oyo Province," N.A.I.

14. Ibid.; see also and Morton-Williams 1956:319.

15. Although there are women and there is possession *(orisa gigun)* in some non-Oyo Ogun cults, sources in Ketu (which is near the setting of Morton-Williams's account) told me that in this region the Ogun belonging to the blacksmiths and hunters (the specific terms in which Morton-Williams describes Ogun in this case) never possesses people. Moreover, Ogun's is an entirely male cult in the Oyo regions mentioned in Morton-Williams's account.

16. Ogboni is a secret society of male and female elders. In many communities, it actively counsels the king.

17. Scholarly sources report variously that the king has "witchcraft" (Thompson 1972:254), that he is the "head of the witches" (Babayemi 1982:10), and that he actively respects and cooperates with the witches (Abimbola, personal communication, 19 October 1990). The Alepata of Igboho told me that the "witches" *(aje)* do good things for the town and that he meets with them regularly.

18. See, for example, "Report to support recommendations for a Subordinate Native Authority and a Sub-Treasury for the Village Areas of Igboho, Kishi and Igbetti," p. 4—in Oyo Prof. I, file no. 4162, undated (printed between 1940 and 1944), N.A.I.

19. His counterpart in the Oyo capital, who led in the worship of the royal graves there, was a priestess addressed as "Father," on the grounds that she is the embodiment of Sango (Abraham 1962:19).

20. Memorandum by the Minister of Justice and Local Government, Executive Council (57) 372, dated 30 July 1957. Property of the Executive Council: Western Region/Chieftaincy Matters, Oyo Division. File no. 288/13; N.A.I.

21. The fact that the woman so readily abandons a commandant in favor of a king is also suggestive in light of the gendered contrast between Ogun and Sango.

22. "Report to support recommendations for a Subordinate Native Authority and a Sub-Treasury for the Village Areas of Igboho, Kishi and Igbetti," p. 4 (see n. 18).

23. See Matory (1986, 1991) for a similar structural analysis of "containment" and its sexual coordinates in Yoruba religion. See also Apter (1992).

24. Annual offerings to the blacksmiths' Ogun are made on one day of the Egungun festival.

Chapter 4. A Ritual Biography

1. A 25-year-old scholarly debate in the Yorubanist literature addresses the relative importance of agnatic and cognatic elements in Yoruba kinship, as well as the relative salience of lineage and coresidence in collective identity and action (see summaries in Barber [1991:156–58] and Eades [1980:49–51]). The "agnatic kinship system" of the Oyo kingdom and a number of northern Yoruba towns, writes Eades, "has never been questioned" (1980:46, 50). What remains clear is that efforts at ahistorical generalization across Yoruba groups are counterproductive and that local, multifactor analyses belie simple

classificatory tags. Standard anthropological labels require specific explanation in the local case.

2. Maternal and paternal relatives are addressed as Bàbá ("father") or Ìyá ("mother"), according to their sex. Elder maternal and paternal relatives of one's own generation are called Ẹ̀gbọ́n ("elder sibling [or cousin]") regardless of their sex, and junior persons of one's generation are called Àbúrò ("junior sibling [or cousin]"). Persons of the junior generation are all classified as one's ọmọ, or "children."

3. During the 1952–54 chieftaincy dispute, the candidates disagreed over how many sublineages there were. One named the three sublineages as Oyèbọ̀ọ́dé, Òtú, and Agánnà (or Aláàtípó). The other identified Oníkẹ́kẹ́ as one sublineage and both Otu and Oyeboode sublineages as parts of a single Alàbàjà sublineage (see Oyo Prof. 1, file no. 1048/13, pp. 15, 18, 23, National Archives, Ibadan).

4. Reports from an Oyo-Yoruba town closer to Ibadan suggest that the husband's contribution is usually much smaller than what the wife herself has supplied from her earnings in service to another women trader (Sudarkasa 1973:118).

5. The norm of de facto gender segregation among the egbe is so ingrained that it tends to govern the membership of even the emergent professional associations of, for example, female accountants and lawyers.

6. "Ọmọ̀ọ̀ mi tí ń wá ọkọ, ọ̀dọ́ olókó ló wà,
Má jẹ́ẹ́ kí wọ́n dó nídòòkídòó
Ọmọ tó wà lọ́dọ̀ọ̀ mi tó ń lọ ilé ìwé,
Má jẹ́ẹ́ kí wọ́n dó ní ìdòó kídòó.
Má jẹ́ẹ́ kó lọ́kọ búúú."

7. These estimates are based on averages before the structural adjustments in the import market had elevated crop prices.

8. "Ni ẹnu ọ̀nà ti ìyàwó yóò ba gba wole, a gbọ́dọ̀ fi èéfó igbá kan sibẹ. Aṣa náà ni lati jẹki iyawo fi ẹsẹ rẹ tẹ igbá yi fọ́ si ọ̀nà pupọ. Idi rẹ ni pe awon Yoruba gbàgbọ́ pe iye ọ̀nà ti igbá náà ba ti fọ si, iye ọmọ náà ni iyawo yóò bí. Nitori náà awọn ara ile ọkọ yóò ti wa èéfọ́ igba ti ara rẹ ti kan gba a, ti a o fi ese kan ti yóò si funka si ọna aimoye" (tones and diacritics reproduced exactly from the original text).

9. For example, it is said that some women fọdí fún ọkọ wọn jẹ—"They wash their bottoms [i.e., vaginas] for their husbands to eat"; that is, the woman cooks her husband's food in special water used first to rinse her vagina. Thereafter, it is believed, her husband cannot stray sexually or neglect her material demands.

10. In keeping with the negotiated character of religious identity in Yorubaland, most Muslim women are not secluded. Indeed, some Muslim women in Lagos and Ibadan are wealthy traders, who invest their money not only in their children but in the highly prestigious hajj.

11. Also commonly seen are decals featuring the image and words of Abubakar Gumi, a Muslim religious leader and the most vocal opponent of women's political enfranchisement in Nigeria. His opinions favoring the seclusion of women and their exclusion from the national presidency are widely publicized in the Nigerian press.

12. In data recorded during the 1940s, about 46 percent of all marriages (except those ended by death) eventually ended in divorce. A similar proportion of marriages ended in divorce during the 1960s, when about 5 percent of all extant marriages were dissolved annually (Lloyd 1968:79).

13. See chapter 1 for one version of a tale also current in Igboho. See also Matory 1986:83ff., 133ff., 171ff.

14. One reported form of that harnessing involves a chain around the child's ankle.

15. Among the one female and two male conspirators, a man and a woman spent time in prison. The man who escaped is said to have gone crazy. Some say the town-improvement society has banished them all from the town.

Chapter 5. Engendering Power: The Mythic and Iconic Foundations of Priestly Action

1. "Ayé la bá 'Fá
   Ayé la bá 'Màle
   Òsán gangan ni 'Gbàgbó wolé dé" (from Babayemi 1979:67).

2. Consider, for example, àṣírí ("secret," from the Arabic sirr—Gbadamosi 1978:207); àlùjònú ("an evil spirit," from the Arabic al-jinn, which refers to good, evil, or morally neutral creatures of the netherworld); sàráà (a sacrificial offering to the orisa or a type of marriage free of bridewealth, apparently assimilating two Arabic terms—ṣadaqah, meaning "alms," and ṣadaq, referring to bridewealth, or gifts from the husband to the wife upon marriage and divorce; Noha Aboul-Magd Forster and Samira Sisson, personal communication, 9 February 1991); báríkà ("Congratulations!" from the Arabic baraka, meaning "grace"—[see Gbadamosi 1978:207]); àdúrà ("prayer," from the Arabic al-du'ā—ibid.). Although the paradigmatic referent of this last term in modern Yoruba is Christian prayer, the term derives from the Arabic (ibid.); lukudi ("moneymaking magic") derives from the Hausa word for cowry, kud'i (see Lovejoy 1974:566).

3. Bascom's informants define saraa by contrast to conventional sacrifice (ẹbọ) as the form of offering that "traditionalist" diviners prescribe for Muslim and Christian clients who wish to distinguish themselves from orisa-worshipers (Bascom 1969a:60–61).

4. A variety of specifically Yoruba Muslim forms of divination have developed alongside "traditional" forms. Although they have much in common, Yoruba Muslims are anxious to attribute distinct origins to them. Both are patronized by members of all religions (see Bascom 1969a:12; Abdul 1970). Ryan (1978:163) even implies that "traditionalist" diviners are especially popular in predominantly Muslim towns.

5. Idowu (1963:100) records panegyrics that call Sonponnon "The Muslim, king of the Mosque."

6. Certain ritual occasions in most Yoruba towns—such as Ìrómò in Igede-Ekiti and Èfè among the southwestern Yoruba—license groups of women to compose and publicly sing songs of personal and social criticism.

7. "Omi ni èsìn wa;
   Nínú ilée wa bá a bímọ tón oooo,
   Lèmọmù lè má kóo."

8. "Àwa náà yíò ṣe Yemoja;
   Àwọn Onígbàgbó ń ṣe Ìgbàgbó;
   Àwa náà yíò ṣe Yemoja."

9. See Appendix IV. It is unclear when these passages entered Sango's local panegyrics. What is clear is that in the late 1980s they were sung publicly with full knowledge that a religiously divided community was listening.

10. For example, a young man might say of a woman who interests him sexually, Màá jẹ iṣu yẹn!—"I'm going to eat that yam!"

11. Recorded in May 1988, during a recitation to a multireligious gathering in the palace of the Onigboho, chief of Oke-Igboho quarter of Igboho. Traditionally, he derives

his sanction to rule from the *orisa* Yemoja, all of whose possession priests, unlike Sango's, are real women. For the Yoruba text, see Appendix I, *Oriki Yemoja*, verses 4–5.

Ìyáà mi ń pani, a lóbìnrin ni.

Omi alagbalúbú omi òréré yèlú Yemoja tí í gbódò jèjì àgbò.

12. His panegyrics also identify him as *Àjàlá tó mọ orí*—"Ajala who molds heads."

13. Some say that Saki is actually the original home of Ogun (Abimbola 1975:175 n).

14. The reader should not confuse "Ògùn," as in "the River Ògùn," with the god "Ògún." The two words are distinct in tonal pattern and meaning.

15. See also the court records of Suit No. I/108/85, before the Honourable Justice Y. Olayiwola Adio on 10 July 1986, in which it is claimed as proof of the Onigboho's supremacy in the town that the Onigboho used to invite the rulers of Ṣẹpètèrí, Ṣakí, Kísí, and Ìgbẹtì to attend "customary rites and they use[d] to invite him to their own places for the same purpose." High Court of Oyo State, Ibadan Judicial Division.

16. I call the late Mr. Afolabi "King" (*oba*) here because his subjects and his panegyrics identify him as that. I do not thereby wish to take sides in the local chieftaincy tussle.

17. See Prince (1961). Morton-Williams (1960:35) reports the explicit belief in Oyo that Yemoja is the mother of the witches, and, researching among a number of southwest Yoruba groups, Thompson infers that Yemoja herself is a witch (1976, chapter 14:2–5).

18. A slap with this ring knocks down but does not ordinarily kill the victim.

19. For example, the phrase "*láti ọwọ́*" denotes literary authorship.

20. Oyo Prof. 1, file no. 1048/13, p. 9; National Archives, Ibadan.

21. Babayemi records a nickname of Alaafin: *A boju lu kara bi ajere*, meaning "[The one who] has eyes all over his body like a perforated pot." The nickname is used to indicate the great reconnaissance available to Alaafin through his roving deputies, the *ilari*.

22. Roasting pots (*ajere*) and baskets are sometimes the vessels in which Sango priests carry burning coals on their heads during possession (see Frobenius 1968 [1913]:216; Verger 1970 [1957]:305).

23. A pseudonym, like most of the names in the account that follows.

24. Mr. Akinbami (a pseudonym) died in 1989, after the completion of my fieldwork. His son has regularly worked jobs outside the town, to which he has returned since the end of my fieldwork.

25. See Matory (1986:149–64) on the sacred symbolism of royal and plebeian, bourgeois architecture.

26. Madam Oladunni passed away in late 1991. As in several priestesses' names below, I have recorded and tone-marked not only personal names but the *oriki* by which intimates know them.

27. The Yemoja calabashes of the two present *arumi*'s most recent predecessors—Akee and Oyeyemi—are still with their children. However, neither Akee's nor Oyeyemi's children are *orisa*-worshipers, and they no longer visit Onigboho House. Therefore, if they do not return the calabashes to the palace, Oladunni believes, their children will start dying, and it will be left to the diviner to discover their neglect of Yemoja as the cause.

28. Most reasonably prosperous Igboho residents mark graves with cement platforms and tombstones.

29. He received the palm nuts by some other form of inheritance that his descendants cannot explain. He does not appear to have been a *babalawo*, or Ifa diviner—the normal professional user of palm nuts.

30. These shrines belong to the nonpossession priests (*mogba*), who are the official heads of the cult and who are responsible for initiating possession priests. The mortar

(*odó*) appearing in the photo is in the shrine of the *mogba*'s house in Ìsàlẹ̀ Ọ̀gẹ̀dẹ̀, Igboho, where one of the initiations discussed in chapter 6 occurred.

Chapter 6. Re-dressing Gender

1. Note that Yoruba does not distinguish verbally between "husband" and "groom" or between "wife" and "bride." The translation "bride" has the virtue of highlighting the fact that *iyawo* indicates the junior status of the addressee relative to the speaker or of the referent relative to the point of reference. To put it another way, a person is not addressed or referred to as the *iyawo* of anyone who is junior to her with respect to residence in the house.

2. I use the term "literal" advisedly, not to imply that the marriage between common husbands and wives possesses some ultimate and fully concrete form but to identify this type of marriage as the prototype by which most people will initially understand the term "bride" when it is raised in the context of Sango-worship. Of course, my ultimate argument is that this prototypical bride herself is transformed by the activities of the Sango priesthood.

3. In her influential article "How Man Makes God in West Africa," Barber writes that, in the hierarchical but relatively fluid social structure of another Oyo-Yoruba town, "Men make themselves, by attracting supporters; and in such a society it is also conceived that men make their gods by being their supporters" (1981:740). Barber thus illuminates an indigenous sociological dimension of the "madeness" of the *orisa*.

4. Verger published an extensive account of one Sango initiation in Sakete (in present-day People's Republic of Benin) in the mid-twentieth century (1981:36–43). Salami describes the initiation in an unmentioned locale (1990:59–66). Both of these sources are in Portuguese. They differ in some important details from what I witnessed in Igboho, Nigeria, in 1988, although the similarities are far greater. Johnson published a brief account of the initiation based on late nineteenth-century testimony in Oyo town (1921:34–35). His account differs radically from what I observed and heard in Igboho, although he mentions a variety of leaves still in use among Yemoja-worshipers in the town.

5. For another interesting discussion of Yoruba religious secrecy, see Barber (1981:439–40).

6. The reported scheduling and duration of initiations vary (see Salami 1990:59–66; and Verger 1981:36–43).

7. In 1988, the Nigerian naira was devalued in relation to major foreign currencies, with which Nigerians had previously purchased large quantities of foreign grain. After the devaluation, foreign food became expensive in naira terms, making the crops of domestic farmers more competitive and allowing local farmers to raise their prices.

8. Recall that in passing on her witchcraft (*aje*) a retiring "witch" is also said to vomit up the substance of her power in order to allow her successor or recruit to swallow it or part of it.

9. See Appendix V for the significance of these items in the ceremonial naming of infants.

10. On this day of the initiations I have attended in the Brazilian Candomblé, the three-day-old food offerings to the god, as well as the shaved hair and clipped nails of the initiand, are deposited in the river. I do not know if a similar practice obtains in Igboho or elsewhere in Yorubaland.

11. See Matory (1991:576–631) for a more complete description of the rites and personalities involved in the initiations I observed.

12. I equivocate in my citation of de Saussure because his view that the sense of a sign relies specifically on relations of *contrast* within the sign system speaks inadequately to the compelling quality of *linkage* and *relationship* that gives "brideliness" its distinctive power. See "The Internal Logic of Brideliness" later in this chapter.

13. This is a compound of names peculiar to the Oyo royal family (see Johnson 1921:83). "Tela Afonja" therefore probably refers to Sango.

14. Recorded on the "third day" of a male bride's initiation. See Appendix IV for a lengthier sample of the *Ṣàngó pípè*.

15. We saw in chapter 1 that Isola (1991) and Abimbola (personal communication, 19 October 1990) argue that the tale of Sango's hanging proceeds from a deliberate Christian misinterpretation during the 1940s. Despite its origin, it is difficult to ignore so vastly popular and influential a tale in the interpretation of this religion as it stood in the 1980s.

16. As a description of the sexual act, *gun* does not normally apply to human beings. Applied to human beings, this term suggests rape (Wande Abimbola, personal communication, 19 October 1990). Hence, its application here suggests metaphorically the violence and absolute domination implicit in Sango's command.

17. When it rains, women are advised never to sit on an upright mortar, since doing so might provoke Sango's unwelcome penetration—that is, the striking of the woman by lightning, which is conceived of as penetration by a "thunder axe."

18. In the worldly house, that "senior co-wife" is usually also the groom's mother.

19. Recall that *iyawo* may mean "bride" or "wife."

20. Bloch (1989) also discusses a case in which the money associated with an ancient politico-religious order acquires a sacred value in anchoring contemporary kin groups against fissiparous forces. Indeed, the new money is used to expiate departures from kin unity.

Chapter 7. Conclusion: Dialogue, Debate, and the *Chose du Texte*

1. See Carneiro (1964:98–102) concerning one of several Brazilian precedents to these conferences.

2. Offering an earlier alternative to the "pantheon" models, Barber (1981) had observed the blending of *orisa* identities due to worshipers' parallel efforts to build up their particular divinities by attributing to them the panegyrics of other divinities.

3. *Adé* (pl., *adés*) in Portuguese differs in both pronunciation and meaning from the Yoruba *adé*, which means "royal crown."

4. See Willett 1967; Fagg and Pemberton 1982; Drewal, Pemberton, and Abiodun 1989; and figure 9 in this volume. Priesthoods of the Oyo god Sango remain the exemplary patrons of such art forms even outside the present heartland of Oyo culture—in Egbado and Ekiti, for example. Extant artifacts date back to the eighteenth century.

Appendix I. *Oriki Yemọja* (Yemọja Panegyrics)

1. Or, as Karin Barber interprets it, she showed her toughness by ruining the host's food, as the *orisa* Sonponnon is also said to do—he rolls it in the mud (personal communication, 18 July 1990; Barber 1981:733). Consider also line 82.

2. Alternatively, "The river is her headquarters," or, "The river is her homestead."

3. Water that is so expansive (and deep) that it appears as dark as indigo dye.

4. *Olómú* is rendered as *olómó* in this recitation.

5. *Oódán* is Oyo-North dialect for *odúndún*.

6. *Abíyá* is rendered as *abéyá* in this recitation.

Appendix II. A Partial Genealogy of the Oyebǫǫde Priests

1. I have chosen to tone-mark names and personal *oriki* here in order to preserve the form and meaning of those rarely spoken outside of Oke-Igboho.

Appendix III. Yemoja in the Kingdom of Sango: The Ritual Calendar

1. This assertion duplicates an old distinction extant in the present Oyo capital as well.

2. Surprisingly, they did not present at the Yemoja calabash of the *elégùn Sàngó* Oyerogun, who had accompanied them all morning. Although she belongs to Oyeboode line of Onigboho House, it was always the townwide Sango priesthood, and not the Yemoja priesthood, that attended rites in her house.

3. The oracular cowries rest in front of and under the mat, right rear, in figure 9.

4. See Bascom (1969a:130) for other examples of the punning implicit in Yoruba medicinal and religious rites.

5. *Òrúwa* (or *òrúwo*) is said to cure malaria (Buckley 1985:221).

6. Yemoja's most characteristic food offering—*ègbo*, or hominy—is made of corn, which takes a pivotal role in this wordplay. A verb sharing the morphological root of *àyàmu*—*yàgbàdo*—describes the wrenching of the corncob from the stalk. Parts of the corn plant are therefore especially redolent instruments of this ritual manipulation.

7. *Òpòtó* is used ritually to attract people to a newly established market, apparently because *òpò* means "plenitude."

8. The *ìrokò* tree is in many places identified as an *orisa*; diviners instruct barren and witch-afflicted people to leave offerings among its roots and in its trunk.

Appendix IV. *Sango Pipe* (Sango Panegyrics)

1. This is a compound of names peculiar to the Oyo royal family (see Johnson 1921:83). "Tela Afonja" therefore probably refers to Sango, the essence of Oyo kingship.

2. Someone named Oyadolu would be a child born with the assistance of Sango's mythic wife Oya. Such a person would worship and, in mythic references, be closely identified with Oya. Like local descriptions of anthropomorphic shrine sculpture, local exegeses of tales and verse about the *orisa* often conflate the gods with their past human worshipers and servitors.

Appendix V. The Naming Ceremony

1. When anger remains inside a person it may become mystically effective and harm its unprotected object.

Bibliography

Abdul, M. O. A. 1970. "Yoruba Divination and Islam." *Orita* 4 (1): 17–25.

Abimbọla, Wande. 1976. *Ifa: An Exposition of the Ifa Literary Corpus*. Ibadan: Oxford University Press (Nigeria).

———. 1975. *Sixteen Great Poems of Ifa*. Zaria: Gaskiya Corporation (UNESCO).

———. 1973. "The Literature of the Ifa Cult." In *Sources of Yoruba History*, ed. S. O. Biobaku, pp. 41–62. Oxford, England: Clarendon.

Abiọdun, Rowland. 1989. "Woman in Yoruba Religious Images." *African Languages and Cultures* 2 (1): 1–18.

Abraham, R. C. 1962. *Dictionary of Modern Yoruba*. London: Hodder and Stoughton.

Aderele, T. A. 1982. "Report of Public Inquiry into the Headship Tussle among Alepata, Onigboho and Ona-Onibode, All in the Irepo South Local Government Area, held on 1st to 3rd June, 1982. Transcript and report of a judicial inquiry held under the auspices of Oyo State of Nigeria." Ibadan: Chieftaincy Affairs Division, Oyo State Government Secretariat.

Afọlabi, Ọba Jeremiah, and Pa. Phillip Babalọla. 1972. *The History of Igboho*. Trans. Atoyebi. Mimeograph.

Agbaje-Williams, Babatunde. 1983. *A Contribution to the Archaeology of Old Oyo*. Ph.D. dissertation, Department of Archaeology, University of Ibadan.

Ajayi, J. F. Ade. 1965. *Christian Missions in Nigeria, 1841–1891*. London: Longmans.

Ajuwọn, Bade. 1989. "Ògún's Ìrèmòjé: A Philosophy of Living and Dying." In *Africa's Ogun*, ed. Sandra Barnes. Bloomington: Indiana University Press.

Akinrinṣọla, Fọla. 1965. "Ogun Festival." *Nigeria* 85: 84–95.

Akintoye, S. A. 1971. *Revolution and Power Politics in Yorubaland 1840–1893*. New York: Humanities Press.

Amadiume, Ifi. 1987. *Male Daughters, Female Husbands: Gender and Sex in an African Society*. London: Zed Books.

Apter, Andrew. 1992. *Black Critics and Kings: The Hermeneutics of Power in Yoruba Society*. Chicago: University of Chicago Press.

Ardener, Edwin. 1975 (1972). "Belief and the Problem of Women." In *Perceiving Women*, ed. Shirley Ardener, pp. 1–18. New York: John Wiley and Sons.

Asiwaju, A. I. 1976. *Western Yorubaland under European Rule 1889–1945: A Comparative Analysis of French and British Colonialism*. London: Longman.

Atanda, J. A. 1979 (1973). *The New Oyo Empire: Indirect Rule and Change in Western Nigeria 1894–1934*. London: Longman.

———. 1970. "The Changing Status of the Alafin of Oyo under Colonial Rule and

Independence." In *West African Chiefs*, ed. Michael Crowder and Obaro Ikime, pp. 212–30. Ile-Ife, Nigeria: University of Ife Press.

———. 1969. "The Iseyin-Okeiho Rising of 1916: An Example of Socio-Political Conflict in Colonial Nigeria." *Journal of the Historical Society of Nigeria* 4 (4): 497–514.

Awẹ, Bọlanle. 1977. "The Iyalode in the Traditional Yoruba Political System." In *Sexual Stratification*, ed. Alice Schlegel, pp. 144–60. New York: Columbia University Press.

———. 1975. "Notes on Oriki and Warfare in Yorubaland." In *Yoruba Oral Tradition*, ed. Wande Abimbọla, pp. 267–92. Ile-Ife, Nigeria: Department of African Languages and Literatures, University of Ife.

———. 1972. "The Economic Role of Women in Traditional African Society: The Yoruba Example." In *La Civilisation de la femme dans la tradition africaine*. Colloquium in Abidjan, Ivory Coast, 3–8 July 1972.

———. 1964. "The Ajele System: A Study of Ibadan Imperialism in the Nineteenth Century." *Journal of the Historical Society of Nigeria* 3 (1): 47–60.

Awolalu, J. Ọmọṣade. 1979. *Yoruba Belief and Sacrificial Rites*. Bristol, England: Longman.

Babayẹmi, S. O. 1982. "Oyo Palace Organisation." A paper presented at the Institute of African Studies Seminar, 16 June.

———. 1979. *The Fall and Rise of Oyo c. 1760–1905: A Study in the Traditional Culture of an African Polity*. Ph.D. dissertation, Centre for West African Studies, University of Birmingham, England.

———. 1971. "Upper Ogun: An Historical Sketch." *African Notes* 6 (2): 72–84.

Bach, Daniel C., and Mouftaou Laleyẹ. 1986. "Vie politique et construction de l'État." In *Le Nigeria Contemporain*, ed. Daniel C. Bach, pp. 77–95. Paris: Centre National de la Recherche Scientifique.

Bada, Chief Reverend S. O. n.d. *History of Saki*. Saki, Nigeria: Bada's Compound.

Bakhtin, M. M. 1981. *The Dialogic Imagination*, ed. Michael Holquist. Trans. Caryl Emerson and Michael Holquist. Austin: University of Texas Press.

Barber, Karin. 1991. *I Could Speak until Tomorrow: Oriki, Women, and the Past in a Yoruba Town*. Washington, D.C.: Smithsonian.

———. 1990. "*Oriki*, women and the proliferation and merging of *orisa*." *Africa* 60 (3): 313–37.

———. 1981. "How Man Makes God in West Africa: Yoruba Attitudes toward the *Orisa*." *Africa* 51 (3): 724–45.

Barnes, Sandra T. 1980. *Ogun: An Old God for a New Age*. Philadelphia: Institute for the Study of Human Issues.

Barnes, Sandra T., and Paula Girshick Ben-Amos. 1989. "Ogun, the Empire Builder." In *Africa's Ogun*, ed. Sandra T. Barnes, pp. 39–64. Bloomington: Indiana University Press.

Bascom, William R. 1969a. *Ifa Divination*. Bloomington: Indiana University Press.

———. 1969b (1944). "The Sociological Role of the Yoruba Cult- Group." *American Anthropologist* (n.s.) 46 (1), part 2. New York: Kraus Reprints.

———. 1969c. *The Yoruba of Southwestern Nigeria*. New York: Holt, Rinehart and Winston.

———. 1956. "Yoruba Concepts of the Soul." In *Men and Cultures: Selected Papers of the Fifth International Congress of Anthropological and Ethnological Sciences* (Philadelphia, 1–9 September), ed. Anthony F. C. Wallace, pp. 401–10. Philadelphia: University of Pennsylvania Press.

Basso, Keith. 1976. " 'Wise Words' of the Western Apache: Metaphor and Semantic

Theory." In *Meaning in Anthropology*, ed. Keith A. Basso and Henry A. Selby, pp. 93–121. Albuquerque: University of New Mexico Press.

Bastide, Roger. 1978. *The African Religions of Brazil*. Trans. Helen Sebba. Baltimore: Johns Hopkins University Press.

Baudin, Rev. P. 1885. *Fetichism and Fetich Worshipers*. Trans. M. McMahon. New York: Benziger Brothers.

Baum, Robert M. 1993. "Homosexuality and the Traditional Religions of the Americas and Africa." In *Homosexuality and World Religions*, ed. Arlene Swidler, pp. 1–46. Valley Forge, Pa.: Trinity Press International.

Beattie, John, and John Middleton, eds. 1969. *Spirit Mediumship and Society in Africa*. New York: Africana Publishing.

Beier, Georgina. 1980. "Yoruba Pottery." *African Arts* 13 (3): 48–53, 92.

Beier, H. U. 1955. "The Position of Yoruba Women." *Présence Africaine* (n.s.) 1–2 (April–July): 39–46.

Beier, Ulli. 1980. *Yoruba Myths*. Cambridge, England: Cambridge University Press.

Belasco, Bernard I. 1980. *The Entrepreneur as Culture Hero: Preadaptations in Nigerian Economic Development*. New York: Praeger.

Berger, Iris. 1976. "Rebels or Status-Seekers? Women as Spirit Mediums in East Africa." In *Women in Africa*, ed. Nancy J. Hafkin and Edna G. Bay, pp. 157–81. Stanford: Stanford University Press.

Berry, Sandra. 1985. *Fathers Work for Their Sons: Accumulation, Mobility, and Class Formation in an Extended Yorùbá Community*. Berkeley and Los Angeles: University of California Press.

Besmer, Fremont E. 1983. *Horses, Musicians, and Gods: The Hausa Cult of Possession-Trance*. South Hadley, Mass.: Bergin and Garvey.

Bibeli Mimọ (*The Holy Bible* in Yoruba) (n.d.—1900 edition). Dallas: International Bible Association.

Biobaku, Saburi. 1960. "Madame Tinubu." In *Eminent Nigerians of the Nineteenth Century*, a series of studies originally broadcast by the Nigerian Broadcasting Corporation. Cambridge, England: Cambridge University Press.

———. 1952. "An Historical Sketch of the Ẹgba Traditional Authorities." *Africa* 22 (1): 35–49.

Bloch, Maurice. 1989. "The symbolism of money in Imerina." In *Money and the Morality of Exchange*, ed. J. Parry and M. Bloch, pp. 165–90. Cambridge, England: Cambridge University Press.

Boddy, Janice. 1989. *Wombs and Alien Spirits*. Madison: University of Wisconsin Press.

Boserup, Ester. 1970. *Women's Role in Economic Development*. New York: St. Martin's Press.

Bourdieu, Pierre. 1977. *Outline of a Theory of Practice*. Trans. Richard Nice. Cambridge, England: Cambridge University Press.

Brain, Robert. 1976. *Friends and Lovers*. London: Hart-Davis, MacGibbon.

Brown, David Hilary. 1989. *Garden in the Machine: Afro-Cuban Sacred Art and Performance in Urban New Jersey and New York*, 2 vols. Ph.D. dissertation, American Studies, Yale University.

Buckley, Anthony D. 1985. *Yoruba Medicine*. Oxford, England: Clarendon.

———. 1982. *Yoruba Medicine*. Ph.D. dissertation, Centre for West African Studies, University of Birmingham, England.

———. 1976. "The Secret—An Idea in Yoruba Medicinal Thought." In *Social Anthropology and Medicine*, ed. J. B. Loudon, pp. 396–421. London: Academic Press.

Butler, Judith. 1990. "Gender Trouble, Feminist Theory, and Psychoanalytic Discourse." In *Feminism/Postmodernism*, ed. Linda J. Nicholson. New York and London: Routledge.

Cabrera, Lydia. 1974. *Yemayá y Ochún: Kariocha, Iyalorichas y Olorichas*. Madrid: Chicherikú.

Carneiro, Edison. 1964. *Ladinos e Crioulos*. Rio de Janeiro: Editôra Civilização Brasileira.

Chanock, Martin. 1982. "Making Customary Law: Men, Women, and the Courts in Colonial Rhodesia." In *African Women and the Law: Historical Perspectives* (Boston University Papers on Africa, no. 7), ed. Margaret Jean Hay and Marcia Wright, pp. 53–67. Boston: Boston University, African Studies Center.

Clapperton, Hugh. 1829. *Journal of a Second Expedition into the Interior of Africa, from the Bight of Benin to Soccatoo*. London: John Murray.

Clarke, Peter B. 1982. *West Africa and Islam: A Study of Religious Development from the 8th to the 20th Century*. London: Edward Arnold.

Clarke, William H. 1972 (1871). *Travels and Explorations in Yorubaland 1854–1858*, ed. J. A. Atanda. Ibadan: Ibadan University Press.

Collier, Jane Fishburne, and Sylvia Junko Yanagisako, eds. 1987. *Gender and Kinship: Essays toward a Unified Analysis*. Stanford: Stanford University Press.

Comaroff, Jean. 1985. *Body of Power, Spirit of Resistance: The Culture and History of a South African People*. Chicago: University of Chicago Press.

Comaroff, John L., and Jean Comaroff. 1987. "The Madman and the Migrant: Work and Labor in the Historical Consciousness of a South African People." *American Ethnologist* 14 (2): 191–209.

Costa Lima, Vivaldo. 1981. "Os Obás de Xangô." In *Olóòrìṣà*, ed. Carlos Eugênio Marcondes de Moura, pp. 87–126. São Paulo: Agora.

———. 1977. *A Família-de-Santo nos Candomblés Jeje-Nagôs da Bahia: Um Estudo de Relações Intra-Grupais*. Master's thesis in Human Sciences, Federal University of Bahia.

Counihan, Carole M. 1985. "Transvestism and Gender in a Sardinian Carnival." *Anthropology* 9 (1–2): 11–24.

Cunha, Manuela Carneiro da. 1985. *Negros, estrangeiros: os escravos libertos e sua volta à Àfrica*. São Paulo: Editôra Brasiliense.

Curtin, Philip D. 1969. *The Atlantic Slave Trade: A Census*. Madison: University of Wisconsin Press.

Curtin, Philip D., Steven Feierman, Leonard Thompson, and Jan Vansina. 1978. *African History*. Boston: Little, Brown and Company.

Dantas, Beatriz Góis. 1988. *Vovó Nagô e Papai Branco: Usos e Abusos da Àfrica no Brasil*. Rio de Janeiro: Graal.

———. 1982. "Repensando a pureza Nagô." *Religião e Sociedade* 8: 15–20.

Daramola, Olu, and Adebayo Jeje. 1975 (1967). *Àwọn Àṣà àti Òrìṣà Ilẹ̀ Yorùbá*. Ibadan: Oníbọn-Òjé Press.

Davis, Angela. 1985. "Sex-Egypt." In *Women: A World Report*, ed. Anita Desai, Toril Brekke, et al., pp. 325–48. London: Methuen.

Davis, Natalie. 1978. "Women on Top: Symbolic Sexual Inversion and Political Disorder in Early Modern Europe." In *The Reversible World*, ed. Barbara A. Babcock, pp. 147–90. Ithaca, N.Y.: Cornell University Press.

Dennett, R. E. 1910. *Nigerian Studies*. London: Macmillan.

Dennis, Carolyne. 1987. "Women and the State in Nigeria: The Case of the Federal Military Government 1984–85." In *Women, State, and Ideology: Studies from Africa and Asia*, ed. Haleh Afshar, pp. 13–27. Albany: State University of New York Press.

A Dictionary of the Yoruba Language. 1979 (1950). Ibadan: Ibadan University Press.

Drewal, Henry John. 1989. "Art or Accident: Yoruba Body Artists and Their Deity Ogun." In *Africa's Ogun*, ed. Sandra T. Barnes, pp. 235–60. Bloomington: Indiana University Press.

Drewal, Henry John, John Pemberton III, and Rowland Abiodun. 1989. *Yoruba: Nine Centuries of African Art and Thought*, ed. Allen Wardwell. New York: Center for African Art/Harry N. Abrams.

Drewal, Margaret Thompson. 1992. *Yoruba Ritual: Performers, Play, Agency*. Bloomington: Indiana University Press.

———. 1989. "Dancing for Ogun in Yorubaland and Brazil." In *Africa's Ogun*, ed. Sandra T. Barnes. pp. 199–234. Bloomington: Indiana University Press.

———. 1986. "Art and Trance among Yoruba Shango Devotees." *African Arts* 20 (1): 60–67, 98–99.

———. 1977. "Projections from the Top in Yoruba Art." *African Arts* 11 (1): 43–49, 91–92.

Dudley, Billy. 1982. *An Introduction to Nigerian Government and Politics*. Bloomington: Indiana University Press.

Durkheim, Emile. 1983. *The Division of Labor in Society*. Trans. George Simpson. New York: Macmillan. [Original written in French, 1893.]

Eades, J. S. 1980. *The Yoruba Today*. Cambridge, England: Cambridge University Press.

———. 1975. "The growth of a migrant community: the Yoruba in Northern Ghana." In *Changing Social Structure in Ghana*, ed. J. R. Goody, pp. 37–57. London: International African Institute.

Ellis, A. B. 1964 (1894). *The Yoruba-Speaking Peoples of the Slave Coast of West Africa*. Chicago: Benin Press.

Epega, D. Olarimwa. 1931. *The Basis of Yoruba Religion*. Lagos: Ijamido Printer.

Étienne, Mona, and Eleanor Leacock, eds. 1980. *Women and Colonization: Anthropological Perspectives*. New York: Praeger/J. F. Bergin.

Euba, Titi. 1985. "The Ooni of Ife's Are Crown and the Concept of Divine Head." *Nigeria* 53 (1) (January-March): 1–18.

Evans-Pritchard, E. E. 1970. "Sexual Inversion among the Azande." *American Anthropologist* 72 (6): 1428–34.

Fadipe, N. A. 1970. *The Sociology of the Yoruba*. Ibadan: Ibadan University Press. Written originally as a Ph.D. dissertation (1939), University of London.

Fagg, William, and John Pemberton III. 1982. *Yoruba Sculpture of West Africa*, ed. Bryce Holcombe. New York: Knopf.

Falola, Toyin. 1984. *The Political Economy of a Pre-Colonial African State: Ibadan, 1830–1900*. Ibadan: African Press.

Faniyi, Dejo. 1975. "Ekun Iyawo: A Traditional Yoruba Nuptial Chant." In *Yoruba Oral Tradition*, ed. Wande Abimbola, pp. 677–99. Ife: Department of African Languages and Literatures, University of Ife.

Fernandez, James W. 1986. *Persuasions and Performances*. Bloomington: Indiana University Press.

Fisher, H. 1973. "Conversion Reconsidered: Some Historical Aspects of Religious Conversion in Black Africa." *Africa* 43 (1): 27–40.

Foucault, Michel. 1980 (1978). *The History of Sexuality*, vol. 1: *An Introduction*. Trans. Robert Hurley. New York: Random House.

———. 1977. *Discipline and Punish*. Trans. Alan Sheridan. New York: Pantheon.

Francis, Paul. 1984. " 'For the Use and Common Benefit of All Nigerians': Consequences of the 1978 Land Nationalization." *Africa* 54 (3): 5–28.

Frobenius, Leo. 1968 (1913). *The Voice of Africa*, vol. 1. New York: Benjamin Blom.

Fry, Peter. 1986. "Male Homosexuality and Spirit Possession in Brazil." *Journal of Homosexuality* 11 (3/4): 137–53.

———. 1982. *Para Inglês Ver: Identidade e Política na Cultura Brasileira*. Rio de Janeiro: Zahar.

Gadamer, Hans-Georg. 1975. *Truth and Method*. New York: Crossroad Publishing.

Garber, Marjorie. 1992. *Vested Interests: Cross Dressing and Cultural Anxiety*. New York: Routledge.

Gates, Henry Louis, Jr. 1988. *The Signifying Monkey: A Theory of Afro-American Literary Criticism*. New York: Oxford University Press.

Gbadamọsi, T. G. O. 1978. *The Growth of Islam among the Yoruba*. Atlantic Highlands, N.J.: Humanities Press.

Gilliland, Dean S. 1986. *African Religion Meets Islam: Religious Change in Northern Nigeria*. Lanham, Md., and London: University Press of America.

Gleason, Judith. 1987. *Ọya: In Praise of the Goddess*. Boston: Shambala.

Greenblatt, Stephen. 1980. *Renaissance Self-Fashioning: From More to Shakespeare*. Chicago: University of Chicago Press.

Hafkin, Nancy J., and Edna G. Bay, eds. 1976. *Women in Africa*. Stanford: Stanford University Press.

Hebdige, Dick. 1979. *Subculture: The Meaning of Style*. London and New York: Methuen.

Henfrey, Colin. 1981. "The Hungry Imagination: Social Formation, Popular Culture and Ideology in Bahia." In *The Logic of Poverty: The Case of the Brazilian Northeast*, ed. Simon Mitchell, pp. 58–108. London: Routledge and Kegan Paul.

Herskovits, Melville J. 1966 (1948). "The Contribution of Afroamerican Studies to Africanist Research." In *The New World Negro*, ed. Frances S. Herskovits, pp. 12–23. Bloomington: Indiana University Press.

Hoch-Smith, Judith. 1978. "Radical Yoruba Female Sexuality." In *Women in Ritual and Symbolic Roles*, ed. Judith Hoch-Smith and Anita Spring. New York: Plenum Press.

Hoch-Smith, Judith, and Anita Spring, eds. 1978. *Women in Ritual and Symbolic Roles*. New York: Plenum Press.

Hogendorn, Jan, and Marion Johnson. 1986. *The Shell Money of the Slave Trade*. Cambridge, England: Cambridge University Press.

Horton, Robin. 1975. "On the Rationality of Conversion—Part II." *Africa* 45 (4): 373–99.

Hubert, Henri, and Marcel Mauss. 1964. *Sacrifice: Its Nature and Function*. Trans. W. D. Halls. Chicago: University of Chicago Press.

Ibigbami, K. I. 1978. "Ogun Festival in Ire Ekiti." *Nigeria* 126–27: 44–59.

Idowu, E. Bọlaji. 1970. "The Challenge of Witchcraft." *Orita* 4 (1): 3–16.

———. 1963. *Olódùmarè: God in Yoruba Belief*. New York: Praeger.

Isichei, Elizabeth. 1983. *A History of Nigeria*. London: Longmans.

Isọla, Akinwumi. 1991. "Religious Politics and the Myth of Sango." In *African Traditional Religions in Contemporary Society*, ed. Jacob K. Olupọna, pp. 93–99. New York: Paragon House.

Jay, Nancy. 1990. *Throughout Your Generations Forever: A Sociology of Sacrificial Religions*. Unpublished manuscript. Harvard University Divinity School.

Johnson, Rev. Samuel. 1921. *The History of the Yorubas*. Lagos: CSS Bookshops. Originally written 1899.

———. 1880. Letter from Johnson to Wright. Annual Report, January 1880. Church Missionary Society Archives CA2/056, Nigerian Mission. University of Birmingham, England.

Jones, David. 1988. *Poets with Adzes: An Introduction to Yoruba Religious Art*. Ipswich, England: Ipswich Borough Council.

Kandiyoti, Deniz. 1988. "Bargaining with Patriarchy." *Gender and Society* 2 (3): 274–90.

Karp, Ivan. 1989. "Power and Capacity in Rituals of Possession." In *Creativity of Power*, ed. W. Arens and Ivan Karp, pp. 91–109. Washington, D.C.: Smithsonian.

Kimambo, Isaria, and C. K. Omari. 1972. "The Development of Religious Thought and Centres among the Pare." In *The Historical Study of African Religion*, ed. T. O Ranger and I. N. Kimambo. Berkeley and Los Angeles: University of California Press.

Krige, Eileen Jensen. 1974. "Women-Marriage, With Special Reference to the Lovedu— Its Significance for the Definition of Marriage." *Africa* 44 (1): 11–37.

Laitin, David D. 1986. *Hegemony and Culture: Politics and Religious Change among the Yoruba*. Chicago: University of Chicago Press.

Lakoff, George, and Mark Johnson. 1980. *Metaphors We Live By*. Chicago: University of Chicago Press.

Lambek, Michael. 1980. "Spirits and Spouses: possession as a system of communication among the Malagasy-speakers of Mayotte." *American Anthropologist* 7 (2): 318–31.

Lan, David. 1989 (1985). *Guns and Rain*. Berkeley: University of California Press.

Lander, Richard, and John Lander. 1832. *Journal of an Expedition to Explore the Course and Termination of the Niger*, vol. 1. London: John Murray.

Landes, Ruth. 1947. *City of Women*. New York: Macmillan.

———. 1940. "A Cult Matriarchate and Male Homosexuality." *Journal of Abnormal Social Psychology* 35 (3): 386–97.

Lawuyi, Olatunde B. 1987. "The Sex Symbolism in Sango Worship." *Afrika und Übersee* 70: 245–56.

Leighton, Alexander H., Raymond Prince, and Rollo May. 1968. "The Therapeutic Process in Cross-Cultural Perspective—a Symposium." *American Journal of Psychiatry* 124 (9): 1171–83.

Leiris, Michel. 1989. *La possession et ses aspects théâtraux chez les Éthiopiens de Gondar*. Cognac: Fata Morgana.

Lévi-Strauss, Claude. 1976. *Structural Anthropology*, vol. 2. Trans. Monique Layton. New York: Basic Books.

———. 1966. *The Savage Mind*. Chicago: University of Chicago Press.

Levtzion, Nehemia. 1968. *Muslims and Chiefs in West Africa: A Study of Islam in the Middle Volta Basin in the Pre-Colonial Period*. London: Oxford University Press.

Lewis, I. M. 1986 (1971). *Ecstatic Religion*. London: Routledge.

Lewis, I. M., Ahmed Al-Safi, and Sayyid Hurreiz, eds. 1991. *Women's Medicine: The Zār-Bori Cult in Africa and Beyond*. Edinburgh: Edinburgh University Press.

Lloyd, Peter C. 1968. "Divorce among the Yoruba." *American Anthropologist* 70: 67–81.

———. 1960. "Sacred Kingship and Government among the Yoruba." *Africa* 30 (3): 221–37.

Lovejoy, Paul E. 1974. "Interregional Monetary Flows in the Precolonial Trade of Nigeria." *Journal of African History* 15 (4): 563–85.

Mabogunję, A. L. 1961. "The Market-Woman." *Ibadan* 11: 14–17.

———. 1958. "The Yoruba Home." *Odu* 5: 28–36.

Mabogunję, A. L., and M. O. Oyawoye. 1961. "The Problems of the Northern Yoruba Town: The Example of Shaki." *The Nigerian Geographical Journal* 4 (2): 1–10.

MacCormack, Carol, and Marilyn Strathern, eds. 1980. *Nature, Culture and Gender*. Cambridge, England: Cambridge University Press.

Mageo, Jeannette Marie. 1992. "Male Transvestism and Culture Change in Samoa." *American Ethnologist* 19 (3): 443–59.

Mann, Kristin. 1985. *Marrying Well: Marriage, Status, and Social Change among the Educated Elite in Colonial Lagos*. Cambridge (Cambridgeshire), England: Cambridge University Press.

Matory, James Lorand. 1994 (forthcoming). "Rival Empires: Islam and the Religions of Spirit Possession among the Oyo-Yoruba." *American Ethnologist* (in press).

———. 1993. "Nagôs e Índios: Tattered Memories of Africa in an Afro-Brazilian Religion." A lecture presented to the Center for the Study of World Religion, Harvard University, 4 May.

———. 1991. *Sex and the Empire That Is No More: A Ritual History of Women's Power Among the Oyo-Yoruba*. Ph.D. dissertation, Department of Anthropology, University of Chicago.

———. 1988. "Homens Montados: homossexualidade e simbolismo da possessão nas religiões afro-brasileiras." In *Escravidão e Invenção da Liberdade*, ed. João José Reis. São Paulo: Editôra Brasiliense.

———. 1986. *Vessels of Power: The Dialectical Symbolism of Power in Yoruba Religion and Polity*. Master's thesis in anthropology, University of Chicago.

Mauss, Marcel. 1967. *The Gift*. Trans. Ian Cunnison. New York and London: W. W. Norton.

Mba, Nina. 1989. "Kaba and Khaki: Women and the Militarized State in Nigeria." In *Women and the State in Africa*, ed. Jane L. Parpart and Kathleen A. Staudt. Boulder, Colo.: Lynne Rienner Publishers.

Mintz, Sidney W., and Richard Price. 1976. *An Anthropological Approach to the Afro-American Past: A Caribbean Perspective*. Philadelphia: Institute for the Study of Human Issues.

Morton-Williams, Peter. 1967. "The Yoruba Kingdom of Oyo." In *West African Kingdoms in the Nineteenth Century*, ed. Daryll Forde and P. M. Kaberry, pp. 36–69. London: Oxford University Press.

———. 1964a. "An Outline of the Cosmology and Cult Organization of the Oyo Yoruba." *Africa* 34 (3): 243–61.

———. 1964b. "The Oyo Yoruba and the Atlantic Slave Trade." *Journal of the Historical Society of Nigeria* 3 (1): 25–43.

———. 1960. "Yoruba Responses to the Fear of Death." *Africa* 30 (1) 34–40.

———. 1956. "The Atinga Cult among the South-Western Yoruba: A sociological analysis of a witch-finding movement." *Bulletin de l'I.F.A.N.*, series B 18 (3–4): 315–34.

Mudimbe, V. Y. 1988. *The Invention of Africa: Gnosis, Philosophy, and the Order of Knowledge*. Bloomington: Indiana University Press.

Munn, Nancy D. 1973. "Symbolism in a Ritual Context: Aspects of Symbolic Action." In

Handbook of Social and Cultural Anthropology, ed. John J. Honigmann, pp. 579–612. Chicago: Rand McNally.

Nadel, S. F. 1954. *Nupe Religion.* London: Routledge and Kegan Paul.

———. 1937. "A Ritual Currency in Nigeria—A Result of Culture Contact." *Africa* 10 (4): 488–91.

Nina Rodrigues, Raimundo. 1945. *Os Africanos no Brasil,* 3d ed. São Paulo: Companhia Editôra Nacional.

———. 1935. *O Animismo Fetichista dos Negros Bahianos.* Rio de Janeiro: Civilização Brasileira.

Nwogugu, E. I. 1974. *Family Law in Nigeria.* Ibadan: Heinemann Educational Books (Nigeria).

Oboler, Regina Smith. 1980. "Is the Female Husband a Man? Woman/Woman Marriage among the Nandi of Kenya." *Ethnology* 19: 69–88.

O'Brien, Denise. 1977. "Female Husbands in Southern Bantu States." In *Sexual Stratification,* ed. Alice Schlegel, pp. 109–26. New York: Columbia University Press.

Ogunde, Herbert. 1982. *Jaiyesimi* (a booklet published and distributed in conjunction with the film of the same title). Lagos (Yaba): Pacific Printers.

Ogundipẹ-Leslie, 'Mọlara. 1985. "Women in Nigeria." In *Women in Nigeria Today,* ed. S. Bappa, J. Ibrahim, A. M. Imam, F. J. A. Kamara, H. Mahdi, M. A. Modibbo, A. S. Mohammed, H. Mohammed, A. R. Mustapha, N. Perchonock, and R. I. Pittin, pp. 119–31. London: Zed Books.

Ojo, G. J. Afọlabi. 1966. *Yoruba Culture: A Geographical Analysis.* London: University of London Press.

Okediji, O. O., and F. O. Okediji. 1966. "Marital Stability and Social Structure in an African City." *The Nigerian Journal of Economic and Social Studies* 8 (1): 151–63.

Olupọna, Jacob K. 1991. *Kingship, Religion, and Rituals in a Nigerian Community.* Stockholm: Almqvist and Wiksell International.

———. 1983. *A Phenomenological/Anthropological Analysis of the Religion of the Ondo-Yoruba of Nigeria.* Ph.D. dissertation in religion, Boston University.

Omari, Mikelle Smith. 1984. *From the Inside to the Outside: The Art and Ritual of Bahian Candomblé.* Los Angeles: Museum of Cultural History, University of California at Los Angeles.

Ong, Aihwa. 1988. "The Production of Possession: Spirits and the Multinational Corporation in Malaysia." *American Ethnologist* 15 (1): 28–42.

Oppong, Christine, ed. 1983. *Female and Male in West Africa.* London: George Allen and Unwin.

Oroge, E. Adeniyi. 1971. *The Institution of Slavery in Yorubaland with Particular Reference to the 19th Century.* Ph.D. dissertation, Centre for West African Studies, University of Birmingham, England.

Ortner, Sherry B. 1974. "Is female to male as nature is to culture?" In *Woman, Culture and Society,* ed. M. Rosaldo and L. Lamphere, pp. 67–88. Stanford: Stanford University Press.

———. 1973. "On Key Symbols." *American Anthropologist* 75 (5): 1338–47.

Ortner, Sherry B., and Harriet Whitehead, eds. 1981. *Sexual Meanings: The Cultural Construction of Gender and Sexuality.* Cambridge, England: Cambridge University Press.

Oyemakinde, Wale. 1983. "The Management of Chieftaincy Affairs in Nigeria." *African Notes* (Ibadan) 9 (1): 27–34.

Parrinder, Geoffrey. 1972 (1953). *Religion in an African City*. Westport, Conn.: Negro
    Universities Press.
Parry, J. 1986. "The *gift*, the Indian gift and the 'Indian gift.'" *Man* 21 (3): 453–73.
Parry, J., and M. Bloch, eds. 1989. *Money and the Morality of Exchange*. Cambridge,
    England: Cambridge University Press.
Peacock, James. 1978. "Symbolic Reversal and Social History: Transvestites and Clowns
    of Java." In *The Reversible World: Symbolic Inversion in Art and Society*, ed. Barbara A.
    Babcock, pp. 209–24. Ithaca, N.Y.: Cornell University Press.
Peel, J. D. Y. 1990. "The Pastor and the *Babalawo*: The Interaction of Religions in
    Nineteenth-Century Yorubaland." *Africa* 60 (3): 338–69.
———. 1984. "Making History: The Past in the Ijesha Present." *Man* (n.s.) 19: 111–32.
———. 1983. *Ijeshas and Nigerians: The Incorporation of a Yoruba Kingdom 1890s-1970s*.
    Cambridge, England: Cambridge University Press.
———. 1978. "Olaju." *Journal of Development Studies* 14: 139–65.
Pepper, Stephen C. 1942. *World Hypotheses*. Berkeley and Los Angeles: University of
    California Press.
Pesman, Dale. 1991. "Reasonable and Unreasonable Worlds: Some Expectations of
    Coherence in Culture Implied by the Prohibition of Mixed Metaphor." In *Beyond
    Metaphor: The Theory of Tropes in Anthropology*, ed. James W. Fernandez. Stanford:
    Stanford University Press.
Potash, Betty. 1989. "Gender Relations in Sub-Saharan Africa." In *Gender and
    Anthropology*, ed. Sandra Morgan, pp. 189–227. Washington, D.C.: American
    Anthropological Association.
Prince, Raymond. 1966. "Possession and Social Cybernetics." In *Trance and Possession
    States*, Proceedings of the Second Annual Conference of the R. M. Bucke Society, 4–6
    March, Montreal, ed. Raymond Prince, pp. 157–65.
———. 1961. "The Yoruba Image of the Witch." *Journal of Mental Science* 57: 795–805.
Ribeiro, René. 1969. "Personality and the Psychosexual Adjustment of Afro-Brazilian
    Cult Members." *Journal de la Société des Américanistes* 58: 109–20.
Risério, Antônio. 1988. "Bahia com 'H.'" In *Escravidão e Invenção da Liberdade*, ed. João
    José Reis, pp. 143–65. São Paulo: Editôra Brasiliense.
Robertson, Jennifer. 1992. "The Politics of Androgyny in Japan: Sexuality and
    Subversion in the Theater and Beyond." *American Ethnologist* 19 (3): 419–42.
Rosaldo, Michelle Z., and Louise Lamphere. 1974. *Woman, Culture and Society*. Stanford:
    Stanford University Press.
Rosaldo, Renato. 1980. *Ilongot History 1883–1974*. Stanford: Stanford University Press.
Ryan, Patrick J. 1978. *Imale: Yoruba Participation in the Muslim Tradition: A Study in Clerical
    Piety*. Missoula, Mont.: Scholars Press.
Ryle, Gilbert. 1949. *The Concept of Mind*. New York: Barnes and Noble.
Sahlins, Marshall. 1985. *Islands of History*. Chicago: University of Chicago Press.
———. 1981. "The Stranger King." *Journal of Pacific History* 16 (3): 107–32.
Salami, Sikiru (King). 1990. *A Mitologia dos Orixás Africanos*, vol. 1. São Paulo: Editôra
    Oduduwa.
dos Santos, Juana Elbein. 1976. *Os Nàgô e a Morte: Pàde, Àsèsè e o Culto Égun na Bahia*.
    Petrópolis, Brazil: Vozes.
dos Santos, Juana Elbein, and Deoscóredes M. dos Santos. 1969. "Ancestor Worship in
    Bahia: The Égun-cult." *Journal de la Société des Américanistes* 58: 79–108.

de Saussure, F. 1983. *Course in General Linguistics*. Trans. Roy Harris. London: Gerald Duckworth.

Schlegel, Alice, ed. 1977. *Sexual Stratification*. New York: Columbia University Press.

Schneider, David. 1968. *American Kinship: A Cultural Account*. Englewood Cliffs, N.J.: Prentice-Hall.

Shepherd, Gill. 1987. "Rank, Gender and Homosexuality: Mombasa as a Key to Understanding Sexual Options." In *The Cultural Construction of Sexuality*, ed. Pat Caplan. London: Tavistock.

Smith, Rev. Edwin W., and Captain Andrew Murray Dale. 1920. *The Ila-Speaking Peoples of Northern Rhodesia*. London: Macmillan and Co.

Smith, Robert. 1988. *Kingdoms of the Yoruba*, 3d ed. Madison: University of Wisconsin Press.

———. 1965. "The Alafin in Exile: A Study of the Igboho Period in Oyo History." *Journal of African History* 6 (1): 57–77.

Soumonni, Elisée. 1986. "Histoire et Historiographie." In *Le Nigeria Contemporain*, ed. Daniel C. Bach, pp. 45–64. Paris: Centre National de la Recherche Scientifique.

Ṣoyinka, Wọle. 1976a. *Myth, Literature and the African World*. Cambridge, England: Cambridge University Press.

———. 1976b. *Ogun Abibimañ*. London and Ibadan: Rex Collings.

Strathern, Marilyn. 1987. "Introduction." In *Dealing with inequality: Analysing gender relations in Melanesia and beyond*, ed. Marilyn Strathern, pp. 1–32. Cambridge, England: Cambridge University Press.

Stichter, Sharon B., and Jane L. Parpart, eds. 1988. *Patriarchy and Class: African Women in the Home and the Workforce*. Boulder, Colo. and London: Westview.

Sudarkasa, Niara. 1977. "Women and Migration in Contemporary West Africa." *Signs* 3 (1): 178–89.

———. 1973. *Where Women Work: A Study of Yoruba Women in the Marketplace and the Home*. Museum of Anthropology, University of Michigan Publication 53. Ann Arbor: University of Michigan Press.

Thomas, L. L., J. Z. Kronenfeld, and D. B. Kronenfeld. 1976. "Asdiwal Crumbles: a critique of Lévi-Straussian myth analysis." *American Ethnologist* 3 (1): 147–73.

Thompson, Robert Farris. 1983. *The Flash of the Spirit: African and Afro-American Art and Philosophy*. New York: Random House.

———. 1976. *Black Gods & Kings: Yoruba Art at U.C.L.A.* Bloomington and London: Indiana University Press.

———. 1973. "An Aesthetic of the Cool." *African Arts* 7 (2): 40–43, 64–67, 89–91.

———. 1972. "The Sign of the Divine King." In *African Art and Leadership*, ed. Douglas Turner and Herbert M. Cole, pp. 227–60. Madison: University of Wisconsin Press.

———. 1969. "Abatan: A Master Potter of the Egbado Yoruba." In *Tradition and Creativity in Tribal Art*, ed. Daniel Biebuyck, pp. 120–82. Berkeley and Los Angeles: University of California Press.

Trimingham, J. Spencer. 1968. *The Influence of Islam upon Africa*. London: Longmans Green and Co.

Turner, Victor. 1969. *The Ritual Process*. Ithaca, N.Y.: Cornell University Press.

———. 1967. *The Forest of Symbols*. Ithaca, N.Y.: Cornell University Press.

Valeri, Valerio. 1985. *Kingship and Sacrifice: Ritual and Society in Ancient Hawaii*. Trans. Paula Wissing. Chicago: University of Chicago Press.

Verger, Pierre. 1970 (1957). *Notes sur le Culte des Òrìṣà et Vodun à Bahia, la Baie de tous les*

Saints, au Brésil et à l'ancienne Côte des Esclaves en Afrique. Mémoires de l'Institut Français d'Afrique Noire 51. Dakar: Institut Français d'Afrique Noire. Reprinted by Swets and Zeitlinger, Amsterdam.

Verger, Pierre Fatumbi. 1981. *Orixás*. São Paulo: Editôra Corrupio.

———. 1967. *Àwọn Ewé Òsanyìn: Yoruba Medicinal Leaves*. Ile-Ife, Nigeria: Institute of African Studies, University of Ife.

Wafer, James William. 1986. *Sacred and Profane Love in Islam*. Master's thesis in anthropology, Indiana University.

Webster, J. B. 1968. "Attitudes and Policies of the Yoruba African Churches towards Polygamy." In *Christianity in Tropical Africa*, ed. C. G. Baeta. London: Oxford University Press.

White, Hayden. 1973. *Metahistory*. Baltimore: Johns Hopkins University Press.

Whitehead, Harriet. 1981. "The bow and the burden strap: a new look at institutionalized homosexuality in native North America." In *Sexual Meanings: The Cultural Construction of Gender and Sexuality*, ed. Sherry B. Ortner and Harriet Whitehead, pp. 80–115. Cambridge, England: Cambridge University Press.

Wikan, Unni. 1977. "Man Becomes Woman: Transsexualism in Oman as a Key to Gender Roles." *Man* (n.s.) 12: 304–19.

Willett, Frank. 1967. *Ife in the History of West African Sculpture*. New York: McGraw-Hill.

Index

For ease in reference, standard English letter-by-letter alphabetization has been used, although Yoruba alphabetization requires that a high-tone vowel precede that mid-tone vowel, which precedes that low-tone vowel, and a letter marked with an inferior dot would follow that letter without the dot. Complete Yoruba diacritic markings are provided for main entries; the diacritics have been dropped for other mentions of Yoruba words (see "Note on Orthography" at the beginning of this book).

J. Lorand Matory is assistant professor of anthropology and of Afro-American studies at Harvard University. He has taught at Williams College and held research appointments with the W. E. B. Du Bois Institute for Afro-American Research at Harvard University, the Department of Anthropology at Princeton University, the Field Museum of Natural History in Chicago, and the National Museum of Natural History in Washington, D.C. He has conducted extensive field research in Nigeria, Brazil, and African-inspired religious communities in the northeastern United States.